Empirical Research towards a Relevance Assessment of Software Clones

Dissertation

Submitted by **Saman Bazrafshan**

on

25th November 2016

to the

University of Bremen

Faculty of Mathematics and Computer Science

in partial fulfillment of the requirements for the degree of

Doktor der Ingenieurwissenschaften

Supervised by

Prof. Dr. rer. nat. Rainer Koschke *University of Bremen, Germany*

and

Prof. Dr. rer. nat. Stefan Wagner *University of Stuttgart, Germany*

Bibliografische Information der Deutschen Nationalbibliothek

Die Deutsche Nationalbibliothek verzeichnet diese Publikation in der
Deutschen Nationalbibliografie; detaillierte bibliografische Daten sind
im Internet über http://dnb.d-nb.de abrufbar.

ISBN 978-3-8325-4509-3

Logos Verlag Berlin GmbH
Comeniushof, Gubener Str. 47,
10243 Berlin
Tel.: +49 (0)30 42 85 10 90
Fax: +49 (0)30 42 85 10 92
INTERNET: http://www.logos-verlag.de

To Mandana Mirhossini and Mohammad Bazrafshan, my parents and my foundation.

To Sara and Siamak Bazrafshan, my sister and my brother, my best friends and my valuable advisers.

To Sahar Pahlevani Jazi, my partner and my faithful companion in any situation.

Words cannot express how much I love you all.

Acknowledgments

Over the past five years I have received support and encouragement from a great number of individuals. Firstly, I would like to express my deepest gratitude to my supervisor Rainer Koschke for his continuous support and patience. His guidance helped me in all the time of research and writing this thesis. I truly appreciate him as a great advisor and even more as a great person. I am also heartily thankful to Stefan Wagner who co-supervised this thesis and helped me with many insightful comments.

My sincere thanks goes to my fellow colleagues of the Software Engineering Group for many interesting discussions and helpful feedback on my work. You guys have a great team spirit and I enjoyed laughing with you just as much as working with you.

I thank my partner Sahar Pahlevani Jazi for always believing in me and having my back throughout writing this thesis and my life in general.

Last but not least, I owe my everything to my dear family who made me who I am today.

Saman Bazrafshan, November 2016

Abstract

Redundancies in program source code—so called software clones—are a common phenomenon. Although it is often claimed that software clones decrease the maintainability of software systems and need to be managed, research in the last couple of years showed that not all clones can be considered harmful. A sophisticated assessment of the relevance of software clones and a cost-benefit analysis of clone management is needed to gain a better understanding of cloning and whether it is truly a harmful phenomenon.

This thesis introduces techniques to model, analyze, and evaluate versatile aspects of software clone evolution within the history of a system. We present a mapping of non-identical clones across multiple versions of a system, that avoids possible ambiguities of previous approaches. Though processing more data to determine the context of each clone to avoid an ambiguous mapping, the approach is shown to be efficient and applicable to large systems for a retrospective analysis of software clone evolution.

The approach has been used in several studies to gain insights into the phenomenon of cloning in open-source as well as industrial software systems. Our results show that non-identical clones require more attention regarding clone management compared to identical clones as they are the dominating clone type for the main share of our subject systems. Using the evolution model to investigate costs and benefits of refactorings that remove clones, we conclude that clone removals could not reduce maintenance costs for most systems under study.

In addition, we performed a controlled experiment on the effect of clone information on the performance of developers fixing cloned bugs. Our findings indicate that the absence of clone information can be compensated through testing and that developers may exploit semantic code relations to uncover cloned defects. However, if cloned defects lurk in semantically unrelated locations, participants also used the search mechanism of an integrated development environment to find certain keywords. Based on that observation we present an approximative code search allowing to search for arbitrary code fragments in a system's history. We evaluated our technique for real-world defects of various large and realistic systems showing that it scales and may help in detecting situations where a defect-correcting change was not propagated to all necessary parts of the system.

Zusammenfassung

Redundanzen im Quelltext von Softwareprogrammen, sogenannte Softwareklone (kurz: Klone), sind ein regelmäßig auftretendes Phänomen. Ein weit verbreiteter Glaube ist, dass Softwareklone die Wartbarkeit von Softwaresystemen negativ beeinflussen und sich Softwareentwickler aus diesem Grund aktiv um diese Klone kümmern sollten. Im Gegensatz zu dieser Annahme hat die jüngste Forschung auf diesem Gebiet gezeigt, dass nicht alle Klone als schädlich zu klassifizieren sind. Eine hinreichende Bewertung der Effekte von Klonen auf die Wartbarkeit von Software sowie eine Kosten-Nutzen-Analyse von aktivem Klonmanagement sind der Schlüssel zu einem besseren Verständnis von Softwareklonen.

Diese Arbeit führt Techniken zur Modellierung, Analyse und Evaluation verschiedener Aspekte von Softwareklonen während der Evolution eines Softwaresystems ein. Es wird eine Abbildung von nicht identischen Klonen zwischen aufeinander folgenden Versionen einer Software vorgestellt. Diese Abbildung löst das Problem einer möglichen mehrdeutigen Abbildung von nicht identischen Klonen aus vorangegangenen Arbeiten. Obwohl das vorgestellte Verfahren zusätzliche Daten verarbeitet, um eine Mehrdeutigkeit zu verhindern, ist es effizient genug und kann zur retrospektiven Analyse großer Softwaresysteme verwendet werden.

In dieser Arbeit werden mehrere Studien beschrieben, in denen das Abbildungsverfahren zum Einsatz kommt, um verschiedene Aspekte von Softwareklonen sowohl in Open-Source-Systemen als auch in industriellen Systemen zu untersuchen. Die Ergebnisse dieser Studien zeigen, dass nicht identische Klone der dominierende Klontyp sind, da sie in den untersuchten Systemen die Mehrheit aller erkannten Klone darstellen. In Hinblick auf eine Kosten-Nutzen-Analyse während der Evolution eines Systems hat sich gezeigt, dass die Kosten von Quelltextrefaktorisierungen in den meisten Fällen höher sind als mögliche Nutzen.

Diese Arbeit stellt darüber hinaus ein kontrolliertes Experiment vor, das den Einfluss von Kloninformationen auf die Korrektur von geklonten Defekten untersucht. Beobachtungen deuten darauf hin, dass fehlende Kloninformationen durch sorgfältiges Testen als auch durch die Berücksichtigung semantischer Quelltextbeziehungen kompensiert werden können. Befanden sich die geklonten Defekte jedoch in semantisch voneinander unabhängigen Orten im Quelltext, griffen viele der Teilnehmer zusätzlich auf vorhandene Suchmechanismen der Entwicklungsumgebung zurück, um mit Hilfe specifischer Schlüsselwörter nach Klonen eines bereits entdeckten Defekts zu suchen. Basierend auf dieser Beobachtung stellt diese Arbeit einen

Suchalgorithmus und dessen Implementierung vor, die es erlauben, nach gleichen oder ähnlichen Quelltextausschnitten in der gesamten Historie eines Systems zu suchen. Die Implementierung wurde für reale Defekte in großen und ebenfalls realen Softwaresystemen evaluiert. Die Ergebnisse dieser Evaluation zeigen, dass der Suchalgorithmus sowohl für große Systeme skaliert als auch in der Lage ist, die Suche nach unvollständig durchgeführten Korrekturen von Defekten zu unterstützen.

Table of Contents

Part I

Prelude

Chapter 1

Introduction

Software is an important part of modern life and its relevance is steadily increasing day by day. There is a very wide range of applications for all kinds of situations that depend on appropriate software to run correctly. Accordingly, demands can be fairly high and complex which implicates likewise high and complex demands to software and its development. In addition, software is very often intended to be used for a long period of time, and therefore, cannot be considered a classical throwaway product. For that reason, continously working on the source code of a software system is an integral part of its lifecycle. Work that is performed after delivery to correct defects, improve certain attributes, or to adapt the functionality to new or changed requirements is denoted as software maintenance.

Boehm showed in a large scale empirical study that the effort needed to develop and deploy the initial version of a software system is relatively small compared to the effort spent on its subsequent maintenance [37]. The effort needed to perform specific maintenance tasks, for instance, adding new functionality to the code base, is strongly depending on a software's source code quality. The higher the code quality the higher the chances to successfully use and maintain software over a long period of time. In contrast, low code quality will most probably cause slinking software erosion until the system is not maintainable anymore. Code segments that are known or assumed to reduce software quality, thus, increasing maintenance effort are denoted as bad smells. Fowler and Beck ranked different bad smells in their so called *stink parade of bad smells* based on the harmfulness of each smell on the code quality and judged code clones to be the worst [81]. This claim initiated or at least inspired the field of code clone research.

Code clones are redundancies in the source code, that is, identical or similar code fragments occurring in the source code multiple times at different locations. Various studies showed that code clones are a common phenomenon in software systems, often caused by copy-and-paste programming. Copy-and-paste programming is usually performed by developers to speed up the development process by reusing existing code. The main advantages are that existing code is generally assumed to be more reliable since it is part of an already running system and that reusing it is faster compared to starting from scratch every time—even if the existing code is used as a starting point only and needs to be adapted to suite the desired functionality. Nonetheless, these are basically short-term benefits that come along with a possible threat to software maintenance in the long term. Concerns are that maintenance activities such as code comprehension, actual changes to the code, and testing have to be performed multiple times for code duplications—in the worst case for each single clone instance. This approach may increase maintenance effort and, moreover, may be error-prone as the developer has to be aware of all clone instances to avoid unwanted inconsistencies when performing changes. Due to these drawbacks Fowler and Beck suggest to refactor cloned code by removing them using appropriate abstractions.

In contrast to the initial claim of Fowler and Beck clone research has shown that code redundancies cannot be considered a threat to software maintenance in general [139, 150, 187]. Thus, it is rather a question of whether and how to actively manage clones instead of trying to avoid or remove them all. Clone management refers to detecting, tracking, and analyzing code duplications to gather valuable information that helps to make a well-founded decision regarding costs and benefits of specific clone instances. To support developers to keep track of and handle clones, plenty of clone management tools have been introduced that detect clones, support refactorings and change propagation as well as monitoring to prevent unwanted inconsistencies. The efficiency of such tools has been successively improved over the years so that even very large systems can be efficiently analyzed. Still, clone management has not yet become an integral part of the daily work of developers [102].

It is desirable that clone management supports the user to identify and refactor harmful clones only, however, in reality the user is exposed to a vast number of clone instances because results provided by state-of-the-art clone tools are based on only structural similarity. Assessing every code clone from the result set manually is neither feasible. An automated relevance ranking of detected clones based on a cost-benefit analysis would eliminate or at least mitigate this problem. The studies presented in this thesis investigate this issue from different perspectives.

1.1   Problem Statement

> *"Cloning Considered Harmful" Considered Harmful*
>
> — Kapser & Godfrey [139]

Even though research has shown that clones have a negative effect on maintainability in certain cases, overall there is still not sufficient evidence that cloned code causes indeed more maintenance effort than appropriate abstractions in general. Therefore, it is essential to support developers distinguishing between relevant and irrelevant clones with respect to costs and benefits for software maintenance.

1.1.1   Clone Rates

Focusing on automated clone detection research proved the existence of code clones in software in its early stages. Nonetheless, the extent of cloning remained rather blurry, because varying clone-rate numbers ranging between about 20% and about 60% have been reported for different software systems under study [24, 75]. Reasons for the disparity of detected clone rates are that different clone-detection techniques have been used among studies and that the studies have commonly been based on quite small datasets. Therefore, findings can neither be compared with one another nor unified to build a more comprehensive dataset. A better understanding of the extent of cloning helps to pin down the impact of clones on software maintenance—small clone rates most probably indicate that the impact is rather arguable whereas high clone rates imply the opposite. Thus, a large scale analysis of clone rates in software systems is needed to answer this very basic question.

1.1.2   Clone Evolution

Using an adequate model keeping track of clones throughout multiple versions of a software represents their individual evolution paths within the version history of the source code. We refer to a version as a snapshot of a program's source code at a given time. Accordingly we denote a version at a particular point of time i as v_i. Information on the evolution of clones enables the quantitative and qualitative analysis of certain characteristics which are not available by considering a single snapshot of the source code only. Attributes provided by the evolution are mainly related to changes applied to clones, that is, how clones have been changed over time in terms of size, complexity, and location. Previous studies on clone evolution provided valuable insights already but focused on identical clone instances only. Similar clones have been widely neglected by research yet. Hence, we need to track and analyze similar clones to assess to what extent they occur in software systems and how they differ from identical clones.

1.1.3   Relevant Clones

Despite ongoing improvements in clone detection and other clone management tools, such as tools to graphically visualize various attributes of cloned code, there are still challenges that make active clone management impractical in daily business. The main hindrance is the large number of clone data detected and presented to the user. Yet, no characteristics of clone fragments could be identified to be useful in ranking the large amount of clones supporting users to filter and concentrate on the interesting clones only. Such a ranking may uncover that a large share of detected clones is not of interest in many situations. Experiences with traditional clone detection techniques show that ranking clones appropriately is complex. Probably, further characteristics of clones need to be investigated, to realize an automated filtering and ranking. Accordingly, code redundancies need to be investigated using additional strategies as well. Retrospective analysis of clones removed deliberately or accidentally by developers might uncover characteristics that have been crucial from their point of view to classify a clone as unwanted and refactor the corresponding source code fragments. Another factor that has been disregarded in the past is whether evidence can be found that such clone removals pay off in the long run. To investigate this factor, it is required to track and analyze source code affected by clones beyond clone removing refactorings.

Besides considering relevant characteristics of cloned code, a relevance ranking of detected clones ideally considers demands and work habits of developers since developers are the ones supposed to use clone management tools in the first place. Only little effort has been spent in clone research to investigate human interaction when dealing with clones. Especially human-based controlled experiments are well suited and yet widely neglected to extend previous work on the use of clone information from a developers point of view.

1.2   Terminology

> *Clones are segments of code that are similar according to some definition of similarity.*
>
> — Ira Baxter (2002)

The statement by Ira Baxter at an international workshop towards the detection of software clones reveals a vagueness and difficulty of giving a precise and universal definition of code clones. Although his statement points out the important qualifier of similarity, it fails in giving a specification of it. In fact, there is no generally accepted specification of what a software clone exactly is [135]. Research in the field of software clones brought up different interpretations mainly based on the underlying detection approach used to find clones that are relevant in a specific context. Basically, a clone can be considered the redundant occurrence of any kind of software artifacts, such as source code or requirement specifications. The main focus of this thesis, however, is on duplicated source code as this work investigates the effect of clones on the maintainability of source code. However, the similarity between code fragments forming clones of each other is not uniquely defined as indicated in "some definition of similarity" by Ira Baxter.

In this section we will introduce the fundamental terminology required to understand the phenomenon of cloning. This will help us in characterizing software clones and drawing a working definition for this thesis. This thesis was created in the *Software Engineering Group* at the *University of Bremen*. Accordingly, the following concepts and terminologies have been developed and introduced together with other researchers of the same working group and can be found in various publications by Falke, Göde, Harder, and Koschke.

1.2.1   Token

A token is the smallest lexical unit of the respective programming language. Among the tokens of a programming language are keywords, identifiers, literals, operators, and preprocessor statements. Whitespaces and comments are excluded in our definition. Each token has a type denoting the lexical unit it represents, for instance, the type *identifier* in case it represents a variable name. Additionally, it may also hold a value corresponding to its actual character sequence appearing in the source code, for instance, *"foo"* in case of a variable name. Since each lexical unit can be represented by a token, the source code of each source file, and therefore, of a whole software system can be represented by sequences of tokens. In this thesis we use a token-based clone detector to investigate different facets of software clones.

1.2.2   Code Fragment

A code fragment denotes a unique and contiguous code sequence located in a single source file. Based on the definition of a token, a code fragment can also be understood as a unique and contiguous sequence of tokens. Accordingly, each code fragment is defined as a triple

$$fragment(file, start, end)$$

with the following attributes:

- **file:** unique file in which the code fragment is located

- **start:** index of the first token which is part of the code fragment

- **end:** reference to the last token which is part of the code fragment

Thus, all fragments between *start* and *end* are part of the code fragment. Since stating the start and end position by pointing to the first and last token of a code fragment is comprehensible only to some extent for humans, these attributes are used in the algorithms only. To present results to a user these values are replaced by more understandable line and column information.

A software clone consists of at least two similar code fragments, but may also consist of several similar code fragments forming a group. In the context of cloned code we will use the term *clone fragment* when referring to a code fragment as one instance of a software clone.

1.2.3   Clone Pair

A clone pair denotes a software clone consisting of exactly two code fragments. Hereby, the clone fragments may be identical or just similar to a certain extent. The similarity between the fragments is used to specify a clone pair type (we will describe clone types in more detail in Section 1.2.5). Hence, a clone pair is described by the following triple:

$$clone\_pair(fragment_A, fragment_B, type)$$

Using the concept of clone pairs to describe software clones in a system, code fragments are grouped into multiple clone pairs.

Example 1.1 – If three different clone fragments $fragment_A$, $fragment_B$, and $fragment_C$ are found to be identical, than their clone relation can be expressed by three clone pairs consisting of $fragment_A$ and $fragment_B$, $fragment_A$ and $fragment_C$, and $fragment_B$ and $fragment_C$, respectively. □

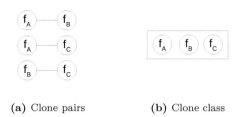

(a) Clone pairs   (b) Clone class

Figure 1.1 – Comparing the representation of clone relations between clone fragments using clone pairs 1.1a and clone classes 1.1b based on Example 1.1.

1.2.4 Clone Class

Clone pairs are well suited to represent software clones consisting of exactly two clone fragments. They are not well suited, however, if a clone relation is to be drawn between more than two clone fragments, because several clone pairs are needed to represent all the relations. More precisely, $n \times (n-1)/2$ clone pairs are necessary to draw all clone relations between n clone fragments. An example is given in Example 1.1. To be able to represent the clone relation among more than two clone fragments in a more compact way compared to clone pairs, clone fragments may be grouped in clone classes. A clone class includes a group of clone fragments of the same clone type—which is equivalent to the transitive closure over all clone pair relations of the clone fragments. Thus, a clone class is defined as

$$clone\_class(fragment_1, ..., fragment_n, type)$$

.

with n being the number of fragments that are clones of each other and $n > 1$. The compact representation of clone relations among clone fragments is important since the major share of studies found that the systems under study showed that code fragments are often cloned multiple times. In addition, the concept allows a more intuitive representation by using one entity that spans all code fragments being clones of each other at one spot. Figure 1.1 compares clone pairs and clone classes using Example 1.1 as given before.

1.2.5 Clone Type

A clone type is used to specify the degree of similarity between two or more clone fragments that are clones of each other. In this thesis, we consider four different clone types introduced by Bellon and colleagues [33]. For all clone types the relation between the clone fragments of a clone pair is symmetric:

$$clone\_pair(f_A, f_B, type) = clone\_pair(f_B, f_A, type)$$

In addition, the relation is transitive for type-1 and type-2 (described below) clones:

$$clone\_pair(f_A, f_B, type) \wedge clone\_pair(f_A, f_C, type) \Rightarrow clone\_pair(f_B, f_C, type)$$

```
1   int sum = 0;              1   int sum = 0;
2   sum = sum + 2;            2   sum = sum + 2;
3   // Comment                3
4   return sum;               4   return sum;
```

(a) fragment_A   (b) fragment_B

Figure 1.2 – A type-1 clone. The light grey box indicates a difference between the fragments, however, comments and whitespaces are commonly ignored by clone detectors.

That is, the existence of clone pairs $clone\_pair(f_A, f_B, type)$ and $clone\_pair(f_A, f_C, type)$ requires the clone pair $clone\_pair(f_B, f_C, type)$ to exist as well.

Type-1 Clones

Clone fragments form a type-1 clone if they are completely identical which is why they are often also referred to as identical or exact clones. The token sequences of clone fragments have to be the same regarding their type as well their value to be type-1 clones of each other. Only comments and whitespaces are disregarded during the comparison since they generally do not appear as tokens. Figure 1.2 shows an example of a clone of type 1.

Type-2 Clones

In contrast to type-1 clones, the token sequences of clone fragments being clones of type-2 of each other are not required to be identical regarding their token values but token types only. By disregarding the token values in the comparison, clones of type 2 abstract from literals, identifiers, and operators. Therefore, type-2 clones are often introduced in the source code by renamings performed to adapt code to different contexts. Clones of type 2 can be further distinguished in type-2 clones with consistent and inconsistent renaming, respectively. A consistent renaming denotes type-2 clones for which identifiers and literals were changed consistently between clone fragments, that is, each identifier or literal of *fragment$_A$* can be assigned to one identifier or literal of *fragment$_B$*— resulting in a bijective mapping of them. This relation does not exist for inconsistently renamed type-2 clones, thus, identifiers or literals may be renamed differently within a clone fragment. Baker presented an algorithm to detect consistently renamed type-2 clones [13]. An example of a type-2 clone with consistent renaming is given in Figure 1.3. Figure 1.4 shows the same example, but with an inconsistent renaming of identifiers.

Type-3 Clones

In contrast to clones of type 2, clones of type 3 may exhibit further differences between clone fragments than renamings. Changes leading to type-3 clones are basically source code insertions, deletions, and modifications or a combination of the preceding. There is

```
1   int  sum = 0;              1   int  result = 0;
2   sum = sum + 2;            2   result = result + 2;
3   // Comment                3
4   return sum;               4   return  result;
```

(a) *fragment$_A$*   (b) *fragment$_B$*

Figure 1.3 – A type-2 clone with consistent renaming. The dashed boxes indicate renamings.

```
1   int  sum = 0;              1   int  s = 0;
2   sum = sum + 2;            2   result = s + 2;
3   // Comment                3
4   return sum;               4   return  result;
```

(a) *fragment$_A$*   (b) *fragment$_B$*

Figure 1.4 – A type-2 clone with inconsistent renaming.

no limitation towards the type of differences caused by such changes, but rather to their extent. That is, most clone detection tools use some kind of threshold limiting the size of unequal tokens allowed between clone fragments such that they are still considered clones of each other. Type-3 clones with only little modifications as well as type-2 clones are also referred to as near-miss clones—indicating that they are close to being identical clones.

Often type-1 and type-2 clones become to type-3 clones due to modifications that interrupt the sequence of equal tokens at certain locations within the clone fragments. These interruption of unequal token subsequences are commonly referred to as gaps. Accordingly, type-3 clones are called gapped clones as well. Clones of type 3 can be understood as clones assembled by a number of neighboring type-1 and type-2 clones with non-cloned code (gaps) in between of these. There are different techniques that use this fact by first detecting clones of type 1 and 2 followed by a postprocessing step to identify which of the detected clone fragments can be put together when tolerating gaps of a certain size to build larger type-3 clones.

Type-3 clones are often of high interest to researchers and developers because it is assumed that an inconsistent or incomplete propagation of changes, for example, a bug fix, to all instances of a type-1 or type-2 clone is an origin of type-3 clones. Figure 1.5 shows an example of a type-3 clone.

Type-4 Clones

While clones from type 1 to 3 are defined based on syntactic similarity using their token sequences, clones of type 4 share the same or similar semantic, though, being syntactically different. Unfortunately, the semantic equivalence of clone fragments is

```
1   int sum = 0;
2   sum = sum + 2;
3   // Comment
4   return sum;
```

(a) fragment_A

```
1   int sum = 0;
2   int i = 2;
3   sum = sum + i;
4
5   return sum;
```

(b) fragment_B

Figure 1.5 – A type-3 clone. Due to the additional line in fragment_B (denoted by a light grey box) the fragments exhibit differences other than comments and whitespaces.

```
1   int sum = 0;
2
3   for(int i=0; i<=100; i++) {
4       sum = sum + i;
5   }
6   return sum; // Comment
```

(a) fragment_A

```
1   int sum = 0;
2   int counter = 0;
3
4   while(counter < 101) {
5       sum += counter;
6       counter++;
7   }
8   return sum;
```

(b) fragment_B

Figure 1.6 – A type-4 clone.

not feasible using automated approaches. Only little research, for instance, towards an automated detection, is directed to this clone type compared to the preceding types. In this thesis we do not consider this clone type as there is no reliable way of locating such clones yet. A common reason of type-4 clones is the use of different concepts of a programming language to solve the same task. Conditional loops are a good example of using different syntactical constructs to implement the same logic. An example of the use of different loops that are semantically the same, thus, being type-4 clones of each other is given in Figure 1.6.

1.3   Contributions

The contributions of this thesis are severalfold. In the following an overview according to the research problems is given.

1.3.1   Clone Rates

We conducted a large scale analysis of code clones in 9,872 open-source projects written in the programming languages C, C++, C# and Java, summing up to 310 MLOC to answer the question of the extent of cloning in software systems more comprehensively. Furthermore, we search for correlations among file or project size and clone rate. Using statistical analysis we estimate the means and variances of clone rates and their likely type of frequency distribution [159].

1.3.2   Clone Evolution

In this thesis, we investigate in which ways the evolution of non-identical clones differs from the evolution of identical clones. By analyzing several open source systems we draw comparisons between identical and non-identical clones. To investigate the evolution of clones, we present an extension of the clone mapping technique suggested by Göde [87] that is capable of mapping non-identical clones between consecutive versions in the context of their clone class. Based on the introduced mapping, we present quantitative and qualitative empirical data on the evolution of identical and non-identical clones. Moreover, we investigate the impact of different parameter settings of a clone detector on the evolution of both clone types [26, 27].

1.3.3   Clone Removals

We conducted a comprehensive study on clone removals to extend previous research in this field. Analyzing not only deliberate but also accidental removals of code duplications in software systems, we investigated several characteristics of clone removing refactorings [29].

   We used the information of clone removing refactorings in a follow-up study to investigate source code that was affected by such a refactoring over a certain period of time [28, 31]. To do so, the evolution model by Göde [87] has been adopted to track arbitrary source code fragments in multiple versions of a software system and has been implemented in the clone-visualization tool CYCLONE. Investigating source code that has been introduced in consequence of refactorings performed to remove existing code duplications over multiple versions allows to analyze different aspects, e. g., the change frequency of such code, to provide valuable insights towards a more accurate cost-benefit analysis of code clones compared to corresponding abstractions.

1.3.4   Usability of Clone Data

We performed a human-based controlled experiment to analyze the approach and performance of developers in common bug-fixing tasks in case clone information are provided by a tool. We set up the experiment such that we ensured the clone tool provided mainly helpful data but still real-world software has been selected as subject systems to emulate a realistic scenario. A controlled experiment provides data on how developers use clone data which helps to gain insights towards the issue of delivering just relevant clone information to the user. Among other findings, the results of the experiment showed that developers often tend to search for specific keywords when trying to find locations of duplicated bugs [30].

   Suiting the observations of the human-based study, we presented an approach for efficiently finding approximate matches of an arbitrary code fragment in the version history of a program's source code and implemented it in the tool APPROX. The underlying algorithm combines concepts used in approximate text search as well as clone detection. Before, code search just allowed for searching in single versions either defining single keywords or a complete source code line, however, it was not possible to search for similar code fragments encompassing multiple lines. Evaluating our approach for real-world defects of various large and realistic programs having multiple releases and branches, we report runtime measurements and recall using varying levels of tolerated differences of the approximate search [32].

1.4   Project Context

Most parts of this thesis were performed in the context of the project "Empirical Research on approaches and development of tools towards cost-effective clone management" funded by the *Deutsche Forschungsgemeinschaft*[1] *(DFG)*. Various algorithms presented in this thesis were developed in the context of the *Bauhaus*[2] project. The *Bauhaus* project started 1997 as a research collaboration between the Institute for Computer Science of the University of Stuttgart and the Frauenhofer Institute for Experimental Software Engineering in Kaiserslautern (IESE). Today, it is a collaboration between the University of Bremen, the University of Stuttgart and the commercial spin-off *Axivion*[3]. The *Bauhaus* project is a versatile toolkit for program analysis aiming at supporting engineers in maintaining a software system.

All technical achievements of this thesis were applied to and tested with a large number of realistic open-source software systems as well as with the *Bauhaus* project itself which is an industrial system.

1.5   Related Publications

A main share of the contents of this thesis was already published. This section lists these publications and the chapters indicating where the respective content occurs within this thesis. The articles (2) and (5) has been submitted to journals but are still in a peer-review process at the time this thesis were finished. All publications listed were mainly created by the author of this thesis. except for (1) and (2) which were collaborative work with others.

(1) **Software-Clone Rates in Open-Source Programs Written in C or C++ [159]**
    International Workshop on Software Clones, 2016
    Chapter 3

(2) **A Large-Scale Statistical Analysis of Software Clone Rates and Localization in Open-Source Programs Written in C, C++, C#, or Java [162]**

---

[1] http://www.dfg.de/en/
[2] http://www.bauhaus-stuttgart.de/bauhaus/index-english.html
[3] http://www.axivion.com/

Transactions on Software Engineering, 2016
Chapter 3

(3) **Evolution of Near-Miss Clones [26]**
International Working Conference on Source Code Analysis and Manipulation, 2012
Chapter 4

(4) **An Empirical Study of Clone Removals [29]**
International Conference on Software Maintenance, 2013
Chapter 5

(5) **No Clones, No Trouble? [28]**
International Workshop on Software Clones, 2013
Chapter 5

(6) **Clone removals and their return on investment [31]**
Journal of Software: Evolution and Process, 2015
Chapter 5

(7) **Effect of Clone Information on the Performance of Developers Fixing Cloned Bugs [30]**
Conference on Source Code Analysis and Manipulation, 2014
Chapter 6

(8) **Approximate Code Search in Program Histories [32]**
International Working Conference on Reverse Engineering, 2011
Chapter 7

1.6   Thesis Outline

This thesis is organized in four main parts.

Part I presents an introduction to the topic of this thesis and gives a working definition to the notion software clones. Chapter 2 provides an extensive overview of previous work on software clones. It contains root causes for their existence, effects they have on a system, existing detection approaches, and further clone management activities. Based on the analysis of previous research we point out open questions which are answered in subsequent sections of this thesis.

Part II provides the techniques introduced to extract clone data needed to investigate the aforementioned research questions. It also presents the different case studies performed within the scope of this thesis using these techniques. Our comprehensive analysis of clone rates in open-source software is presented in Chapter 3. Chapter 4 is concerned with the extraction of data related to the evolution of identical and non-identical clones over time. Our approach to identify clone removing refactorings and track code fragments that have been introduced in the course of these is presented in Chapter 5. Our controlled experiment on the effect of clone information on the performance of developers when fixing cloned defects is described in Chapter 6. Chapter 7 presents an efficient algorithm to detect approximative matches to user-defined code fragments in the entire history of a software system and our case study on its use and feasibility.

Part III provides the conclusions of this thesis. A summary of all findings and suggestions for future research are given in Chapter 8.

Chapter 2

Related Research

Software clones have been subject to many studies and are still an active field of research showing their importance to software maintenance. This chapter summarizes previous work on this topic. While some of the previous research is presented to describe the state-of-the-art, the work presented in this thesis is built upon and extends the other share of previous research. Based on the findings of the latter share, research questions will be elaborated that are subject of and will be answered in the course of this thesis. The outline of this chapter is as follows.

Section 2.1 states the root causes for cloning before its effects on software systems are examined in Section 2.2. Section 2.3 summarizes related research on clone rates and locality in software systems showing that cloning is an existing phenomenon. Clone detection techniques are described in detail in Section 2.4. Research on how to map and track cloned code across multiple versions of a system is presented in Section 2.5. Related work regarding changes applied to clones and patterns derived from these is presented in Section 2.6. Section 2.7 gives on overview of studies on the evolution of clones while Section 2.8.3 focuses on clone removals in particular. Further clone-management tasks are described in Section 2.8. Human-based studies are introduced in Section 2.9. Finally, Section 2.10 summarizes related work on the more general problem of detecting arbitrary code fragments.

A large number of publications have been presented in the field of software clone research. For a general overview reference is made to the surveys by Koschke [157] and Roy and colleagues [226], [229] and most recently by Roy, Zibran, and Koschke [231].

2.1 Causes

Although, software clones are still assumed to possibly decrease software quality and hence to be harmful in certain cases, they can still be found in rather large numbers in today's software. There are several root causes why developers either intentionally or unintentionally create cloned code. A very basic programming activity often yielding in clones is copy and paste programming. The idea of copy and paste programming is

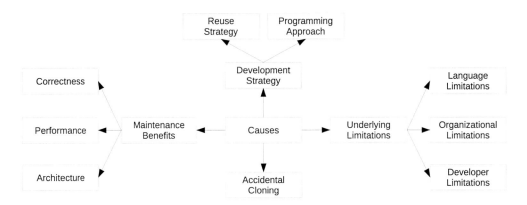

Figure 2.1 – Overview of the root causes and their relations as presented in this thesis.

to reuse existing solutions rather than reimplementing things that are supposed to be similar from scratch—true to the motto "Do not reinvent the wheel".

Among other publications on causes for software clones, Roy and Cordy [226] introduced four categories to describe the most common ones. In the following, we will adapt their classification to summarize reasons for cloning in software presented by previous studies. Figure 2.1 gives an overview of the causes and their relations as presented below.

2.1.1   Development Strategy

Developers may introduce software clones in a system based on the general programming approach followed.

Reuse Strategy

Cloning can be used as a simple mechanism to reuse existing source code and either leave it as is, adapt it to the context it is pasted to, or use it as a template for new functionality by applying further modifications. This approach of copying, pasting, and modifying existing code fragments is often an easy way to implement functionality for which similar solutions exist already. The customization of consciously copied code has been investigated by Kasper and Godfrey [139] who found three cloning patterns *forking*, *templating*, and *customization*. *Forking* denotes a cloning activity that is used to bootstrap development of similar solutions that are assumed to evolve independently from each other in the future. Since the clone fragments evolve independently, changes to one of the clone fragments does not necessarily need to be adapted to the other fragments too. In contrast, *templating* denotes the creation of clones due to a missing abstraction mechanism. That is, existing functionality is meant to be directly copied but appropriate abstractions are unavailable. Finally, the *customization* pattern relates to situations when existing code is similar to new requirements to a certain degree only, but does not meet them such that a plain copy could be used. Therefore, a copy of the existing code is used as starting point and tailored to meet the new set of requirements afterwards.

Programming Approach

The reuse strategy may be applied as an interim solution also. That is, developers clone existing code several times before performing a refactoring of the clone fragments. By delaying a refactoring of cloned code the variabilities of the clones can be captured more reliably. Trying to predict these is difficult and probably leads to an unnecessarily generic and flexible as well as complicated solution.

In some cases two software systems are merged to produce a new one encompassing the functionality of each of the single systems. In cases where both subsystems provide similar functionality the merging of them will result in the new system containing redundancies that have been created independently—possibly from different developers—from each other.

Very large software clones will likely be created when tools are used to generate code automatically. Such tools often use the same or similar formal specifications that generate the same or similar code fragments accordingly. A generative programming approach is commonly used to easily generate code that is highly repetitive instead of manually writing the recurring code fragments, for instance, to build graphical user interfaces. Though, these clones are not created by developers directly and often will not be maintained by them either.

Finally, a team of developers may agree on certain code conventions during the development of a system resulting in clones due to the fact that similar functionality is implemented in a defined way. Often rather small but repetitive code structures are affected by such guidelines, for instance, logging and exception handling or API usage.

2.1.2   Maintenance Benefits

In contrast to the wide spread assumption that software clones could harm the source code quality of a system, researchers indicate that clones can be beneficial in some situations.

Correctness

The reuse strategy of cloning existing solutions may be considered beneficial in terms of correctness. That is, it is a fast way of exploiting source code that is already known to be reliable. This holds especially for creating identical and near-miss clones of existing functionality. Based on the expected correctness of existing functionalities, the risk of introducing new defects is reduced. Accordingly, Cordy [55] reports that clones frequently occur in financial software systems as there are frequent updates and feature requests. However, changes are rather small and developers are asked to copy and adapt existing code because of the high risk in terms of monetary consequences in case of a defective system. Moreover, approaching new versions of such critical systems by cloning existing code reduces test effort by reusing code for which corresponding tests already exist. For example, Cordy reports that 70% of the effort on software development in the financial domain is spent on testing. In another study, Kim and colleagues [148] cite simple cloning as a method to implement cross-cutting concerns.

Similarly, Kasper and Godfrey [139] observed that cloning was used by developers to avoid adapting existing code to meet new requirements. The developers assessed the risk of breaking existing functionality by changing the corresponding source code too high and rather chose to leave such code as is [99]. Instead, clones have been introduced to implement new behavior. Godfrey and Tu [98] found that this approach is also used to guarantee downward compatibility of certain modules, for instance, drivers. Zhang and colleagues [271] conducted an interview which confirmed this observation as 42.9% of developers participating reported to avoid changing and with that possibly breaking existing functionality by creating clones of the corresponding code fragments.

Performance

In certain cases cloned code may contribute to the performance of a system. Using cloning the number of method calls can be decreased by copying and pasting relevant code fragments to the corresponding locations in the source code [11]. Refactorings, for instance, performing an *Extract Method*, that would remove these redundancies and replace the clone fragments by method calls to a newly introduced code fragment are undesired in these cases. Method calls are too costly in highly optimized systems in particular. For example, embedded and real-time software systems. The only alternative to cloning in such systems is using compilers offering automated inlining of the code. However, an appropriate compiler is not always available or cannot be used due to other dependencies.

Architecture

Kapser and Godfrey [139] found software clones to be used in order to keep the software architecture clean and understandable. Using abstractions such as polymorphism may complicate the implementation of functionality that could be realized more straightforwardly using clones. This finding contradicts the assumption of clones decreasing the code quality in terms of understandability in certain cases at least.

Related to the architecture design, developing product variants is strongly related to the creation of clones also. If functionality is missing in an existing system that is specifically required in a certain domain and it is not predictable whether future requests will make a common abstraction a possible solution, an independent instance of the system is created and adapted to the corresponding requirements [74]. This strategy is widely used to develop software product lines. The instances of software product lines share a common code base among each other.

2.1.3   Overcoming Underlying Limitations

Sometimes creating software clones is the only option due to different kinds of limitations. These limitations can be of technical but also of organizational or social nature.

Language Limitations

Limitations and shortcomings of a programming language often force developers to create cloned code. Such limitations and shortcomings are mainly due to missing or insufficient abstraction mechanisms, e.g., inheritance or generic types [139, 148, 150]. Especially in older programming languages such as assembly or COBOL further concepts, e.g., parameter passing, may be missing which enforces the creation of clones. Consequently, developers are required to redundantly implement related code fragments as idioms. Patenaude [21, 217] and colleagues showed that such idioms create rather small clones on the one hand, but on the other hand they potentially occur frequently. Similarly, frameworks and other technical aspects beyond the programming language may make cloning inevitable.

Organizational Limitations

Besides the choice of a programming language and other technical factors, cloning may be caused by architectural design decision. Dependencies between certain subsystems may not allow gathering code fragments providing similar functionality at a single place. For instance, this could be the case, when the packages requiring similar functionality do not share access rights to any existing location and introducing a new package for this purpose only is to costly or disagrees with the desired architecture. Thus, the functionality has to be implemented at both packages by cloning the corresponding code.

Moreover, access rights may cause software clones when a developer is not able to modify parts of the existing implementation, for instance, third-party libraries maintained by someone else. Asking for permissions usually takes a certain amount of time, if granted at all, and is disregarded in favor of creating clones that overwrite the original implementation and provide the desired functionality right away [271]. The same approach was found to be used when defects needed to be fixed but the defective code fragments were not accessible to the developers [139]. Except for access rights, the interaction within a team and between individual developers can also be a factor encouraging a cloning strategy, for example, to avoid discussions [271].

Organizational limits often relate to time and budget available to finish tasks as well. These factors may put developers under certain pressure such that they prefer to use fast ways in implementing features. Code quality in terms of finding abstractions and writing reusable code that could be advantageous in the future fade from the spotlight. That is, creating clones is often less complex and, hence, less time consuming—at least in the short term. In an developer interview conducted by Zhang and colleagues this assumption was confirmed by the participants [271]. Similarly, the performance of some developers is assessed by the amount of code they write in a particular time. This may encourage them to create clones because an appropriate abstraction of several clone fragments probably contributes less code [11, 75].

Developer's Limitations

In comparison to being compelled to copy code based on technical limitations, there are also limitations regarding the experience, skills and motivation of developers causing software clones. Reusing existing code may be induced by an unawareness or simple ignorance of best practices. That is, they just do not know how to use abstractions, for instance, polymorphism or even basic method extraction, or prefer to copy and paste instead—since it is less complicated and time consuming in the short-term. Furthermore, there may be an inability to understand and, therefore, extend existing code already providing the desired functionality. As a result duplications are facilitated. Though, most publications clearly suggest to avoid cloning because it is considered bad practice still and give advice to avoid clones [81, 192]. Experience show that the less skilled developers are the more they tend to clone existing code [271].

Cloning can also be used to experiment while introducing new features without taking the risk of breaking the existing code [139]. Following this explorative approach, the relevant code fragments are temporally copied and modified independently from the production code. As soon as a proper and final solution is found and appropriate abstractions are apparent, the clones can be removed and the modifications applied to the production code [148, 150]. Figuring out correct implementations using explorative programming was named a reason to create clones by 42.9% of the developers interviewed by Zhang and colleagues [271]. Although, such clones are meant to exist a limited time only, there is the risk that their refactoring is omitted because of time pressure or a certain laziness to refactore code actually working. Hence, these clones will remain in the system.

2.1.4   Cloning By Accident

Apart from development strategies and technical or organizational limitations that are considered intentional cloning, software clones may be created unintentionally as well. Common code and programming patterns that are idiomatic contribute to the unintentional creation of cloned code. Although, such code fragments are not necessarily created by copy-and-paste programming they occur quite frequently throughout the source code of a system [139]. Examples of such idioms are among others: usage of API and library protocols or logging.

Finally, working on the same system with several developers (in a team) may yield in redundancies when individual developers implement type-4 clones independently from each other without being aware of it. Missing knowledge about activities of other developers bears also the risk of inconsistent changes to already existing clones [18, 24, 91, 134].

2.2   Effects

There are different causes for the creation of software clones showing that developers copy and paste both intentionally and unintentionally and that cloning cannot always be avoided for different reasons. Since it is certain that duplicated code occurs in real life, the main question is what effects they have on a system. In particular, it is valuable to determine whether their consequences are negative. Indeed, there are plausible arguments that redundancies in the source code decrease the code quality and increase maintenance effort, accordingly. Fowler and Beck initiated an intensive research on software clones by arguing that duplications are harmful in general and should, therefore, be removed whenever possible. For this reason, code cloning is the number one code smell on their stink parade of bad smells in software [81].

Hordijk and colleagues [114] gathered empirical data from existing research to shed light on the effects of software clones on maintainability. Based on their review a hypothesized causal model as shown in Figure 2.2 was presented. The casual model identifies four different aspects of code duplication that have an effect on software maintenance, in particular on the occurrence of errors and the overall changeability of software. The four aspects can be divided into two groups based on which maintenance activity they affect. If code duplications cause changes related to cloned code, the authors talk about *Co-Changes* or *Inconsistent Changes* according to whether clone fragments need to be changed in the same way or not. In contrast, clones that affect the effort required for code analysis rather than for changing clone fragments are categorized *Code Comprehension* or *Code Size*. In addition to the four categories, they also draw a direct link between code duplication and the changeability of a system. The direct relationship refers to studies investigating a correlation between clones and the change rate of code assuming that cloned code causes more changes. We believe that these direct links are either due to consistent or inconsistent changes that fall under the *Co-Change* or the *Inconsistent Change* pattern, respectively. Thus, we will use the four patterns *Co-Change, Inconsistent Change, Code Comprehension*, and *Code Size* presented in the hypothesized causal model to discuss the consequences of cloning on the correctness and the changeability of software systems.

2.2.1 Co-Change and Inconsistent Change

A *Co-Change* pattern describes situations where at least two clone fragments of the same clone class need to be changed in the same way due to the same change request. That is, they are changed consistently and, hence, it is guaranteed they remain clones of each other after the changes are performed. It may also happen that clone fragments change in the same way due to completely different change request. However, such accidentally consistent changes are rather unlikely and can be disregarded. The opposite is the case for the *Inconsistent Change* pattern. That is, at least two clone fragments of the same clone class are changed differently in consequence of the same change request.

Both change patterns may increase maintenance effort. *Co-Changes* obviously cause more effort since changes need to be applied to multiple clone fragments on each change request related to cloned code. *Inconsistent Changes* are assumed to be error-prone, because unintended inconsistencies in clones may create new bugs or, on the other hand, miss the propagation of a bug fix to all clone fragments. Inconsistent changes may also increase the effort needed for future consistent changes to all clone fragments of a clone class.

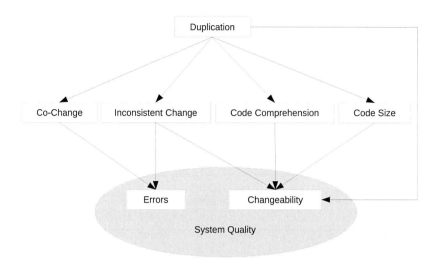

Figure 2.2 – Hypothesized casual model of the effects of software clones on the maintainability of a system by Hordijk and colleagues [114].

Different studies have been conducted to provide empirical data towards the frequency of consistent and inconsistent changes to cloned code [7, 18, 93, 149, 150, 164, 250, 266]. Based on the analyses of various software systems, findings show that both the *Co-Change* and the *Inconsistent Change* patterns occur frequently. Rates between 36% [150] and 74% [7] for consistent changes were reported. Numbers reported on inconsistent changes were smaller, ranging from 13% to 55%. Aversano and colleagues investigated the number of unintended inconsistencies that were resolved later [7]. They found between 13% and 16% of such change patterns which can be considered delayed applications of the *Co-Change* pattern, however. In contrast to the previous studies, Göde and Koschke [93] as well as Wang and Godfrey [262] found that inconsistent changes to clone fragments outnumbered the consistent ones. Nonetheless, changes to cloned code were rare all in all [93].

Studies also investigated in which situations change pattern occur more frequently. Kim and colleagues compared clones they assessed refactorable to those being difficult or not to refactor, concluding that refactorable clones tend to live longer and require consistent changes more frequently [149, 150]. Findings by Kim and colleagues were confirmed by Saha and colleagues in a large study on changes to clones at release level [233]. Geiger and colleagues found files with high clone coupling to be changed more often in the same version on average compared to other files [83]. However, they did not investigate whether the changes actually affected cloned or non-cloned code and if the same changes were performed in other files as well. Observing changes to clones at different granularity, Aversano and colleagues found that more class-level clones were consistently changed compared to clones of block and method granularity [7]. Focusing on method level, Lozano and colleagues reported that methods are changed more often during periods in which they contain cloned code than during periods they do not

[186, 187]. Contrary to other findings, their results also suggest that the *Co-Change* pattern occurs less frequently for method pairs during periods in which they have a cloning relation than during periods in which they have not. Finally, Mondal and colleagues investigated to what degree co-changes are scattered over the source code [201]. Analyzing twelve software systems the results were different with respect to the programming language of the systems. For Java and C changes to cloned code had a higher dispersion and the opposite was the case for systems written in C#.

The relation between consecutive changes to the same clone class was investigated by Göde and Harder [91]. They introduced the term of a change pair denoting reoccurring co-changes to the same clone class. Analyzing three systems their results showed that change pairs occurred in only 6% to 17% of all subject genealogies, thus, indicating they are very rare. Distinguishing between consistent and inconsistent changes, it was found that 37% to 41% of the change pairs consisted of two consecutive consistent changes. Change pairs formed by consistent changes followed by an inconsistent change occurred slightly less with 29% to 33%. Consecutive inconsistent changes constituted the smallest group with only 18% to 22% of occurrences—most of them being intentionally inconsistent.

Krinke conducted a study on co-changes in five open-source systems reporting that roughly half of the changes to clones were applied consistently where the other half were applied inconsistently [164]. Furthermore, he found that most inconsistencies remained in the systems. Göde replicated and extended this study and found frequent inconsistent changes as well, but many of them made consistent by late propagation [87]. Both suggested that some of the inconsistent changes probably caused defects, but did not empirically verify this fact. This assumption, however, could not be observed in a follow-up study by Göde and Koschke [94]. Analyzing the evolution of three software systems, it was found that only about 13% of all genealogies changed at all and from these slightly less than 15% could be verified of being unintentionally changed inconsistently. Based on these findings the authors conclude that bugs due to inconsistent changes to cloned code are rather infrequent. A similar result was presented by Monden and colleagues comparing the number of defects per line in files containing cloned code to files without clones [205]. It was found that files with small clones are less faulty than files without any cloned code. On the other hand, files containing clones that are 200 lines of size at least had the highest defect density measured.

Li and colleagues analyzed whether inconsistent identifier naming of clone fragments is related to bugs [179, 180]. They assume that inconsistent changes, for example, due to adapting copied code to different contexts, probably lead to these defective identifier names. Using their clone detection tool CP-MINER they were able to find such bugs in four subject systems. After automatically detecting inconsistent identifier namings, they found that more than 90% of these inconsistencies were intended and did not lead to unwanted program behavior by asking the original developers about the findings. The remaining inconsistencies were unintended, but in most cases no bugs though. In fact, they applied to coding style and could be fixed to increase the code quality in terms of maintainability. In total, only 21 of their findings caused erroneous program behavior, however, indicating that inconsistent cloning may introduce defects. Similarly, Aversano and colleagues investigated the relation of bugs and late propagations of changes to cloned code assuming that late propagation may indicate that clone fragments were missed accidentally which could be a source for defects [7]. Indeed, they were able to show that some of the late propagations were bug fixes. Their results were confirmed by Thummalapenta and colleagues who analyzed four open-source systems concluding that bugs are more likely to occur in clones that undergo late propagations [250]. The relation between inconsistent changes and bugs in a system was also shown by Jürgens and colleagues [130]. Manually detecting unintended inconsistencies in cloned classes they reported on 10% to 37% where actual bugs.

Another approach to identify a correlation between software clones and defects is to use information recorded in an issue tracking system or in commit messages of a software repository. Rahman and colleagues investigated the likelihood of defect-correcting activities occurring in cloned code compared to non-cloned code by extracting information from an issue tracker [223]. They linked recorded bugs to changes in the source code and found most bugs located in non-cloned code. However, considering the clone rate, non-cloned code tended to be less error-prone than cloned code. Barbour and colleagues focused on the relation of late propagation and defects by inspecting commit messages for two open-source systems [19]. Mapping the recorded defects to the detected late propagations, it was found that especially late propagations for which temporally changes were reverted and all fragments of a clone class were changed at the same time but differently introduced bugs.

The results indicate that both change patterns impose a challenge on developers since being commonly applied. Though, exact numbers presented in the studies partially differ from each other or are contradictory.

2.2.2   Code Size and Code Comprehension

Code Size is directly related to the amount of code redundancy. Assuming that clones can be removed by an appropriate abstraction, $n - 1$ clone fragments can be saved for a clone class containing n fragments [10]. Besides the increase of source code lines, the size of executables is also affected by cloned code. Although, the size of executables is of no interest in most domains nowadays since modern hardware is powerful and cheap at the same time, some domains care about the size of executables. For instance, embedded systems often depend on very small sized executables [35]. However, savings through code refactoring are difficult to estimate precisely, because the abstraction may differ from the original clone fragments due to dependencies and other reasons. That is, the resulting code fragment may actually be bigger than the clone fragment was before [16]. Moreover, it is not always possible to remove clones due to different limitations (as described earlier in this section).

The source code size of a system is related to code comprehension again. That is, developers need to read and understand more code, e.g., to locate functionality they are looking for. Apart from just understanding the code, the likelihood of defects decreases the better developer understand existing code. Unintended inconsistent changes to cloned code are related to defects also. Developers need to know whether and where clones of certain code fragments exist before deciding whether a change needs to be propagated to different code locations in the same or at least a similar way. Finally, in some situations it may also be necessary for developers to understand why a code fragment is cloned, which is an activity caused by duplicated code only.

Interestingly one of the first studies directed towards the relation of the size and comprehension of code to software clones showed that refactoring cloned code may lead to even more code [16]. Balazinska and colleagues used an automated approach to replace code duplications by applying a certain pattern. Though the technique successfully removed clones in their example, the clone fragments were so small in size and number that the abstraction was actually larger in size—probably also increasing complexity. However, results may show the opposite for larger clone fragments that occur more frequently in a system.

Latoza and colleagues performed a survey in which they interviewed developers [172]. The main problems stated by the participants regarding software clones and their effect on code comprehension relate to finding all occurrences of cloned code and correctly performing consistent changes according to the *Co-Change* pattern. Results also confirmed that clones may be introduced due to issues with code ownership. Nonetheless, there was no precise definition of clones used for the interview, that is, the participants used the term clone in a very broad way and not based on syntactical similarity only, for instance, denoting similar functionality implemented through different programming languages or algorithms.

There are no other studies correlating code comprehension to software clones based on empirical data. The reason is probably that code comprehension is inherently difficult to measure. Therefore, there is no final conclusion on the relationship. Nonetheless, there is still the claim that code redundancies decrease the understandability of source code. More research is needed to verify or disprove this claim.

2.3 Clone Rate and Locality

Clone rates and the dispersion of clones in a software system (clone locality) are important aspects to assess the urgency of clone research. Looking at the clone rate of a system, it is straightforward that every drawback that is related or even caused by duplicated code weighs more heavily the more clones exist in a system. Regarding the locality of clones, it makes a difference whether clones are mostly local or rather spread over various source code locations. For instance, clones may be in the same class, same file or same directory. Related to that, a general conjecture is that the farther away clones are, the higher are the chances that a developer fails in updating them consistently. If the clone rate for most software systems were extremely low and clones occur at close by source code locations only, it would be arguable whether clones can have a considerable impact on software quality and maintainability and are worth being investigated at all. On the other hand, high clone rates and randomly spread clone fragments may justify effort spent to manage clones actively.

Baker conducted an empirical study on the extent of duplicated code using the clone detection tool DUP [11]. DUP is a token-based clone detector capable of locating type-1 and type-2 clones with consistent parameter renaming. In a postprocessing step the clone rate is computed together with an estimated possible reduction of source code by eliminating code duplications. The estimation of the amount of code by which the code base could be shrunk is based on the assumption that any number of clone fragments may be replaced by one code fragment of the same size. An analysis based on two large subject systems summing up to 1.1 million lines of code resulted in 2,487 and 5,550 clone instances, respectively, which constitute about 20% of the source code for each system. Moreover, it was found that about 12% of the source code was duplicated code that could be eliminated by refactoring.

Baxter and colleagues presented the first clone detector using an abstract syntax tree (AST) to detect arbitrary clone fragments [24]. The approach basically consists of three steps: In the first two steps sub-tree clones and statement sequence clones are detected subsequently using hashing functions. In the last step more complex non-identical clones are detected by visiting the parents of the already located clones in the AST and checked if the parent is a clone as well.

Baxter and colleagues applied their AST-based clone detector on three subsystems of an industrial process-control system written in C consisting of 400K source lines of code [24]. Baxter and colleagues were able to confirm previous clone rates by Baker [11] by detecting approximately 12.7% cloned code on average over all subsystems of the subject system. Moreover, they found clone rates of 28% in three of these subsystems, indicating that clone rates also vary over different system parts.

Ducasse and colleagues [75] analyzed four software systems written in four different languages, namely C, Smalltalk, Python, and COBOL, to validate their claim of language independence. In total, 751K lines of code have been investigated resulting in relatively high clone rates ranging from 8.7% to 59.3% LOC reported for a commercial payroll system. Though, the results are not too surprising because two out of the four subject systems were known to contain a large amount of cloned code beforehand.

In an empirical study, Roy and Cordy investigated different properties of function clones, including language, clone size, clone location, and clone density, in twenty open-source C, Java and, C# systems using NICAD as clone detector [230]. In a follow-up [228], the authors extended this study by adding eight open-source systems written in the Python scripting language and compare the results obtained for the systems written in Python to those obtained for the systems written in compiled languages. Analyzing the overall clone rate of the subject systems it was found that for Java 7.2%, for C# 6.0%, for C 1.1%, and for Python 7.4% of the lines of code on average are exact clones. Numbers for non-identical clones vary from 2.8% for C to 24.9% for C# depending on the selected degree of similarity between clone fragments. In general, the lower the selected level of similarity the higher the percentage of cloned code. Observing the location of clones, the results show that exact clones occur in 32.1% of all files in the Python systems, 15% of the files in the C systems, 46% of the files in the Java systems, and 29% of files in the C# systems. In addition, Roy and Cordy measured clone density of the files and found that on average 14.1% of the files in the C systems have 10% to 20% of their content as exactly cloned methods. The highest density was found for Java systems with 37.8% of files containing more than 10% exact function clones. The C# and Python systems are in between at 25.1% and 24.0%, respectively. For all systems under study, the average clone rates of exact clones located in the same file vary from 0% LOC for C systems over 8.9% LOC for the Python systems to 17.6%

Table 2.1 – Previous Studies on Clone Rates

%	System	LOC	Citation
19	two different systems	≈ 1,100K	Baker [11]
28	a process-control system	≈ 400K	Baxter and colleagues [24]
59	four different systems	≈ 751K	Ducasse and colleagues [75]
21	31 different systems	≈ 8,849K	Roy and Cordy [228, 230]
25	24 different games	≈ 3,205K	Chen and colleagues [52]

and 18.6% LOC for Java and C# systems, respectively. The numbers of exact clones within the same directory are much higher for each system ranging from 24.4% LOC for C# to 62.4% LOC for Java systems. Average numbers of exact clones located in different directories range from 19.5% LOC for Java to 57.0% for C# systems. Cloned code that is located in different directories is further distinguished in the following categories: clones located in the same grandparent directory, in the same subsystem, and in different subsystems. Considering exact clones yielded in 29.7% to 57.7% LOC in the category *same grandparent directory*, 14.6% to 49.6% LOC in the category *same subsystem*, and 15.7% to 27.6% LOC in the category *different subsystem*. We gather similar statistics in Chapter 3, but for a much larger set of projects.

Recently, a related study has been presented by Chen and colleagues who concentrated on clone characteristics in open-source games [52]. The authors analyzed 24 games written in C, Java, or Python with sizes ranging from 1K LOC to 844K LOC. The clone rate was found to be 4.6% to 24.9% of the source code for exact clones and up to 39.6% considering non-identical clones also. Distinguishing between programming languages, a clear trend could be observed indicating that remarkably more clones existed in the C-based games. Looking at the localization of clones, Chen and colleagues reported that up to 50% of files were associated with exact clones and even up to 74% considering non-identical clones as well. Finally, the authors investigated the clone density of the subject systems concluding that most files contain small portions of cloned lines of code only.

Research Questions

The importance of a system's clone rate was recognized in the early stages of clone research already. Various case studies have been conducted by researchers to measure to what extent source code is redundant. Findings of these studies reported clone rates around 20%, in extreme cases even 59% percent, for particular systems. Table 2.1 summarizes the subject systems of these studies together with their size and the reported clone rate.

The major shortcoming of previous studies on the clone rate is that they are based on rather small corpora regarding the number of software systems and the number source code lines analyzed. Göde and colleagues emphasized that detected clone rates are strongly depending on the clone detection parameters used and that small changes to these may already have a strong influence on the results [97]. Since many studies do not describe their study setup in detail when it comes to the clone detection parameters, results of different case studies cannot be compared or combined also. To the best of our knowledge, there is no empirical study that has investigated more than 31 systems and more than 8,849K source lines of code, respectively. Considering that the clone rate can be determined completely automated and there are detection tools that scale very well even for large projects, the number of subject systems is rather small yet. Therefore, it is left unclear whether findings based on the investigation of those systems are representative for a much larger range of different software systems in terms of domain and size.

Question 1 – *What is the average clone rate of projects in open source?*

To contribute to a more representative answer on the extent of clone rates in terms of analyzing a wide range of software systems of different size and from different domains, we conducted a comprehensive study including 9,666 open-source projects written in C, C++, C#, or Java, summing up to 310 MLOC. We use statistical analysis to estimate the means and variances of clone rates in open-source projects and their likely type of distribution.

Question 2 – *Is there a difference in the average clone rate among C, C++, C#, and Java open-source programs?*

We search for correlations among clone rates and programming languages. Our case study encompasses four common programming languages and results may oncover differences between these with respectto the extent of cloning.

Question 3 – *Does clone rate (of files and projects) depend on size?*

Analogously to searching for correlations among clone rates and programming languages, we also search for potential correlations between clone rate and project size.

Question 4 – *Do clones tend to be local in project source trees?*

As part of our large scale analysis on clone rates, we look at the location of clones too, that is, whether clones are mostly local or rather spread over very different locations of a project. Code localization has not been finally treated in studies yet. Previous results reported show a large variance among different systems and statistical significance tests were not used. Whether these results hold for a larger set of programs and also for arbitrary code fragments rather than only cloned functions is not clear.

Our empirical study on clone rates and clone dispersal in open-source software is described in Chapter 3.

We note that our numbers cannot easily be compared to those of Roy and Cordy, because their clone detector detects only function clones whereas ours arbitrary code fragments.

2.4   Detection

Copy-and-paste programming is a common practice to speed up software development, to reuse existing and reliable code, or to use existing code as starting point for new functionality [148, 172].

To be able to decide whether software clones in a system are harmful or not or basically of interest they have to be detected first. For example, all clone fragments of a clone class have to be located before a developer is able to apply an intended consistent change to all of them. As participants of an interview by Latoza and colleagues [172] stated, it is a problem to detect all occurrences of a clone fragment manually. Considering large systems it is probably not feasible to locate code duplications manually at all, because it would be by far too time consuming. Accordingly, the need for automated clone detectors was recognized in the early stages of clone research. In the last years an abundance of clone detection techniques and tools has been presented and also used in a variety of studies. Many of them have been sufficiently tested meanwhile and were proven to be efficient—even for very large systems and corpora. Yet, the clone detection tools often implement different approaches to detect duplicated code implicitly giving their own working definition of similarity—according to the question what a software clone exactly is. A very basic difference is the code representation they work on. That is, different levels of code abstraction are used to detect clone fragments. In the following we will introduce the basic idea of clone detection based on the different level of code abstraction used as underlying representation. A more detailed comparison of the existing clone detection approaches and tools is given in [17, 229].

2.4.1   Text-based

Text-based clone detection tools work directly on the pure text of a software, thus, representing the lowest level of possible abstraction. That is, the target source code is considered as sequence of characters. Code fragments are compared to each other to detect subsequences of identical or similar character sequences located at different positions in the code base and of maximal length. That is, two or more subsequences of characters are clones of each other when they are identical or similar to some extent and cannot be extended by neighboring characters such that they are still identical or similar to each other. Textual clones do not need to represent a structural entity of the programming language allowing to locate arbitrary clone fragments. Detectors either use no or just a few basic code transformations and normalizations (such as removing blank lines or contiguous whitespace) before starting the actual comparison process. Figure 2.3 shows an example of code fragments that are identical except for comments and whitespaces. Not ignoring them may result in clone detectors not identifying the code fragments as clones.

Operating directly on the source code, with a minimum of transformations, has various advantageous as well as some disadvantageous. The benefits of text-based techniques are strongly related to the fact that the source code is considered plain text. Thus, the detection algorithms can be language independent and even string processing techniques from other domains can be used here [225]. Furthermore, the

```
1   void swap(int i,
2              int j) {
3
4       int temp = i
5
6       i = j;
7       j = temp;
8   }
```

(a) *fragment_A*

```
1   void swap(int i, int j) {
2       int temp = i
3       i = j;
4       j = temp;
5   }
```

(b) *fragment_B*

Figure 2.3 – Two code fragment that are identical except for layout differences due to the use of blank lines and whitespaces. Text-based clone detectors may not detect these fragments as clones when they do not abstract from layout using code transformations.

source code does not necessarily be syntactically correct allowing the processing of the code at any state of development and detecting arbitrary clone fragments independent from syntactic units of a programming language such as methods or loops. Finally, text-based clone detectors provide high recall [33]. The recall of a detection technique denotes the number of detected clone fragments by a tool compared to the total number of existing clone fragments in a subject system.

The main drawback of text-based detection techniques is the rather low precision of results [33]. The precision of clone detectors denotes the number of detected relevant clone fragments, in terms of their relevance to developers for certain tasks, compared to the total number of detected clone fragments. One attribute that facilitates this issue is missing syntactic information that could be used to align clone fragments to syntactic units of the source code, for instance, methods.

Johnson introduced one of the first text-based clone detectors [123, 124]. He used a string matching algorithm based on fingerprints presented by Karp and Rabin [141, 142] which is very efficient. Fingerprints are computed for each source line in a file and clones are identified by detecting identical fingerprints. Fingerprints have been used by Manber to locate cloned code also [189].

Source code lines have been used by Ducasse and colleagues to detect code clones as well [75]. Analogously to fingerprints, every source line is compared to every other source line using a hash function. To increase performance, each line is partitioned using a hashing approach first and, afterwards, is compared to lines in the same partition only. Using dotplots to visualize detected clones—each pair of identical lines is represented by a dot—patterns can easily be found. For instance, a diagonal in the dotplot indicates multiple consecutive cloned source code lines that can be summarized to a larger sequence. Regarding the independence of text-based techniques towards programming languages, the authors reported they were able to adapt their technique to new languages in less than 45 minutes. Moreover, they used code transformations to remove comments and white spaces to increase recall while preserving precision.

Another technique is used by Marcus and colleagues who use occurrences of similar identifier names in fragments to detect potential duplications [190]. To compare identifiers they use a technique from information retrieval named latent semantic indexing, that is, the software system is statically analyzed to determine similar identifiers between source code entities, e.g., functions.

To overcome the problem of missing syntactic information when applying text-based clone detection, Cordy, Synytskyy, and Dean proposed a hybrid approach using a robust island grammar [57, 246]. The island grammar is used to identify and isolate syntactic units before a text-based clone detector is run to find relevant clones across these units. A downside of this approach is that it is not language independent due to the necessary island grammar. The authors successfully applied the approach to various programs and improved it over time [56, 227].

Roy and Cordy also presented a text-based clone detector called NICAD [230]. NICAD uses a textual line-based comparison by means of longest common subsequence (LCS) to compare syntactic blocks (functions in their case) in the pretty-printed and normalized source code.

2.4.2 Token-based

The next level of code representation used to detect software clones are tokens. Tokens are the smallest syntactic unit of the underlying programming language (see Section 1.2.1). Instead of working directly on the source code by comparing characters and strings, token-based techniques first perform a lexical analysis of the whole source code transforming it into a sequence of tokens. After tokenizing is finished, each source file is represented by a sequence of tokens. These sequences are used to create an appropriate data structure allowing for efficient detection of duplications, that is, scanning for identical or similar subsequences of tokens. Compared to pure text, tokens provide additional information that make token-based clone detection more robust against differences in formatting and spacing as well as to abstract from concrete values of identifiers and literals.

Different algorithms have been presented showing that suffix trees can be efficiently constructed in linear time and space while representing all suffixes of a software system in a compact fashion [10, 129, 134]. Branches in a suffix tree represent suffixes sharing the same prefix which in turn represent a cloned sequence. Thus, suffix trees are suitable for efficient clone detection using characters or tokens. Baker presented one of the first token-based techniques based on suffix trees able to abstract from identifiers and implemented it in the clone detection tool DUP [10, 11, 12]. Similarly to line-based clone detection on text, DUP is also line-based while using token sequences instead of sequences of characters and strings. To detect parameterized clone fragments, denoting a consistent renaming of identifiers among clone fragments of the same clone class, she introduced the concept of functors. A functor can be considered a hash function that characterizes each token sequence of a given source line uniquely. Capturing identifiers and literals as parameters to such functors allows to abstract from their concrete values while preserving their order of occurrence. The order is encoded by references to the right-most previous occurrence of an identifier. Using functors a so called *p-suffix tree* is constructed enabling the detection of consistently renamed type-2 clones as described in Section 1.2.5.

Among others, commonly used token-based clone detection tools have been presented by Kamiya and colleagues (CCFINDER) [134] and by Li and colleagues [179, 180] (CP-MINER). The first token-based incremental clone detector based on a generalized suffix tree was presented by Göde (ICLONES) [86, 88, 92, 93]. The incremental detecting approach is used to find clones in multiple versions of a program where results of a version's analysis are reused during the analysis of the consecutive version. This way it is not necessary to re-detect clone fragments of source code that did not change between two versions. In contrast, changes are considered by updating the generalized suffix tree accordingly. Afterwards, new clones can be extracted from the adapted parts of the tree.

Alternatively to suffix trees, suffix arrays can be used for efficient token-based clone detection. Hofmann showed that suffix arrays require less time and space to be computed than suffix arrays [113]. Basit and colleagues presented an approach that uses suffix arrays allowing users to tailor token strings for better clone detection [20]. That is, the flexible tokenization enables suppressing certain token classes that are irrelevant, for instance, access modifiers in Java. The concept of flexible tokenization was introduced by Kamiya et al. [134]. Techniques using suffix trees and suffix arrays provide the same results, however, suffix arrays are more efficient regarding time and space. In this theses suffix arrays were used since being efficient enough for the conducted studies and due to a missing incremental approach based on suffix arrays.

Apart from applying token-based comparison techniques to detect software clones in terms of identical or similar functionality, tools have been introduced to uncover plagiarism [220, 236]. Plagiarism detection based on tokens but using a dynamic programming string alignment approach instead of suffix trees was presented by Gitchell [85].

Advantages and disadvantages of token-based detection techniques are basically similar to those using text-based comparison algorithms. Thus, token-based techniques can be applied by using mature string algorithms. The source code does not need to be compilable allowing for clone detection at any time of the development process, just like text-based approaches. In contrast, however, they are not completely independent from the underlying programming language since a lexer is needed. Nonetheless, this downside can be neglected actually, because scanners are available for many languages already and can also be created with little effort otherwise. On the other hand, the additional information carried by the tokens can be used to improve preprocessing of the token sequences before applying the actual clone detection [134]. For example, irrelevant sequences can be identified and removed and values of identifiers and literals can be ignored. The main advantage of token-based clone detection is a very high recall which is even superior to text-based, tree-based, and graph-based approaches. The main drawback of token-based approaches is rather low precision of the results compared to tree-based and graph-based approaches. Missing information regarding the syntax resulting in some clone fragments overlapping the boundaries of syntactic units is one reason. This issue can be mitigated t some extent by preprocessing [57, 85, 246] or postprocessing [112] steps. Both make use of some syntactic information either gathered by counting tokens opening and closing syntactic units or island grammars [206] or a full-range syntax analysis [85].

2.4.3   AST-based

Using a tree-based approach the source code is parsed and an abstract syntax tree (AST) is built. Thus, a parser for the programming language of the subject system is needed. After parsing, the tree is traversed searching for identical or similar subtrees representing cloned code. Compared to token-based approaches using suffix trees, parse trees and ASTs contain more information related to the source code, for instance, regarding the syntactical structure. This information can be used by the detection algorithm to improve the quality of results.

Baxter and colleagues pioneered clone detection using ASTs [24]. They partition subtrees before matching them using a hash function to improve performance. Afterwards, subtrees of the same partition are matched using a tree matching algorithm allowing for some divergences [2]. Earlier, Yang proposed a similar approach using dynamic programming and a generalization of the longest common subsequence algorithm to locate differences between two versions of the same file represented by subtrees [268]. A hybrid approach using ASTs combined with suffix trees was presented by Koschke and colleagues [77, 160]. First, the AST is built, followed by serializing its nodes in preorder traversal. The serialized nodes of the AST are used as input for the suffix tree. Thus, it is possible to extract maximally long AST node sequences considering their syntactic structure to detect clone fragments corresponding to complete syntactical units only. Another hybrid approach based on a combination of AST and suffix trees was introduced by Tairas and Gray [247]. They implemented a plug-in for Microsoft's Phoenix framework that is capable of detecting exact function-level clones as well as parameterized clone fragments with identifier renaming only. A similar approach was also proposed by Greenan [100]. Method level clones are detected based on a transformed AST using a sequence matching algorithm.

Obviously, the main gain in using AST-based techniques is the information about the syntactic structure of a software system. Using syntactical information clone fragments can be detected in the AST that would not have been found by aforementioned techniques. For instance, normalized AST-based approaches are robust against differences in the order of operands that may be inverted in one clone fragment. Variable names and literal values of the source code are disregarded in the AST in order to make code fragments differing in these appear the same. Furthermore, the data flow of a program is ignored which makes the AST vulnerable towards statement reordering. Nonetheless, the precision of AST-based clone detectors is higher compared to text-based and token-based approaches. In contrast, the performance is quite low and the tree matching algorithm rather complex for some AST-based approaches [33]. Moreover, since grounding on the syntax of a system, the source code needs to be syntactically correct, not allowing to perform clone detection at any time during development. Last but not least, an appropriate grammar of the programming language is needed to parse the source code which discards language independence.

2.4.4   PDG-based

We mentioned that AST-based techniques are not robust against reorderings of source code. Reorderings may occur for different reasons. Either unintentionally during modifications on a clone fragments, for example, when cloning is used as templating strategy (see Section 2.1), or intentionally, for example, to camouflage plagiarism. Such clone fragments will not be detected by AST-based nor by text-based or token-based techniques—except for those that can be normalized by rather simple transformations. A program dependency graph (PDG) is a graph representing statements as nodes connected by edges representing all control and data dependencies [80]. Techniques based on PDGs take advantage of the fact that the order of code fragments cannot be changed arbitrarily without changing their semantic. Control and data dependencies have to be preserved in order to guarantee the same behavior before and after a reordering. Holding the control flow and data flow information of a system a PDG carries semantic information.

Clones are represented as isomorphic subgraphs in PDGs. Matching algorithms on these subgraphs are applied for locating similar ones which depict clone fragments of each other. Komondoor and Horwitz introduced a PDG-based clone detector, PDG-DUP, that uses program slicing to isomorphic subgraphs in a PDG [153, 154]. In addition, they presented an approach to group detected clone fragments for automatic method extraction in order to support clone refactorings [151, 152]. Krinke presented an approach to locate similar subgraphs by using k-length patch matching to iteratively find similar subgraphs of maximal length [163]. Liu and colleagues tackled the issue of detecting software plagiarism using PDGs [182]. They presented the plagiarism detection tool GPLAG which uses a lossy filter to reduce the search space for isomorphic subgraphs in a PDG. Another PDG-based detection tool, namely SCORPIO, was presented by Higo and colleagues [110, 111]. Their technique is based on the one presented by Komondoor and Horwitz [153, 154]. To overcome shortcomings in detecting contiguous code clones links between every pair of two nodes whose program elements are consecutive in the source code are introduced. Evaluating the proposed technique on four open-source systems, it was shown that SCORPIO was able to detect more clones without increasing false-positive rates.

PDG-based techniques are capable of detecting code duplication that cannot be uncovered by other approaches and may also improve the quality of results due to the additional information given in a PDG. Though, the creating of the PDG as well as the actual matching of subgraphs is of high complexity. In fact, the problem of similar subgraphs is NP hard, thus, algorithms have to use approximative solutions. Moreover, PDG-based techniques require syntactically correct source code and are language dependent just as AST-based approaches are.

2.4.5   Metric-based

Metric-based approaches do not compare source code or abstractions of it to detect redundancies, instead different metrics for code fragments are gathered and compared in form of numerical vectors. Metrics can be calculated for different syntactic units of a software system, for instance, classes, functions or even single statements. Similarity between metrics vectors is defined as the distance between two vectors, e.g., using *Euclidean distance*. Metrics vectors are either compared pairwise [193] or clustered using appropriate algorithms [4, 5, 198, 199]. Which metrics are used depends on the specific approach but also on programming language and programming paradigm.

An approach based on several metrics for functions was presented by Mayrand and colleagues [193]. They used an intermediate representation language to characterize functions in the source code and calculate metrics from their names, layout, expression, and control flow. Metrics gathered for the detection of similarity were number of lines of code and number of function calls, for example. Similar metrics, e.g., number of lines of code, number of statements and cyclomatic complexity, were used by Patenaude and colleagues [217], too. They focused on metrics specific to Java only to support the software quality assessment of Java software systems. Kontogiannis and colleagues proposed two different ways to use metrics for clone detection [155, 156]. The first approach starts with constructing an AST from the source code. Calculated metrics values are stored as annotations in the corresponding nodes of the AST. From the annotated nodes a reference table is created that contains code fragments sorted by their metrics values which is used to extract similar statements, blocks, and functions. The second approach is based on a dynamic programming technique for comparing blocks. The distance between blocks is calculated by the *Levenshtein distance* which is the least costly sequence of modifications necessary to transform one block into the other—assuming that cheap transformations indicate clones created by copy and paste followed by adapting activities.

Other metric-based approaches were presented by Buss and colleagues [44] and Dagenais and colleagues [60]. Dagenais and colleagues compared only procedures with a similar number of statements to reduce the runtime of pairwise metrics comparison. Specific metric-based clone detection techniques were also proposed for code duplications in web sites [69, 171]. Based on the frequency of HTML entities DiLucca and colleagues proposed an approach for identifying similar static HTML pages [69]. They use the *Levenshtein distance* to calculate differences between entities. Lanubile and Mallardo introduced a semi-automated technique for detecting cloned script functions [171]. Potential function clones are detected automatically using eMETRICS before inspecting the results visually.

The main drawback of metric-based clone detection is that it dependents on the programming language since metrics are gathered for and compared against syntactic units. Syntactic units have to be predefined allowing for detection of specific granularity only, for instance, function level clones. Thus, clones of other granularity are not identified. Thus, the selection of appropriate metrics impacts the results and is not always obvious [240].

2.4.6   Other techniques

A hybrid approach based on the techniques presented by Patenaude and colleagues [217] and Kontogiannis and colleagues [156] was proposed by Balazinska and colleagues [15]. The metric-based approach by Patenaude is used to compute characteristic metrics for each method and find clusters of similar method bodies in the first step. Afterwards, the dynamic pattern matching algorithm of Kontogiannis is used to compare the token sequences for each pair of similar methods to identify cloned methods.

Leitao uses a combination of syntactic and semantic techniques to detect positive as well as negative indicators regarding the similarity of analyzed code fragments for Lisp-like languages [177]. The approach combines the construction of an AST to overcome variations in the textual representation of the source code together with specialized comparison functions ranging from the analysis of text-based properties to semantic ones, for instance, similar call subgraphs and commutative operators. Each comparison function yields a summarized evidence-factor model indicating a clone likelihood. Results of a combination of these functions can be used to generate a global similarity metric or an explanation of differences. This approach is to some extent flexible in the sense of adding support for new programming languages by giving a specification for their syntaxes and new specialized comparison functions. Furthermore, the evidence model can be replaced by some other model of similarity measure.

Wahler and colleagues [258] and Li and colleagues [179] use frequent item sets to locate similar code fragments. Wahler and colleagues used a data mining technique on the AST whereas Li and colleagues summarized statement sequences to item sets which they searched for frequent item set occurrences by an adapted data mining algorithm.

A approach to detect similar trees was introduced by Jiang and colleagues [121]. The structural information within ASTs are approximated within Euclidean space using certain characteristic vectors. AST locality sensitive hashing (LSH) [61] is used to cluster similar vectors, depicting code clones in terms of Euclidean distance.

Another approach focuses on detecting software clones based on assembler code, bytecode, or intermediate languages. Sæbjørnsen and colleagues used disassembled binary executables to compute characteristic vectors for code regions and locate regions with similar vectors [232]. Davis and Godfrey detect contiguous as well as non-contiguous regions in assembler code generated from C, C++, and Java source code [63, 64]. Al-Omari and colleagues worked on an intermediate language of the Microsoft .NET programming framework [3]. A clone detector, SEBYTE, searching for clones in Java bytecode was introduced by Keivanloo and colleagues [145].

Finally, approaches were introduced using hash-based techniques to detect cloned code [123, 124, 239, 254]. They basically generate hash values from the source code and process these to locate duplications. Compared to other techniques their performance and scalability is quite promising.

2.4.7 Beyond Source Code

Clone detection is not only of interest when it comes to source code. We mentioned already that it is also used in text-based plagiarism detection. In the following we list other research attempting to apply clone detection giving a short overview—for details we refer to the original publications.

- Liu and colleagues presented clone detection based on suffix trees for serialized UML sequence diagrams [183]. Later Störrle dealt with different algorithms and heuristics to assess their suitability for detecting UML domain models [245].

- Duplications in Simulink models based development were investigated and applied to industrial models from the automotive domain by Deißenböck and colleagues [67, 68].

- Pham and colleagues [211, 219] and Stephan and Cordy [243] located clones in the graph based Matlab/Simulink models. However, their approach was tested for small models only.

- Redundancies in textual requirement specification documents were first detected by Domann and colleagues [70] and later used by Jürgens and colleagues on real-world requirements specifications [128, 131].

- Rahman and colleagues tried to predict clones among domain entities [224].

- Clones in Spreadsheets were treated by Hermans and colleagues [107].

2.4.8 Applications

The applications of clone detection are generally based on the collection of information to clone fragments and their location in the source code. This information can be used to enhance various maintenance tasks such as generally understanding the system as clone fragments need to be comprehended once only, perform consistent changes, refactor and remove cloned code based on information of occurrences and exact locations. Applying clone detection to consecutive versions of a system or using an incremental clone detector provides information towards the evolution of clones over time. Evolutionary data can be used to uncover aspects that are invisible through single revision clone analysis, for instance, how long a clone fragment exists in the code base or when it was introduced, respectively. These and other factors may also help in assessing the quality of a software system. Moreover, clone detection is an end unto itself in terms of clone research. That is, clone data helps in investigating and ultimately understanding the phenomenon of cloning with all its benefits and downsides. There are several other applications of clone detection. We list the most prominent ones as follows:

Identify Libraries: Multiple use of a code fragment at different locations in the source code suggests its utility in the system. Replacing clone fragments by libraries would help to refactor such clones and avoid new instance of it by supporting the awareness of developers of an already existing solution [43, 62, 196, 197].

Identify Patterns: Similarly to the identification of potential library usage, multiple occurrences of code fragments in the source code may help in discovering relations between the syntactic units and extract functional usage patterns [225].

Aspect Mining: Detecting identical or similar code fragments is required in aspect mining research to detect cross-cutting concerns. Code causing cross-cutting concerns commonly occurs multiple times in a system, thus, clone detection is perfectly suited for this use case [40, 41, 42].

Inter-System Detection: Clones can not only be detected within one system but also between a system and some other source-code corpora. That is, it allows to identify identical or similar code across different systems. Plagiarism detection is one application of inter-system clone detection which has been already described in the previous sections. Another application of clone detection between systems that is growing fast is the detection of copyright infringements and license violations. Open-source projects enjoy growing popularity in the last years and open-source code is commonly used in various other projects. Therefore, automatically detecting potential copyright infringements by running a clone detector against a large corpus of open-source projects is of great interest [11, 39, 134, 259]. Finally, inter-system clone detection allows also to automatically detect malicious code, e.g., a virus, by running it against source code that is known to be harmful or defective to find occurrences in the own system [259].

Code compression: Detecting code clones can be used as starting point of code compression by reducing the size of the source code through clone refactorings. Compact source code is important for applications which are memory critical, for example, mobile devices [51, 66].

Co-change Suggestion: Changing a code fragment that is cloned requires to change its clone instances as well if the clone fragments are supposed to evolve consistently. Thus, while changing a clone fragment it is of value for a programmer to know whether its clone instances need to be changed in the same way and where they are located [188, 191, 202, 204].

2.5   Clone Mapping

During the life cycle of a software system its source code evolves based on changes, for instance, due to bug fixing activities or ongoing feature requests [175, 176]. Such changes may affect clone fragments also. Therefore, results provided by a clone detector for one version of the source code are not necessarily valid in a subsequent version. Updates to the code base require updating clone information accordingly. Mapping clones across multiple versions of a system is useful as it presents the basis to build an evolution model of them. That is, for each clone its ancestor is determined across multiple versions of a software's source code and, afterwards, can be tracked over time. Figure 2.4 illustrates a schematic example of fragments being mapped between two consecutive versions.

Kim and colleagues introduced the term clone genealogy and presented a model to map code clones across multiple versions of a system [150]. Analogously to mapping clones across subsequent source code versions, the term clone genealogy refers to a sequence of clones evolving over a series of versions of source code. They proposed an approach to analyze the history of clones based on the extraction of clone genealogies and introduced the notion of a *Clone Genealogy Extractor* (CGE) accordingly. Their approach to map clones consists basically of two main steps: First, they use a conventional clone detector, namely CCFINDER [134], to detect clones for each version of a system independently from each other. Afterwards, techniques of text similarity and location overlapping are used to map identified clone classes between consecutive

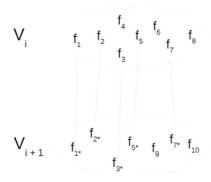

Figure 2.4 – Schematic illustration of fragment mapping between consecutive versions.

versions. Text similarity is defined by the relative proportion of the common token sequences between two classes to the sum of their sizes. Location overlapping refers to a score that is based on how much fragments of one class overlap fragments of another class with respect to their location in the source code. To calculate the location score a line-based tracker was built on top of DIFF.

In contrast to mapping clone classes between versions, Bakota and colleagues proposed an approach to extract the evolution of individual clone fragments. Similarly to Kim and colleagues, they detect all clones of every version separately before performing the mapping of individual clone fragments across different versions. The detection of clones is based on an AST-based technique presented by Koschke and colleagues [160] that is appropriate to identify code clones that form syntactic units, e. g., classes and functions. The actual mapping across multiple versions requires that possible clone candidates have to be of the same syntactic unit, that is, the root of the clone in their respective subtree within the AST has to be of the same type. Based on this constraint a class can only be mapped to a class and a function only to a function. After that, six similarity measures are used to identify which candidates actually match and will be mapped. These measures are: the name of the file containing the candidate, the position of the candidate inside the clone class, the unique name of the head node (if one exists) or the unique name of the first named ancestor in the AST, the relative position of the candidate inside its named ancestor, and at last the lexical structure of the candidate. Attaching an individual weight to each measure, the combination of all measures is used as a score for similarity between two candidates. If there are matches between several candidates with the same calculated score, a mapping is determined randomly among these.

Duala-Ekoko and Robillard introduced a concept to identify locations of code clones using a combination of syntactic, structural and lexical information, and software metrics called clone region descriptors (CRD) [71, 73]. CRDs describe the location of code fragments in the code base in an abstract manner by representing the hierarchical nesting of a clone fragment within its enclosing file, class, method, and block. Computed CRDs are used to locate instances of clone fragments of a particular version in subsequent versions. The approach has been implemented in the tool named CLONETRACKER [72] which is capable of producing CRDs from the output of different clone detectors and notify developers of modifications to clone fragments as well as supporting updates to already documented clones. The CRD approach achieves high performance in tracking clones since it facilitates the identification of clone fragments that have been detected in one version once, in subsequent versions of the same system without redetecting them in every version. For the same reason, the approach is not capable of detecting clone fragments that are moved in the AST or created in a later version. The authors evaluated the performance and usefulness of the approach using three different clone detectors and analyzing five open-source systems. Results show that CRDs can reliably track a large majority of clones across multiple versions of a system.

Another study has been presented by Nguyen and colleagues [213, 215]. They presented CLEVER a software configuration management (SCM) system that supports clone management, for instance, detection and update of clone fragments. The presented approach is based on an abstract syntax tree (AST) of which subtrees are considered code fragments. For each subtree of the AST a structural characteristic vector is computed and used to determine the similarity between different subtrees to identify clone fragments. To avoid costly pairwise comparison local-sensitive hashing (LSH) is used, that is, vectors having a small distance are assigned the same hash by a LSH function. The approach to update detected clones is based on the incremental detection and mapping of clones across multiple versions rather than separately detecting clones in different versions. First, change information of the software repository is used to determine which parts of the source code were changed between two different versions. Afterwards, an AST is built for each of the corresponding source code fragments of both versions and the shortest sequence of operations possible that transforms the AST of one version into the AST of the other one is computed. Based on these change sets clone fragments are updated and tracked across versions. The authors evaluated their clone update and tracking approach using three subject systems and analyzed 2,100 consecutive versions in total. The approach was found to be accurate and efficient as it produced the same output in less time compared to rerunning clone detection for each version. The only drawback is a slight increase of storage costs due to additional information gathered for the updating and tracking of clones.

Similarly to Nquyen and colleagues, Göde presented a clone tracking technique that maps identical clones of consecutive versions during an incremental clone detection process by considering changes to the code base [87]. In a later publication he extended the mapping approach to cover type-2 and type-3 clone fragments also [96]. He approached the problem of non-identical gaps in type-2 and type-3 clones by considering only the common parts for determining the ancestry relationship among non-identical clone fragments. Change information are extracted using a diff-based approach. Since Göde applied a token based clone detector, changes to fragments refer to the addition or deletion of tokens. Depending on the location of a change, the location and bounds of the corresponding clone fragment are adjusted across two versions. Based on these updates individual clone fragments are mapped across multiple versions of the source code. The approach is highly accurate because no heuristics are used (except for those implicitly applied by the diff algorithm), which facilitates a correct mapping even for extensively modified clones. Newly introduced clones in later versions are detected and tracked as well.

Another approach to map not only type-1 and type-2 but also type-3 clones across multiple versions of a system was presented by Saha and colleagues [234]. Clone detection is performed for each subject version separately before clones are mapped. The actual clone mapping is built upon a preprocessing phase in which each function of one version is mapped to its corresponding function in the consecutive version. Functions are matched across different versions using the function signature along with its class name and complete file path, and considering renames and movements of functions. After the preprocessing the actual mapping of clones is performed by matching clone fragments in the context of their containing function. The matching process calculates a similarity score based on the longest common subsequence count (LCSC) metric and the relative locations of clone fragments within the corresponding functions. The LCSC similarity metric is moreover used to map clones that go beyond the bounds of a function, e. g., cloned files. The authors evaluated the proposed framework using three open source projects. They manually analyzed many of the detected genealogies considering predefined change patterns and conclude that their approach is scalable while maintaining high precision and recall. Aspects of the evolution of clones have not been investigated in their study.

Research Questions

Göde [87] and Saha and colleagues [234] presented the first techniques to map non-identical clones throughout the history of a system. Other mapping approaches considered type-1 and type-2 clones only. Saha and colleagues uncoupled the detection of clones from the actual mapping across different versions to be able to utilize the results obtained with an arbitrary non-incremental clone detection tool. Moreover, the technique proposed is mainly intended for the analysis of source code at release level. There might be a significant difference between the source code of different releases which does not suite the intended application of an incremental clone detector—which is particularly intended for mapping clone fragments of more fine-grained levels such as the revision level. The technique presented by Göde does exactly aim at mapping clones in an incremental way, for instance, at revision level. However, the approach used by Göde may lead to an ambiguous mapping in some cases—an example is given below.

Example 2.1 – Considering the scenario shown in Figure 2.5a the fragment f refers to a certain token sequence in the code base of an arbitrary version. The fragments e and f and the fragments h and f are similar to each other based on the given definition of a type-3 clone. In contrast, the fragments e and h are not similar enough to be considered type-3 clones of each other. As a consequence, e and f share different identical blocks and gaps compared to h and f. Therefore, two clone classes are created. That is, the similarity of type-3 clone fragments is not transitive in such cases. Mapping f to its successor in the subsequent version based on its token sequences only, as proposed by Göde, would be ambiguous. This is because Göde's approach

| (a) Detailed illustration | (b) Schematic illustration |

Figure 2.5 – Subfigure (a) shows two example clone classes and their clone fragments in detail—identical and non-identical code blocks between clone fragments of the same clone class. Subfigure (b) gives a schematic illustration of an ambiguous mapping of these clone fragments between two consecutive versions of a system. The clone fragment f of version v_i is mapped to the corresponding fragment f in version v_{i+1} each (denoted by dotted lines). The ancestry of f in version v_{i+1}, however, is ambiguous with respect to their clone class membership.

maps individual fragments without considering their clone class membership. Figure 2.5b shows a schematic illustration of the above described situation for two consecutive versions and the resulting ambiguity in the mapping presented by Göde. □

   Question 5 – *How can an ambiguous mapping of non-identical clones across multiple versions be avoided using an incremental mapping approach?*

In this thesis we introduce a new clone mapping approach capable of mapping type-3 clone fragments between consecutive versions of a system. Our approach extends the incremental clone mapping approach presented by Göde [87] by considering changes to the source code but also clone class information for individual clones. Thus, preserving the benefits of an incremental approach that integrates the mapping of clones into the detection process. Chapter 4 introduces our mapping approach.

2.6   Change Patterns

The detection of clones and their mapping across multiple versions of a system allow to recognize certain patterns that are related to changes to cloned code. Evolutionary clone patterns were subject to different studies that presented change patterns related to individual clone fragments as well as to clone classes.

2.6.1   Clone Fragment Patterns

Bakota and colleagues introduced the notion of code smells which refers to a code fragment that is identified to be harmful based on the way it evolved [14]. To detect such code smells, definitions of four different patterns were presented:

- A *Vanished clone instance* (VCI) denotes changes by which a clone fragment f that existed in version v_i were not mapped onto any clone fragment of the subsequent

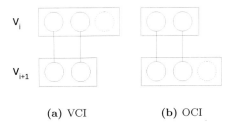

(a) VCI   (b) OCI

Figure 2.6 – VCI and OCI fragment evolution patterns presented by Bakota and colleagues [14]. Occurrences of the changed fragment f are shown as dotted circles.

version v_{i+1}. Either f was removed from the code base in version v_{i+1}, which is actually rated beneficial by the authors, or it has changed so much that the mapping needs to be adapted to detect the ancestry. In contrast, it is regarded critical by the authors if f has changed such that it is not considered a clone with respect to the other fragments of the common clone class anymore. This situation is considered critical as changes that are supposed to be repeated for every fragment of a clone class might not have been performed for all fragments of the clone class due to the missing relationship information. Figure 2.6a shows an example of a VCI change pattern.

- The opposite of the VCI pattern is the *Occurring clone instance* (OCI) pattern. The OCI pattern describes the situation where a clone fragment f gets part of a clone class in version v_{i+1} for which it has not been part of in the previous version v_i. There are two cases leading to the OCI pattern. First, f might be newly created in version v_{i+1} and, hence, did not existed in version v_i. Second, modifications that were applied to the other clone fragments of the clone class before version v_{i+1}, were propagated to f in version v_{i+1}. An example of the OCI change pattern is shown in Figure 2.6b.

- A *Moving clone instance* (MCI) describes a clone fragment f that moves from one clone class cc containing at least three clone fragments (including f itself) to another clone class cc' in a subsequent version. Thus, f is not detected as a clone of the other fragments from class cc anymore. The pattern also requires that f does not occur in clone class cc containing its former clone fragments in any later version. Figure 2.7a illustrates this change pattern. In contrast to the VCI and OCI patterns, MCI describes a long-term pattern since it relates to the evolution of fragments across more than two versions. The MCI pattern occurs due to modifications applied to f either accidentally or intentionally. An accidental modification happens if the developers are not aware of any clones of f or do not know whether the modifications are supposed to be applied to the existing clones of f as well. On the other hand, this can indicate that the fragments are supposed to evolve independently despite their similar structure.

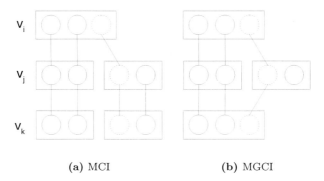

(a) MCI   (b) MGCI

Figure 2.7 – MCI and MGCI fragment evolution patterns presented by
Bakota and colleagues [14]. Occurrences of the changed fragment f are
shown as dotted circles. v_i, v_j, and v_k refer to arbitrary versions with $i < j$
and $j < k$.

- The last pattern introduced by Bakota and colleagues is the *Migrating clone
  instance* (MGCI). It describes an inconsistent change to a clone fragment f such
  that it is in another clone class in every subsequent version v_j for $j > i$ before
  the inconsistent change to f is made consistent in version v_k for $k > j$ and f is
  back in the same clone class as in version v_i. This pattern is also know as *Late
  Propagation*. In contrast to the requirement of the MCI pattern that the clone
  fragment f does not occur in the same clone class as its former clone instances
  again, the MGCI pattern refers to the opposite: a temporary separation of clone
  fragments into different clone classes. Figure 2.7b shows an example of this change
  pattern. Analogously to the MCI pattern it is a long-term pattern as well, however,
  indicating that a modification was accidentally not applied to all clone fragments
  of a clone class but caught up later. Before the missed modification is applied, the
  MGCI pattern is always preceded by either a VCI or MCI pattern.

2.6.2   Clone Class Patterns

Apart from evolution patterns related to individual fragments, evolution patterns have
been introduced targeting the evolution of clone classes. That is, changes to a clone
fragment are assessed in relation to its clone instances in the clone class. Therefore, clone
classes are mapped across multiple versions rather than individual clone fragments.

Kim and colleagues presented the first formal description of clone class patterns
in their study on clone genealogies [150]. They introduced six clone class evolution
patterns to define possible changes to a clone class between two versions, that is, the
cloning relationship between a clone class cc in one version v_i and the clone class cc' it
is mapped to in the subsequent version v_{i+1}. The described patterns are the following:

- Same: No clone fragment of the clone class was changed between the two versions
  v_i and v_{i+1}. That is, changes from v_i to v_{i+1} did not affect the clone fragments.

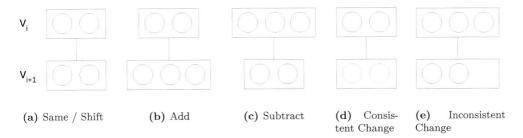

Figure 2.8 – Lineup of the short-term clone class evolution patterns by Kim and colleagues [150]. Dotted circles denote changed clone fragments.

- Shift: The position of at least one clone fragment of cc changed but still overlaps with a clone fragment in cc'. That is, the changes performed from v_i to v_{i+1} did only affect the position of a clone fragment resulting in a shift of that fragment in the code base.

- Add: At least one new clone fragment was added to cc' compared to cc. For instance, due to a newly introduced code fragment in v_{i+1} that is a clone of the clone fragments of cc. This pattern is equivalent to the *OCI* introduced by Bakota and colleagues [14].

- Subtract: At least one clone fragment disappeared in cc'. For instance, if one clone fragment of cc was eliminated from v_i to v_{i+1} by a performed refactoring. This pattern relates to the *VCI* pattern presented by Bakota and colleagues [14].

- Consistent Change: The same modification was applied to all clone fragments of cc in version v_i, thus, resulting in all fragments being part of cc' in version v_{i+1}.

- Inconsistent Change: At least one clone fragment of cc in version v_i was changed inconsistently compared to the other fragments, thus, resulting in all fragments being part of cc' in v_{i+1} except for the inconsistently changed fragment. This change pattern commonly occurs if a modification is unintentionally not applied to a fragment, for instance.

Figure 2.8 shows an example for each evolution pattern introduced by Kim and colleagues. In the model presented by Kim and colleagues evolution patterns do not necessarily occur exclusively. Instead, different types of evolution patterns may overlap and implicate each other. For instance, the *Add* and the *Consistent Change* pattern may occur at the same time and the *Inconsistent Change* pattern always implicates a *Subtract* pattern. The relation among the different patterns as given by Kim and colleagues in their original publication is shown in Figure 2.8 as Venn diagram.

Aversano and colleagues expanded the work of Kim and colleagues by adding further patterns regarding the evolution of clones [7]. They detailed the *Inconsistent Change* pattern presented by Kim and colleagues [150] by investigating the pattern not only for

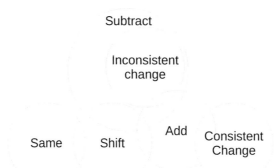

Figure 2.9 – Schematic illustration of the relationship among the short-term clone class evolution patterns introduced by Kim and colleagues [150] (taken from the original publication).

two versions of a system but for multiple. Using a long-term pattern it was analyzed how fragments of the same clone class were maintained by differentiating between inconsistently changed fragments that are continuously maintained independently and those that are made consistent in a later version. Accordingly, they divided the *Inconsistent Change* pattern into the *Independent Evolution* and the *Late Propagation* pattern. The *Independent Evolution* pattern describes two or more clone fragments of the same clone class that evolved differently after an inconsistent change from a version v_i to its consecutive version v_{i+1}. The *Late Propagation* pattern refers to the same situation with the only difference being that the inconsistent change is made consistent with another inconsistent change at a later point in time. This pattern may occur when changes are performed at different stages, for instance.

A similar study on clone class evolution patterns was presented by Thummalapenta and colleagues [250]. They presented three patterns related to consistent and inconsistent changes to clone fragments of a clone class. Analogously to Aversano and colleagues [7] the *Independent Evolution* and *Late Propagation* pattern—which is named *Delayed Propagation* in their study—are described in their study. The *Independent Evolution* and the *Late Propagation* pattern, respectively, presented by Aversano and colleagues and Thummalapenta and colleagues are strongly related to the clone fragment patterns *MCI* and *MGCI*, respectively, introduced by Bakota and colleagues. Examples of the *Independent Evolution* and the *Late Propagation* pattern are given in Figure 2.10a and Figure 2.10b, respectively. In addition to these two patterns, Thummalapenta and colleagues also introduce the *Consistent Change* pattern denoting that changes are applied to all clone fragments of the same clone class immediately throughout their whole lifetime. This corresponds to a sequence of *Consistent Change* patterns as described by Kim and colleagues [150]. Figure 2.10c shows an example of an long-term *Consistent Evolution* pattern.

Göde presented a unified model that represents the evolution of individual fragments, but facilitates deriving clone class evolution patterns also [87]. The *Clone Evolution*

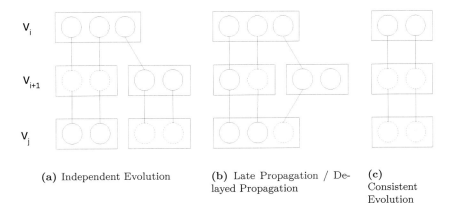

(a) Independent Evolution   (b) Late Propagation / De-   (c)
                                       layed Propagation   Consistent
                                                                 Evolution

Figure 2.10 – Long-term clone class evolution patterns by Aversano and colleagues [7] and Thummalapenta and [250] colleagues. Dotted circles denote changed clone fragments.

Graph (CEG) was derived from this model and is capable of representing short-term as well as long-term patterns for both clone fragments and clone classes. Göde used the tracking of individual clone fragments to detect another long-term pattern which is actually a variant of the *Late Propagation* pattern. The pattern approaches inconsistent changes to fragments of the same clone class that result in the disappearance of at least one fragment of the class. That is, due to the inconsistent changes the disappearing fragment is no clone instance of the other fragments anymore. Such disappearing fragments are being kept track of in the CEG, although not being part of a clone class and, hence, not being actually a clone fragment. These fragments are denoted as *Ghost Fragments* by Göde. By keeping track of *Ghost Fragments* it is possible to detect a *Late Propagation* of these fragments and also to determine their last ancestor when being a clone fragment of a clone class before the inconsistent change took place. Figure 2.11a and Figure 2.11b show the evolution of clone fragments without and with the ghost tracking technique proposed by Göde [87], respectively.

Research Questions

Various studies focused on the evolution of code clones and extracted different change patterns that can basically be categorized as short-term and long-term patterns. Especially the long-term patterns help to open up new possibilities to investigate important characteristics of cloning during software development. In contrast to the other patterns, the *Late Propagation* pattern for non-identical clones has only been targeted by Göde [87, 96]. Göde built his approach to detect the *Late Propagation* pattern for non-identical clones on his clone mapping technique as described in Section 2.5. That is, only the identical parts of a clone fragment are considered. He presented a corresponding clone evolution model and derived a graph from it. However, the technique has only been applied to analyze the evolution of identical clones yet. There

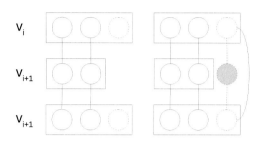

(a) Without *Ghost Frag-*
ment tracking

(b) With *Ghost*
Fragment tracking

Figure 2.11 – Tracking of disappeared clone fragments without and with
the approach presented by Göde [87]. Changed fragments are denoted by
dotted circles. Not tracking disappeared clone fragments results in a *Subtract*
and a later *Add* pattern, though, losing the ancestry information of the
reappearing fragment. Based on the tracking of *Ghost Fragments* (indicated
by dotted lines) the ancestry relation of the disappeared fragment (indicated
by a grey circle) can still be resolved in a later version.

is no empirical study to validate whether the suggested approach is suitable to analyze
the evolution of non-identical clones.

We conduct a comprehensive study to evaluate the *Late Propagation* pattern for non-
identical clones. We found the approach by Göde to be not feasible for large systems
with a high number of subject versions [26].

> **Question 6** – *How may a clone mapping look like that scales in detecting
> the* Late Propagation *pattern for a large number of versions of large-sized
> software systems?*

We present and evaluate a new detection approach for the *Late Propagation* pattern
for non-identical clones. A detailed description of this technique is given in Chapter 4.

2.7   Clone Evolution Analysis

Having access to the evolution of clones opens up new possibilities to analyze certain
characteristics. Evolution patterns can be used to investigate aspects not available by
investigating a single snapshot of a system only. For example, an analysis of the evolution
can reveal which clones are frequently changed and for how long clones exist in the code.
This makes studies on clone evolution a key piece in the puzzle of understanding and
addressing issues of code clones. Based on the introduced techniques to map clones
across multiple versions and to detect change patterns, several studies investigated how
clones evolve to gain further insights into the phenomenon of cloning. Depending on
the patterns considered, each study analyzes and reveals different aspects.

2.7.1   Clone Rate

Laguë and colleagues have been one of first to investigate the evolution of clones by conducting an experiment on the benefits of introducing function clone detection in an industrial software development process [168]. They used a clone detection technique proposed by Mayrand and colleagues [193] that computes the similarity of various metrics for functions. Two additions to the software development process have been presented to evaluate potential advantages of clone detection. The first modification was aimed at keeping the introduction of new clones in the system under control whereas the second one was directed to manage the base of code clones already existing in a system. The impact of these process modifications have been analyzed post mortem over a three year period of software development including six subsequently released versions of the system under study. Laguë and colleagues observed a slight growth of the clone rate in the subject system only as many clones have been removed. Moreover, it was also found that most clones were never changed after their initial creation. They conclude that applying clone detection as a preventive measure would help to keep the clone rate from growing and avoid the effort spent to remove them at a later point in time. In addition, the second process change was found to uncover opportunities for correcting defects before they affect customers.

A method to model clone evolution across multiple versions of a software system based on time series was presented by Antoniol and colleagues [4]. A metric-based clone detection approach was applied to identify clone fragments before modeling clones in terms of time series. Using the history of a system the authors used time series to predict the future evolution of the average number of clones per function. To evaluate the accuracy and performance of this method, a study on 27 subsequent versions of MINISQL has been performed. Results showed that the approach is able to predict the number of clones per function on an average error rate of 3.81%. Antoniol and colleagues used the same approach to conduct a more extensive study of clone evolution in the LINUX KERNEL [5]. Evaluating 19 releases of the system it was found that the clone rate was not relevant for the whole system as well as for the subsystems and tends to remain stable across versions—analogously to the findings by Laguë and colleagues.

Li and colleagues presented CP-MINER, a clone detection tool that uses frequent subsequence mining techniques to identify clones in large software systems [179, 180]. Based on the data mining process statements are first tokenized and then mapped to sequences of numbers in a database. Afterwards, the database is mined to find frequent subsequences that occur at least twice, representing clones. Analyzing the operating systems LINUX and FREEBSD showed an increasing amount of code clones as the systems evolved except for the last versions for which the clone rate remained relatively stable. However, the increase in the earlier versions was mainly caused by a few subsystems, for instance, "driver" and "arch" in LINUX and "sys" in FREEBSD.

The evolution of the LINUX KERNEL has also been studied by Livieri and colleagues [184]. They used the token-based clone detector D-CCFINDER, a distributed version of CCFINDER presented by Kamiya and colleagues [134], which is designed for clone detection in large source code corpora [185]. Examining 136 versions of the LINUX KERNEL they found that the amount of clones was proportional to the system size, whereas most clones were caused by a particular subsystem as reported by Li and colleagues also.

2.7.2   Changing Clones

Based on the mapping approach described in Section 2.5 Kim and colleagues investigated the evolution of type-1 and type-2 clones in two small Java systems [150]. They measured how long a detected clone genealogy existed in the system and found that detected clones were either very volatile—since being eliminated short after their introduction—or hard to remove. In both cases a refactoring is no good option as immediate refactorings of short-lived clones do not pay-off and the long-lived ones cannot be removed by standard refactoring methods. In addition, the change consistency of clone genealogies was anaylzed, that is, clone genealogies to which the *Consistent Change* pattern was applied at least once. Their results indicated that about one third of all genealogies of the subject systems have been changed consistently at least once. Yet, the study did not cover inconsistent changes and the relation of both consistent and inconsistent changes.

Saha and colleagues expanded the work of Kim and colleagues [150] by studying different aspects of clone genealogies at release level [233]. Kim and colleagues focused on the revision level of only two small systems both written in the programming language Java. Saha and colleagues used the same clone genealogy model, but examined how code clones evolve in software systems of varying sizes written in different programming languages. However, they slightly modified the clone genealogy extractor used in the previous study by replacing the location overlapping function by a snippet matching algorithm. The snippet matching algorithm maps a clone class between consecutive versions based on identifier matching. Using this adapted technique, they analyzed 17 open-source systems of varying sizes covering four different programming languages. Their results show that the majority of detected clones were either not changed or changed consistently and that many genealogies remain alive during the evolution. It was also found that the evolution of cloned code is neither remarkably affected by the project size nor the programming language.

Krinke performed a case study analyzing the ratio of consistent and inconsistent changes to cloned code in five open-source systems looking at weekly snapshots over a 200-week period of time [164]. He linked clone information obtained by the detection tool SIMIAN and change information extracted from software repositories to determine which clones were changed consistently and which inconsistently. He found that clones are changed inconsistently about half of the time and that late propagations were rare. Similarly, Göde obtained empirical data by analyzing the history of nine open-source systems over a one year period of time using snapshots on a daily basis also [87]. He reported that either consistent or inconsistent changes to clone classes were more frequent depending on the system and that more than half of the inconsistent changes remained persistent on average—not differentiating between intentional and accidental inconsistencies. Moreover, he found that cloned fragments existed more than a year on average. In a replication study Göde and Rausch analyzed three industrial systems and found that clearly more inconsistent than consistent changes were applied to clone fragments of the subject systems [95].

Göde and Koschke also studied the frequency and risks of changes to clones using the history of three subject systems [94]. They found that 12.2% of the clones were changed more than once and that nearly 14.8% of all changes to clones are unintentionally inconsistent. Based on the results they conclude that the history of clones provides important information to determine their relevance regarding maintenance tasks. Göde and Harder confirmed these findings in a follow-up study [91].

Using the approach described in Section 2.6.2 Aversano and colleagues investigated the consistency of changes to clones as well as the occurrence of the *Late Propagation* pattern by investigating the same two software systems as Kim and her colleagues did [7, 150]. Detecting consistent and inconsistent changes to clones the same procedure was used as by Kim and her colleagues: Clones were detected for each version separately and, afterwards, linked to source code changes extracted from the software repository. Based on the results of this step, every inconsistent changes was manually oracled to determine whether the inconsistently changed fragments evolved independently or were subject to *Late Propagated*. It was found that most clone classes are maintained consistently, whereas the majority of inconsistent changes to clone classes were intended. Most inconsistent changes that were accidental, were rated non-critical by the authors, e.g., changes to the layout. Thummalapenta and colleagues [250] extended the study by analyzing four different open-source software systems—two Java and two C systems. The results confirmed the findings of the previous study by Aversano and colleagues: clones are changed consistently in most cases and in case of inconsistent changes to clone fragments of the same clone class the affected fragments underwent an independent evolution. Inconsistent changes that were only temporarily, corresponding to the *Late Propagation* pattern, occurred rarely.

2.7.3   Clones and Defects

Bettenburg and colleagues used the tracking approach by Duala-Ekoko and Robillard [71] (described in Section 2.5) to investigate changes to clones at release level focusing on inconsistencies [36]. In a case study on two open-source systems they observed 72 releases in total, concluding that the risk of unintended inconsistencies is low and that only a very small number of inconsistent clones introduced defects. In addition, the lifetime of clones was observed and found to be rather high, in contrast to the findings by Kim and colleagues [150].

Aversano and colleagues analyzed the relationship of evolution patterns to bug fixing activities in a case study [7]. From a total of 17 bug fixes, they found four to be consistently propagated to all clone fragments and six to be inconsistently propagated intentionally due to an independent evolution of the fragments. The remaining seven defects were corrected by a late propagation of the corresponding fix—indicating that cloned defects may increase the risk of incomplete bug fixes. Bakota and colleagues came to the same conclusion based on the manual analysis of twelve consecutive versions of *Mozilla Firefox* [14]. Based on the evolution patterns described in Section 2.6.1 they found six changes related to defects and eight related to defects that were corrected by late propagation after an unintended inconsistency.

The correlation between inconsistent changes and defects was also investigated by Thummalapenta and colleagues [250] who found that occurrences of the late propagation pattern were often related to defect-correcting changes. Barbour and colleagues expanded this study [250] by using clone genealogies from two open-source systems to examine late propagations [19]. They found that the late propagation pattern indicates a risky cloning behaviour regarding defects. In a recent study towards the correlation of late propagations and defects Hui Mui analyzed four Java systems using an approach to detect late propagations based on log information provided by software repositories [207]. In contrast to Barbour's findings, it was found that late propagations are not very common and about one quarter of the detected ones cause a bug—concluding that the overall impact is moderate.

2.7.4   Impact on Maintainability

Monden and colleagues were the first to quantify the influence of duplicated code on software reliability and maintainability [205]. They detected code clones in a legacy system featuring more than twenty years of history using the token-based clone detection technique suggested by Kamiya and colleagues [134]. Reliability was defined by the number of defects found, that is, the less defects are found the more reliable the software system is. To estimate the maintainability of a system its number of revisions was used, that is, a system with a high revision number was considered more difficult to maintain compared to systems having low revision numbers—assuming that the number of revisions correlate to the change frequency of a system. Regarding the reliability measure it was found that modules containing cloned code are more reliable than non-clone modules on average except for modules containing clones with more than 200 lines of code which were found to be less reliable as modules without clones. In contrast, modules containing code clones were found to be less maintainable on average than those not containing any clones. Similarly to reliability, the maintainability decreased with an increasing amount of cloned code in a module.

Based on the assumption that a change to a clone fragment probably needs to be propagated to its other clone instances, too, Geiger and colleagues conducted a study on the relation of cloned code and change coupling [83]. Using CCFINDER [134] as clone detector, a framework was presented to examine code clones and relate them to change couplings taken from release history analysis. To relate clones and change couplings coverage values were computed for each and results were represented in a dot plot where each dot refers to a file pair sharing duplicated code. Values for code clone coverage were drawn on the X-axis and values for the change coupling coverage on the Y-axis, thus, dots would concentrate along the diagonal if high clone coverage leads to frequent change couplings and vice-versa. Evaluating the framework by investigating the open-source project MOZILLA revealed cases for which a relation between clones and change couplings was found, however, the relation was not statistically significant.

Another study directed to the relation of code duplications and changes to a system was conducted by Lozano and colleagues [187]. They presented the tool

CLONETRACKER to analyze with what frequency a method that once contained a cloned fragments at some point of time was changed—when containing a clone and when not containing a clone. The tool also counts the number of changes applied to method pairs containing the corresponding clone fragments in one transaction, again considering periods when they contained clones and when they did not. In a small case study using DNSJAVA as subject system the authors found that the amount and density of changes to methods in the cloning period were higher compared to when they did not contain cloned code. To validate the findings Lozano and Wermelinger performed a more comprehensive follow-up study [186]. In contrast to the results of the previous study, it was found that change effort increased only for less than half of the methods despite containing cloned. Nonetheless, in most of these cases the increase of change effort was statistically significant.

The extent of changes to cloned code compared to non-cloned code has been investigated by Krinke [165] who observed the development of five open source systems looking at weekly snapshots over a 200-week period of time. To detect clones the text-based clone detection tool SIMIAN[1] has been used. Krinke determined whether cloned or non-cloned code is more stable during the evolution of a system by counting changed source code lines, that is, whether the amount of changes applied to cloned or non-cloned code is larger. Results have shown that the dominating change performed was deletion of source code, for instance, massive deletions of code duplications. Eliminating these large deletions from the results, non-cloned code was found to be more stable concluding that cloned code does not necessarily increase maintenance effort in this respect.

A similar study was conducted by Hotta and colleagues [115]. In contrast to Krinke [165] they defined and analyzed the change frequency as indicator for maintenance costs. That is, they assumed that duplicated code is more costly regarding software maintenance when changes are more frequently applied to cloned code than to non-cloned code. Since the authors do not count the number of modified source lines but the frequency, the overall number of changes to cloned code is incremented by one if the changed code is completely included by a clone fragment and the overall number of changes to non-cloned code is incremented analogously if the modification was completely subsumed by non-cloned code. In case of changes crossing the border of cloned and non-cloned code both counters are incremented accordingly. Hotta and colleagues analyzed 15 open-source systems and found cloned code to be more stable than non-cloned code supporting the findings by Krinke.

Göde and Harder partially replicated and extended the work of Krinke [165] using a more fine grained measurement setup and different parameter combinations during the clone detection process [90, 104]. The evolution of five subject systems has been evaluated, two of the systems were part of Krinke's study already and two of them were from an industrial sector. By looking at each version available in the corresponding software repositories, changes have been extracted with the most detailed granularity possible using a retrospective analysis approach. Observing the evolution over a time period of up to five years of development, Göde and Harder were able to generally confirm Krinke's findings that cloned code is more stable than non-cloned code.

---

[1]http://www.redhillconsulting.com.au/products/simian/

Investigating why clones are less stable regarding deletions the authors found that instead of frequent intentional deletions, large amounts of cloned code is deleted in the course of general restructuring and clean-up activities. In addition, it was found that clones were not less stable compared to non-cloned code regarding deletions in the industrial systems.

Research Questions

The extent of clones in a software system has been evaluated mainly for type-1 and type-2 clones. Little is known on the evolution of non-identical clones and whether they differ from identical clones in some way. To the best of our knowledge, only Göde and Saha and colleagues conducted studies in which an approach to extract both identical and non-identical clone genealogies across multiple versions of a program was presented [87, 234]. Though, Göde did not gather any empirical data on the evolution of non-identical clones. Saha and colleagues concentrated on evaluating their clone genealogy extractor—characteristics of the evolution of clones have neither been investigated in their study. In addition, previous studies investigated a rather small number of subject systems and only a small section of the evolution of these. Thus, findings need to be validated by more comprehensive studies.

> **Question 7** – *Which clone type yields a higher clone rate?*

We investigate the clone rate of identical (type-1) and non-identical (type-2 and type-3) clones. The clone rate depicts how much of a system's source code is actually cloned. Furthermore, we analyze whether the clone rate of identical and non-identical clones tends to increase or decrease over time.

> **Question 8** – *Are non-identical clones more persistent than identical clones?*

The lifetime of cloned fragments is considered to be one indicator for their impact on maintenance tasks. Cloned fragments that are long-lived are usually claimed to be more relevant regarding software maintenance tasks, e. g., refactorings, because it may not pay off to remove clones proactively if they exist only for a short period a system.

> **Question 9** – *How often do identical clones change into non-identical clones and vice versa?*

During the lifetime of code clones it might be the case that the type of a fragment changes from identical to non-identical or vice versa. We analyze how frequent type changes occur and if they change more often in one particular direction.

> **Question 10** – *Are non-identical clones more frequently changed (consistently/inconsistently) or more often subject to late propagations?*

To investigate whether identical or non-identical clones change more frequently, we investigate consistent and inconsistent changes to cloned fragments. The change frequency of cloned fragments might provide information on the relevance of a clone with respect to maintenance costs—a programmer is most likely more interested in tracking and managing clones that are frequently changed. In addition, we adapted the existing definition of a late propagation to cover non-identical clones and use this definition to investigate if non-identical clones are more often subject to late propagations than identical clones.

To investigate the above questions we partially replicate and extend the study of Göde [87] by quantitatively analyzing nine open-source systems considering four years of each system's history. Based on our mapping approach that maps non-identical clone fragments in the context of their clone classes, data has been gathered that depicts and compares the evolution of type-1, type-2, and type-3 clones to provide further insights. The study and our findings are presented in detail in Chapter 4.

2.8   Management

Clone detection is just one of various activities directed towards dealing with redundancies in the source code. Detecting cloned code on its own does not suffice to mitigate problems caused by cloning nor to exploit potential benefits. Dealing with clones encompasses further activities that are summarized under the term clone management.

> *Clone management summarizes all process activities which are targeted at detecting, avoiding or removing clones.*
>
> — Giesecke (2007)

According to the above statement by Giesecke [84] clone management encompasses a wide range of software development activities. Koschke [158] supports that definition, adding that each of the various tasks provide information necessary to make founded decisions when performing active clone management:

> *To make informed decisions in clone management, we need to understand the reasons for clones, their risks and benefits, and ways to detect, track, present, remove, or consistently change them.*
>
> — Koschke (2008)

In Section 2.4 the detection of clones has already been discussed in detail. Based on the results presented by the clone detection process the location and relationship of clone fragments is available which can be considered a clone documentation of a system. In the following we focus on further clone management activities.

2.8.1   Monitoring

Reporting detected clones represents a snapshot of the current state of a software system. To support developers during their daily work, it is necessary to provide clone information not only at a specified point in time on request, but during the actual work. That is, clone management tools need to be integrated into the development process to provide continuous support. For example, tools can be integrated into IDEs or version control systems. Particularly, developers may be supported by monitoring approaches informing a developer whenever code changes are being applied that are related to redundancies. Such warning systems could help proactive clone management in terms of avoiding clones due to higher awareness of existing functionality, but also improve maintenance of cloned code in terms of decreasing effort for consistent changes or decrease the probability of unintended inconsistencies in the propagation of changes, respectively.

To inform developers whether currently changed code is cloned, different IDE plugins track clones based on the recording of clip-board activities (copy and paste of code) [65, 74, 116]. Jacob and colleagues also suggest to record copy and paste activities. The authors implemented the feature in an own editor—also capable of displaying differences between clones and visualizing changes to clone fragments [119]. Another feature aiming to support the propagation of changes to clones is linked editing as described by Toomim [252]. Different tools implement linked editing as plugins for IDEs [65, 74, 118]. Kawaguchi and colleagues introduced SHINOBI which is an add-on to Microsofts Visual Studio displaying clone instances of a clone fragment on mouse over [143]. There is also tool support to annotate clone fragments using a version control system. This is quite helpful if a clone fragment has been reviewed and its benefits and costs evaluated by a developer who decides not to remove the clone but document his or her findings [214, 215, 212]. Other developers do not have to encounter the same set of clone fragments based on the annotations unless modifications require corresponding updates to an existing review. CEDAR by Tairas and Gray incorporates the results from different clone detectors and displays certain clone properties of the result in an IDE [248].

Duala-Ekoko and Robillard focused on supporting developers avoiding unintended inconsistencies in propagating changes to clone fragments [71, 72, 73]. They introduced the tool CLONETRACKER which tracks clone fragments across consecutive versions and displays a warning to the user when potential inconsistencies to clones are introduced. Similar techniques were presented in other studies as well [54, 65, 263]. De Wit and colleagues were the only ones to extensively evaluate their tool, named CLONEBOARD, concluding that monitoring can be useful but supporting change propagation often requires more complex strategies than existing tools provide yet.

2.8.2   Visualization

Apart from integrating clone detection and its results into an IDE different ways to visualize a clone report have been introduced. Clone visualization helps the user to grasp different aspects of cloning aiding an effective analysis, for instance, an overview of the clone rate in specific modules or the whole system or how clone fragments evolve over time. Most clone detection tools just report clone data either as clone pairs or clone classes in a textual format providing basic information to the clones such as file path and name, exact position (e.g., line and column number), clone type (degree of similarity), and size (e.g., in lines of code or tokens). Visualization tools help to overcome the problem of very large clone findings presented as plain lists with properties—experience show that many systems contain very large numbers of clone fragments—and, hence, improve the usability of clone data provided by detection tools. A recent survey on clone visualization was presented by Basit and colleagues [22].

Early clone visualization used already known approaches like Hasse diagrams or scatter plots to represent similarity between source files and code fragments [58, 124, 125, 185, 255]. An advantage of scatter plots is that they are capable of representing intra- as well as inter-system clones. Fukushima and colleagues used a graph visualization to help identifying scattered clones by connecting clones located in the same file to clusters and then connecting different clusters based on their clone relation [82]. Tairas and colleagues proposed to visualize clones as colored stripes on bars representing source files where clones of the same clone class get the same color [249]. Similar approaches using shapes and colors, e.g., stacked bar charts, line graphs, or tree maps, to encode cohesion and coupling of code duplications were used in other tools as well [9, 103, 122, 129, 260, 272]. Jiang and colleagues proposed a hierarchical approach with respect to the filesystem particularly designed for the analysis of very large systems [122].

Apart from presenting clone fragments and their relations visualization tools have been introduced that allow for interactive use to explore clone data. Basically two approaches were presented: using hyperlinks or filtering. Cordy and colleagues provided an interactive way of exploring clones by using hyperlinks on HTML websites to navigate through the clone information [57]. Other tools support query based filtering to analyze the presented clones [103, 137, 138, 140, 267, 272]. Filtering techniques based on custom made queries help to mitigate the challenge in identifying useful cloning information out of a large volume of textual or graphical data.

The aforementioned approaches target visualization of clone information resulted from single version clone detection only. Studies have shown that visualization support can also aid the analysis of multi-version clone detection. Different techniques and tools have been proposed to visualize clone relations and properties of evolving clones. Adar and Kim presented SOFTGUESS which provides three visualization views to explore clones [1]. Clone evolution is represented by nodes depicting clone fragments which are arranged horizontally from left to right corresponding to a time axis—each column represents a single version. Clone fragments of the same clone class are arranged vertically in the same position and are linked by edges across versions. In addition, SOFTGUESS offers views to visualize more details on a single version, for instance, the distribution of clones in the system and containment relationships, and charting as well as a query mechanisms to filter certain clones. Another multi-perspective visualization tool, CYCLONE, for clone evolution was developed by Harder and Göde [103]. Similarly to Adar and Kim [1], evolutionary data is presented based on the arrangement and positioning of clone fragments and clone classes. However, CYCLONE arranges versions top down with each row representing a single version and edges connecting clone fragments across consecutive versions rather than clone classes. Clone fragments are grouped in rectangles depicting clone classes again. Further functions and views, e.g., filtering, tree map, and charts, allow to analyze specific clone data such as clone type, type of changes (consistent or inconsistent) and clone rate over time. Analogously to the previous two tools, Asaduzzaman and colleagues developed VISCAD for supporting clone evolution visualization [6].

2.8.3   Removal

Clone research got popular with the assumption of cloned code being the worst code smell, thus, harming software quality and maintenance [81]. Accordingly, a major aim of studies has been to mitigate the problem of redundancies in the source code by refactoring clones. Fowler even argued to remove code clones whenever detected and possible and presented a catalog proposing suitable refactoring patterns for removing code duplications [81]. The refactorings listed in that catalog can be categorized in three general types which will be shortly described in the following. Nonetheless, clone removing refactorings may introduce other conflicts and issues which developers prefer to avoid instead of removing cloned code [55].

Low-Level Operations: Low-level refactorings that may be used to prepare the removal of cloned code are among others identifier renaming, splitting of loops, and substitution of conditionals [273]. Especially consistent renaming of parameters and identifiers are commonly used after copy and paste activities to adapt a clone fragment to the new context. Such refactorings are provided by many IDE now, thus, a developer does not need to manually rename all references of identifiers. Additionally, plugins are available aiming to identify inconsistencies in the renamings of identifiers suggesting appropriate adaption [118, 212]. Kerievsky proposed to eliminate code clones by applying the chained constructor refactoring pattern to constructors of the same class [147, 210]. Extracting clones into aspect-oriented patterns was presented by Schulze and colleagues [238]. They proposed the *extract feature into aspect, extract fragment into advice,* and *move method from class to interface* patterns.

General Software Refactorings: Among the various general software refactoring patterns applied to remove clones are *Extract Method, Pull Up Method,* and *Extract Superclass* [109, 174, 237, 269, 273, 274]. The most prominent pattern to remove clones is the *Extract Method* refactoring which replaces two or more clone fragments by a call to a newly created method [24, 78, 132, 152, 255, 273, 274]. Fanta and Rajlich described different scenarios that can be used to remove function level clones using appropriate patterns [78]. To identify which refactoring pattern is best suited to remove certain clones, Higo and colleagues suggest to filter the results provided by a clone detector [108, 109]. Automatically applying patterns to refactor type-3 clones is more challenging, however. Approaches are needed that are capable of abstracting from the differences to allow unifications. Komondoor and Horwitz make use of PDGs to support refactoring of fragments with different statement order, thus, preserving the semantic [151, 152]. Juillerat and Hirsbrunner presented a technique that allows for automated refactoring certain parts of individual statements [132]. A technique that is able to refactor and unify identical as well as non-identical code clones was presented by Krishnan and Tsantalis [166, 167]. The approach identifies maximal identical control structures within detected clones. For non-identical clones differences between clone fragments are examined against a set of preconditions to determine whether they can be parameterized without changing the program behavior. Due to the challenge of preserving semantics in case of non-identical clone fragments, some approaches aim to only suggest or provide semi-automated refactoring [15, 16, 200]. That is, developer interaction is needed to perform or complete a refactoring to make sure the semantic of the code is not changed.

Generics and Templates: Focusing on programming languages that are preprocessed, Baxter and colleagues proposed to extract duplicated code into macros which are invoked at every location where the clones occurred [24]. A parameterization of the macros can be used to eliminate non-identical clones as well. However, macros may be used carefully because they may decrease the comprehensibility of the system.

Basit and colleagues presented studies on the use of generics to remove cloned code [23]. Analyzing two libraries, the Java Buffer Library and the C++ Standard Template Library, they were able to refactor about 40% of the detected clone fragments only. Based on the study results the authors conclude that the use of generics is limited by the constraints of language constructs and meta level parameterizations may perform better since not being as restrictive. In a follow-up study Jarzabek and Li performed a case study on cloning in the JAVA BUFFER LIBRARY [120]. They propose a technique to unify clones in situations in which it is difficult to eliminate them with conventional program design techniques because of missing generic design mechanisms. Their framework concentrates on buffer classes using a generative programming technique on top of the actual programming language which was JAVA. Similarities in classes and methods were delegated to this generic language aiming an appropriate unification while the core functionality was still programmed in the conventional language. Cloned structures are replace by generic structures that are enriched with information on how to obtain instances of the generic structures in a required form. The approach has been evaluated in qualitative and quantitative ways as well as in a controlled experiment. It was found that unifying clones reduced code size which is assumed to reduce conceptual complexity—by 68% in case of the JAVA BUFFER LIBRARY. Moreover, the changeability is supposed to be enhanced by decreasing the code size at rates proportional to the code size reduction.

Though, many studies prupose ways to remove cloned code, only a vague idea of costs and benefits exists. Without substantial research on clone removals and their economic consequences, clone management will remain questionable or even risky and does not become an integral part of the daily work of developers. Therefore, clones that have been automatically detected need to be ranked by the relevance to a specific maintenance task. Studying clones that were actually removed by developers may give indicators for a suitable relevance ranking. Apart from the challenge of ranking clones according to their relevance towards certain tasks, there is only a gain in removing clones if it can be shown that cloned code causes higher maintenance costs than an appropriate abstraction.

Göde presented the first empirical study of code clone removals [89]. Clone removals were identified by a semi-automated approach mainly consisting of three phases. First, clones are detected using a state-of-the-art clone detection tool, before those clones are filtered out that cannot be part of a clone removing refactoring; for instance, clones that were not affected by any changes can be neglected. In the last phase Göde manually assessed the remaining code clones and changes applied to identify refactorings deliberately performed to remove duplicated code. Different aspects of deliberate clone removals were investigated using this framework to get a clue of the developers' view on clones. Analyzing four open-source systems he found a number of intentional clone removals, but the gap to clones detected by a clone detector was remarkable though. Moreover, it was found that the scope of the refactorings hardly ever matched the scope of detected clones indicating that the developers lacked awareness of the extent of clones in the projects, that detected clones subsume smaller inner clones, or that clone tools are not accurate enough. Regarding metrics that might be useful to detect duplications that are good candidates for refactorings the findings did not provide clear results. Finally, Göde analyzed the committers of clone removals and found that the less people were involved in the projects, the more intentional removal of code clones took place.

Bouktif and colleagues presented a first effort model to schedule refactorings aiming at removing code clones in procedural code [38]. A more comprehensive effort model for estimating clone refactoring effort has been proposed by Zibran and colleagues [274]. Considering possible conflicts in scheduling clone refactorings, the authors apply a constraint programming approach to compute an optimal solution of the problem. In a case study with six software systems they found that the model is complete and useful to estimate code clone refactoring effort. Related research towards scheduling and ranking of code clone refactorings has been done by Lee and colleagues [174] as well as Mondal and colleagues [203]. A generic algorithm approach to compute an optimal refactoring schedule for code clones is used by Lee and colleagues. The authors compared their proposed technique to existing solutions concluding that their approach computes more beneficial schedules compared to the others. Mondal and colleagues suggest clones for refactoring based on a defined pattern which covers clone fragments that have changed consistently. Based on the analysis of thirteen subject systems the authors found that clones suggested by the pattern can be considered important candidates for refactoring.

The first analytical cost model to estimate the increase of maintenance costs caused by duplicated source code has been presented by Jürgens and Deißenböck [127]. The model estimates the increase of maintenance effort relative to a system without any cloning rather than computing absolute costs of clones. Based on the assessment of potential effects of cloning and the evaluation of investments in clone management activities they performed a case study on 11 industrial software systems to evaluate their cost model. Results of the study indicate that the impact of code clones varies heavily between systems and is substantial for some of the subject systems—concluding that the benefits outweigh the costs of active clone management for these systems.

Research Questions

The aforementioned studies cover different important aspects of the evolution of clones. Still, there are some limitations that we try to overcome in ours. The results presented by Göde [89] are based on a relatively small amount of data and need to be validated by a more extensive analysis. Furthermore, he considered deliberate clone removals only, however, clones may also be removed accidentally. None of the previous studies analyzed cost-benefit-aspects beyond the removal of a clone.

Question 11 – *How often is duplicated code deliberately and how often accidentally removed?*

Just as Göde [89] did, we investigate whether and with what frequency code clones have been deliberately removed by developers. An answer gives a clue about the programmer's view on managing duplications. Apart from deliberate removals that have been subject of the previous study by Göde, clones might be removed accidentally as a side effect by some other change. We analyzed how often duplicated source code is removed by arbitrary code modifications by chance. Frequent accidental clone removals could be a reason for developers not to manage clones actively as the problem will resolve itself in the long-term.

Question 12 – *Are there clones that are missed by a refactoring?*

Besides analyzing clones that have been removed by refactorings, we also investigate whether or not duplicated code that could have been removed in consequence of a performed refactoring was missed by developers—which was also no subject of Göde's study. Developers may miss clones when performing a suitable refactoring if they are not aware of them. This risk could be mitigated using automated tool support that provides useful information.

Question 13 – *By what type of refactorings is duplicated code deliberately and by what type of refactorings accidentally removed?*

In addition to investigating the frequency of removals, the refactorings applied to resolve duplicated code are compared to clones detected by a state-of-the-art detection tool. As a result of the comparison existing weaknesses in automated detection can be uncovered. Particularly, information on refactorings that were actually not meant to remove cloned code but even so did, might contribute to the improvement of clone management tools by uncovering characteristics that indicate good clone candidates for a removal—focusing exclusively on deliberately removed clones might not reveal these characteristics.

Question 14 – *What type of measurable code characteristics may help in ranking clone candidates for removal?*

Having detected deliberate and accidental clone removals in the evolution of software systems, it would be useful to extract code characteristics that flag clones to be removed. The approach presented by Göde [89] to detect clone removals, which has been adapted in this paper, is only semi-automated. Being able to use code characteristics to further automate the detection process would contribute to the improvement of clone management tools as the information helps to provide meaningful data to the user only. Göde investigated a few preliminary metrics, but his results suggest that those metrics do not clearly indicate good candidates. We will extent his preliminary study by analyzing additional metrics.

Question 15 – *Which effect do clone removals have on software maintenance?*

Tracking and analyzing source code that has solely been introduced to remove clones over time will uncover so far unknown aspects and, therefore, is of great interest. The hypothesis is that the more new code fragments change over time after they have been introduced the more maintenance costs have been saved in the mid and long term since changes have to be performed only once. In addition, the risk of inconsistent changes to different clone fragments is eliminated and does not need to be taken care of anymore— which most probably reduces maintenance costs as well.

We extend previous work on clone removals to validate and extend existing results based on a more comprehensive analysis of clone removals. Besides investigating refactorings that have been performed by developers to remove cloned code, we track and analyze code fragments that have been introduced as a consequence of these refactorings. Results of this analysis will help to improve the understanding of costs and benefits of clone removals, especially considering long-term effects. To the best of our knowledge, this is the first study on software clones to go beyond the removal of code duplications to contribute to a better understanding of costs and benefits of clone management. Chapter 5 describes our empirical analysis of clone removals and their cost-benefit ratio.

2.9   Human-based Studies

The majority of empirical studies on the effect of duplicated code is commonly based on retrospective analysis using source code repositories or defect issue databases. Although such data may provide valuable insights towards the relation of clones and maintainability, other important factors are left out since retrospective analysis considers only the result of a possibly more complex sequence of actions. For instance, a bug fix with preceding tedious localization effort may appear as a simple and small change in the source code. To observe and investigate the benefits of clone-management tools and human interaction in dealing with clones during maintenance activities such as defect reproduction, program comprehension, code changes, and testing, other approaches are necessary. Controlled experiments are appropriate to bridge the gap and help to investigate such aspects in a controllable manner.

Carver and colleagues consider human-based studies an important but yet largely neglected approach to complement findings that are based on analytical studies only [45]. As software repositories contain only snapshots of data and activities, it is only possible to obtain the state of artifacts before and after activities have been performed that produce the snapshots. That is, it is not possible to confidently determine the activities between two versions in a repository. Although, recognizing the value of analytical data, the authors emphasize that speculating about human behavior using such data is not adequate enough. Instead, claims need to be validated more thoroughly focusing on human-based studies. The authors argue that human-based studies could provide insights to the very basic question (among others) whether or not clones are harmful regarding software maintenance.

In an ethnographic study Kim and colleagues analyzed copy-and-paste programming practices of developers to uncover opportunities for assistance [148]. Developers were observed directly or using an instrumented ECLIPSE IDE which recorded their editing operations in combination with a follow-up interview to understand the developers' tasks and confirm the interpretation of the recorded activities. Based on the collected information a taxonomy of copy-and-paste usage patterns has been derived. They observed that developers often recall those clones they have created themselves and adapt them to the pasted context, mainly using them as either syntactic or semantic templates for implementing new functionality. In contrast to an intended application, the authors found copy-and-paste programming was also induced by existing architectural and design decisions. Regarding maintenance tasks arising due to cloning, it was found that developers tend to apply certain changes shortly after pasting code, for instance, renaming of variables, while other changes are performed at a later point in time, such as refactoring multiple copied code segments—in both cases the changes are generally applied consistently to the corresponding copies. However, it is noted that the results indicate that a developer's recollection of performed copy-and-paste actions may be short-lived, somewhat inaccurate, and difficult to transfer to other developers. Based on their findings, Kim and colleagues propose a set of tools to reduce maintenance problems incurred by copy-and-paste programming and to better support the intents of commonly used cloning scenarios.

In another observational study, Chatterji and colleagues addressed the questions on whether and how developers use clone information in bug localization tasks and whether there is any difference between novice and professional developers in this respect [50]. They observed developers in two bug localization tasks in systems they were unfamiliar with. One bug was contained in cloned code, the other one was not cloned (intended as a placebo). The participants were not required to actually fix the defect. The participants received a clone report created by CCFINDER [134] which was available in textual form only. No further clone-management support was given and no integration of the reported data in any type of IDE was available. Most of their participants did not use the clone report correctly—possibly because of insufficient training or missing tool support. Their study indicates that there is a relationship between correct use of the clone report and effectiveness (i.e., those who used the clone report correctly were more effective in detecting defects), as well as that clone-detection ability is heavily reliant on experience, as professionals tended to use the clone report correctly more often than novices. Nonetheless, the design of the study does not truly allow to establish causal relationships. They conjecture that the clone report might not necessarily help developers locate the initial defect in a large software system, but it will help them locate clones of that defect.

The first human-based controlled experiment to evaluate how a developer's performance is affected by clones in specific maintenance tasks has been conducted by Harder and Tiarks [105]. In a controlled experiment with a total number of 33 participants—including students as well as experts in the field of software clones—they analyzed how the removal of a defect is influenced by the fact that it is cloned or not. No clone information, clone tools or other hints related to clones have been given to the subjects. Based on the results they used statistical significance tests to investigate the performance in terms of time and correctness. The results of the statistical tests did not indicate a significant difference in the time needed to correct cloned defects nor the correctness of the solutions. Nonetheless, they observed many cases in which cloned defects were repaired incompletely. That is, often only one occurrence of the cloned defect was located and fixed.

Chatterji and colleagues [49] replicated the controlled experiment by Harder and Tiarks with a different sample of participants. This replication neither yielded any significant difference in the time needed to solve the tasks. In contrast to the original study, however, the replication showed that it was significantly more difficult to correctly fix a cloned bug than a non-cloned one. Moreover, they extended the previous study by an additional task for which the developers were provided with a clone report in textual form and a training on how to use it. The results of this extension indicate that developers perform significantly better when a clone report of the software system is available than without any clone information.

Research questions

The impact of clones has been investigated mostly by retrospective analysis of software systems. Only little effort has been spent to investigate human interaction, that is, human-based studies on the effect of clones in defect localizing and repairing tasks are very rare in clone research. None of the aforementioned studies has sufficiently evaluated the support clone-management tools can offer in such tasks yet. Either the developers were not supported by any kind of clone management tool in these studies or the level of tool support was minimal, that is, only a simple clone report as a textual list of clones without any further integration in an integrated development environment (IDE) was provided. So these studies did not investigate the full potential clone management tools can offer.

> **Question 16** – *Does the time needed to remove a cloned defect decrease when clone information is available?*

It may seem obvious that it may take less time to fix a defect that is cloned when clone information is accessible. Yet, this clone information must be interpreted, filtered, and inspected by a developer, which causes some overhead. By answering this question, we aim at providing evidence as to whether it takes more time to fix a cloned defect without any clone information. Moreover, if a difference exists, we investigate the extent of the difference.

> **Question 17** – *Does the probability of incorrect or incomplete removals of cloned defects decrease when clone information is available?*

A commonly stated threat is that clones may lead to inconsistent or incomplete changes. By answering this question, we aim to provide empirical evidence as to whether the risk of inconsistent changes is reduced by providing clone information.

We think that some design decisions of Chatterji and colleagues [49] regarding the extension part (compared to the original study by Harder and Tiarks [105]) of their study should be reconsidered to allow for a more accurate inspection of the effect of clone information on software maintenance. First, they used a textual clone report as in their previous study [50]. To investigate the effect of clone information on the performance of programmers, a more realistic scenario in terms of daily work and development environment is necessary. Therefore, we provide clone information and clone browsing using a simple tool integrated in an existing and well known IDE. Besides the missing tool support, the participants were most probably biased by a learning effect because the same subjects and software systems were used for the replication part and the extension with all participants required to solve the tasks related to the replication first. Afterwards, they were already familiar with the source code as well as the defective features for both systems because the defects changed only in the fact as to whether they occurred in form of a clone or as a non-cloned abstraction. The learning effect of the subjects probably lead to a better performance in the tasks related to the study extension. Moreover, performance was analyzed for the extension in terms of correctness only. No data were collected that allow for conclusions on the efficiency in terms of time. Finally, Chatterji and colleagues assigned the subjects to two groups such that each participant was required to solve a cloned defect in one of the systems and a non-cloned defect in the other one. To evaluate the effect of clone information on the performance of developers when fixing cloned bugs, it is more appropriate that each participant is required to fix a cloned bug in each system and to switch the order for which of the systems clone information is provided to the participants. We chose exactly this experiment design—each defect occurs twice in both subject systems. This enables us to compare the performance of the programmers repairing a cloned defect once with and once without the help of clone information.

We conducted a controlled experiment that evaluates how a developer's performance—in terms of time and correctness—is affected when clone information is provided while dealing with a common bug-fixing task involving a cloned defect. To overcome the shortcomings of pure textual information, we offer a more realistic tool support in our experiment that provides contextual clone information integrated in an IDE (i.e., only the clones of the currently inspected file are shown) and enables the user to easily browse through existing clones and to identify the location of each clone fragment. This kind of tool support is more realistic for assessing the effect of clone management tools that try to compensate for risks imposed by clones and leverages the user's experience with his or her familiar IDE. We present our controlled experiment in Chapter 6.

2.10 Code Search

Often changes, for instance, correcting a defect, must be corrected not only at one particular place but in many places and in other versions of a system than the current one—possibly even in different development branches. Consequently, we need a technique to efficiently locate all approximate matches of an arbitrary code fragment in the program's history as they may need to be changed as well. This kind of code search is a specialized problem of clone detection as code segments are related to each other based on their similarity—in our case syntactic similarity. There are two main differences to the more general problem of detecting cloned fragments:

(1) The user defines a certain code fragment of which similar fragments are of interest and need to be located. That is, not all existing clones of a system are detected and eventually ranked afterwards, but just specific clone instances of the user-defined code fragment.

(2) It is sufficient if the user-defined code fragment, which represents the code to be searched, occurs just once in the code base of an arbitrary version. Therefore, we are not necessarily searching for cloned code if the user-defined code fragment is not considered a clone fragment itself.

Approximate search is the problem of finding all matches of a query pattern in a larger text, both of which are arbitrary sequences of tokens in our case. Different algorithms have been proposed to solve this problem. Among these are the algorithms by Baeza-Yates and Perleberg [8], [101], Chang and Lawler [47], [48] and Myers [209]. Further algorithms were, for example, presented by Wu and Manber [265] as well as Pevzner and Waterman [218].

Apart from the general problem of finding approximate matches, certain approaches specifically focus on searching large bodies of source code as we basically do. Prominent code search engines include GOOGLE CODE SEARCH and KODERS.COM. Although these search engines scale well, they do not support queries in the form of arbitrary source code fragments. That is, queries have to be specified in a particular language and finding approximate matches is left to the user who needs to formulate the corresponding regular expressions. The same limitations hold for tools like GREP and AGREP.

Lee and colleagues proposed an approach to efficiently find approximate matches of a given code fragment in a large body of source code [173]. This is done by first creating an index that represents the source code and then locating matches of a query code fragment using this index. Although the approach is fast, it requires an AST representation of the source code. This prohibits searching for syntactically incorrect code or code that contains preprocessor directives. Furthermore, the approach is not designed to operate on multiple versions and branches of a system.

Another index-based technique to locate duplicate code fragments has been presented by Hummel and colleagues [117]. Matches are detected based on chunks of n sequential statements. Although the technique is fast in principle, the authors note that runtime is "severely affected" when n is smaller than 5. The approach is not applicable to our scenario since code fragments always have to align with statement bounds. In addition, the technique tolerates only differences in identifiers and literals but does not detect approximate matches where certain tokens occur in one of the fragments only. Finally, both approaches [173], [117] require additional effort for constantly maintaining the index.

Keivanloo and colleagues presented a multi-level indexing approach using hash table-based and binary search to improve Internet-scale real-time code clone search response time [144]. They showed that 32-bit hash values are sufficient in almost all cases and, thus, were able to reduce memory consumption for keeping the hash values. They performed an evaluation on an Internet-scale corpus (1.5 million Java files and 266

MLOC) and found that their approach has response times in the microseconds range on average.

Research questions

The approximate search of code fragments is strongly related to clone detection and could in theory be solved using a modified version of a clone detector. The query fragment would be added to the source code of each version and all classes of similar fragments detected subsequently. After that, one would need to discard all clone classes but those that contain the query fragment. However, first detecting and then discarding the majority of clones is an unnecessary overhead for our use case, which makes clone detection a poor solution to this problem.

> **Question 18** – *How can approximate matches of arbitrary code fragments be detected in an incremental fashion?*

To avoid the overhead of detecting all clones in a software system before discarding the majority of them, an algorithm tailored to search for approximate matches of a given query fragment is needed. The approximate code search introduced in this work reuses some of the concepts of clone detection, especially those targeting an incremental approach since we want to allow searching in the whole history of a program. In this work, we use the algorithm by Chang and Lawler [47] as the basic concept, because it is faster and more robust than the approach by Baeza-Yates and Perleberg [8]. Although, Myers' algorithm [209] is even faster, it contains a preprocessing step [101] which is not considered in the runtime evaluation and which we expect to be expensive in our application. The algorithms by Wu and Manber [265] as well as Pevzner and Waterman [218] were not considered by us due to a missing proof of their claimed runtime. Our approach to detect approximate matches to an arbitrary code fragment in multiple versions of a software system and its implementation in the tool APPROX, are described in Chapter 7.

> **Question 19** – *Can we provide evidence that APPROX can be used to detect incomplete corrections of defects in real-world systems?*

First, we investigate how much time is needed by APPROX to locate all approximate matches of an arbitary code fragment. Since the runtime is likely to be influenced by the parameters used, we also evaluate their effect on the performance. Afterwards, we analyze the approximate matches found in our subject systems to see whether we can find indications of incomplete defect corrections since the use case for APPROX is finding situations where corrections of defects have not been propagated to all affected code fragments.

2.11   Summary

This chapter presented previous research that is most related to the work presented in this thesis. Various subjects and techniques were described related to the extent of cloning, evolution of clones and assessment of clone management. Though, existing work provided valuable insights already, different shortcomings have been pointed out from which research questions were derived. The remaining chapters of this thesis address these questions and provide answers to them in terms of technical implementations and results of empirical analysis gathered in several studies.

Part II

Studies

Chapter 3

Software Clone Rates

Early researchers in clone detection reported a high number of clones in the systems they investigated. Baker reported a clone rate of 19 % for the X Window System sources [11] using a token-based clone detector. Baxter et al. found a clone rate of 28 % in three subsystems of a commercial process-control system consisting of 400 KLOC [24] using a syntax-based clone detection technique. An extreme clone rate of even 59 % was reported by Ducasse et al. for a commercial payroll system [75] using a textual clone detector. Roy and Cordy compared clone rates of eight Python programs ranging in size from 9 to 272 KLOC to programs written in ten C, seven Java and six C# systems varying in size from 4 to 6,265 KLOC [228] and report clone rates in the range of 0.1 and 72.2 % for different thresholds of similarity. Their clone detector uses a textual line-based comparison by means of longest common subsequence (LCS) to compare syntactic blocks (functions in this study) in the pretty-printed and normalized source code. The clone rates of these studies are difficult to compare because different clone detection technologies were applied to different systems with different thresholds for minimal length of a clone (30 SLOC by Baker, 10 SLOC by Ducasse et al, an unpublished length by Baxter et al.). Moreover, it is not clear whether these systems are representative. Nevertheless these clone rates are often cited and used to motivate research in software clones.

The clone rate is an important aspect to assess the urgency of cloned code. The reason for this is straight forward: Every drawback that is related or even caused by cloned code fragments weighs more heavily the more clones exist in a system. If the clone rate for most software systems were extremely low, however, it would be arguable whether clones can have a considerable impact on the overall software quality and maintainability and are worth being investigated at all. On the other hand, high clone rates may justify effort spent to manage clones actively.

Clones may be in the same file, same directory or elsewhere. Related to that, a general conjecture is that the farther away clones are, the higher are the chances that a developer misses their consistent update. Roy and Cordy find in their study that on average, cloned functions tend to be more in different files in the same directory than in different directories [228]. The least fraction of cloned functions is located in the same file. It must be noted, however, that there is a large variance among different systems and statistical significance tests were not used. Whether these results hold for a larger set of programs and also for arbitrary code fragments rather than only cloned functions is not clear.

In this chapter we report on a large scale analysis of clones for 9,666 open-source projects written in C, C++, C#, or Java, summing up to 310 MSLOC to shed light on expected clone rates and locality of clones. We use statistical analysis to estimate the means and variances of clone rates and their likely type of frequency distribution. In addition, we look at the locality of clones, that is, whether clones are mostly local or rather spread over very different parts of a project. We search for correlations among project size and clone rate. In addition to that, our approach for creating a human oracle may be a model for other researchers to create benchmarks for clone research. Findings presented in this chapter will answer the following research questions presented in Section 2.3:

> **Question 1** – *What is the average clone rate of projects in open source?*
>
> **Question 2** – *Is there a difference in the average clone rate among C, C++, C#, and Java open-source programs?*
>
> **Question 3** – *Does clone rate (of files and projects) depend on size?*
>
> **Question 4** – *Do clones tend to be local in project source trees?*

3.1   Study Setup

This section describes our study. We will first describe the projects analyzed and then how the clones were detected using a clone detector whose filters were trained empirically through human oracles. After that we describe our quantitative and qualitative findings and finally our threats to validity.

3.1.1   Source Code Corpora

We analyzed open-source projects from the following four sources:

- **Audris Mockus's data set**: We used a corpus including projects hosted on SourgeForge and GoogleCode gathered by Audris Mockus. The corpus contains projects written in the languages C, C++, C#, Java and Pascal with a commit history of at least 33 commits and a lifespan greater than one year. In addition, projects with limited defect data or without fix-inducing commits have been filtered out—for more details about this corpus, we refer to [270].

- **Iman Keivanloo's data set**: Iman Keivanloo provided us with a corpus that has been crawled focusing on projects from reputable organizations and projects such as Google chromium, Mozilla, and Eclipse[1].

---

[1]Personal communication with Iman Keivanloo, Feb. 26th, 2015

- **Ubuntu Sources**: The Ubuntu sources provide a well known and large data set of programs frequently used and continuously developed in the open-source community. Using the Unix tool *apt-get*, we mirrored the Ubuntu C sources of version 10.04 (downloaded on 12/17/2010) for an earlier study on clone detection [161].

- **GitHub**: While the first three sources provided us with a large number of subject systems written in the languages Java, C and C++, the number of programs written in C# was quite small. To add more programs written in C# we used the GitHub API v3 to clone open-source systems maintained on GitHub. Through this API, we downloaded about 890 projects written in C#. Except for the programming language the only other constraint used for downloading was that each project needed to be at least 1,000 kilobytes in size. The GitHub API requires a fixed size limit in terms of bytes for all project content including graphics and the like and does not allow for queries related to a project's size in terms of lines of code. Our minimum size constraint was selected to filter out very small projects. The GitHub API provides the projects—ordered by name—matching the given criteria.

The different corpora overlapped in a number of projects because they were obtained from different sources. To count every project only once, we removed repeated projects based on different criteria. First, we searched all corpora for projects having the same name, excluding version numbering and minor spelling differences in the project names. That alone, however, is not enough due to possible renaming, e.g., long project names were often replaced by shortcuts. To also detect duplicated projects with different names, we compared all files between corpora through hashing their content. This comparison creates hash values for the token-type sequences of length 200 tokens for every file. A token type categorizes the text, but abstracts from each exact textual representation. For instance, the type of all identifiers is a particular token type *id*, abstracting from the actual name of the identifiers. This abstraction allows us to detect exact copies as well as copies with parameter renaming—that is, type-1 and type-2 clones on file level. For each manually verified match, we then removed the copy that was either smaller in terms of lines of code or—if both were the same size—the older one in terms of development revision. Besides duplicated projects we found that specific libraries (e.g., image processing libraries) are used by a relatively large number of projects among all corpora. The source code of such libraries were contained in the project sources. To rule out bias on the overall detected clone ratio as with duplicated projects, we extracted these libraries once and considered them as a project of their own and removed all of its instances in all containing projects. Finally, generated code was excluded by searching for patterns that are common for generated code, e.g., the term *generated* as part of the file path, file names matching *y.tab.[ch]* or *lex.yy.[ch]*. We manually checked such matches to make sure that the code was really generated.

Unlike the GitHub and Ubuntu corpora, the other two corpora include projects of different programming languages. As mentioned before we focus only on projects written in Java, C, C++ or C# in this study. Therefore, we need to identify which languages

Table 3.1 – Descriptive statistics on analysis projects

corpus	#projects	C	C++	C#	Java	#files	SLOC	#tokens
Ubuntu	6,819	6,819	0	0	0	670,393	204,984,212	1,232,289,476
Mockus	1,482	268	517	106	684	185,873	41,353,791	279,843,288
Keivanloo	476	64	176	20	265	434,847	46,258,975	325,951,455
GitHub	889	8	36	888	21	156,174	17,586,364	112,567,801
Total	9,666	7,159	729	1,014	970	1,447,287	310,183,342	1,950,652,020

are used to implement each project. We used generally used conventions for file name extensions to do so, based on the following patterns:

- **C**: .c, .h, .cc, .hh

- **C++**: .h, .c++, .cpp, .hpp, .cxx, .hxx, .qml

- **C#**: .cs

- **Java**: .java, .groovy, .scala

Projects that are not written in one of the above four languages were dismissed from the subject corpora. For all remaining projects the programming language was determined using the above file-extension patterns and considered during the clone detection process.

Some projects consist of multiple languages. We analyzed the code of multi-language projects separately. That is, we treat the part written in one language as a project of its own. In other words, an *analysis project* in our study is that part of an open-source project that is written in the same programming language. Formally, an analysis project is a pair of an open-source project and a programming language.

Table 3.1 summarizes the corpora under study. Column *#project* lists the number of open-source projects of each corpus. We analyzed 9,666 open-source projects (original projects, not analysis projects). The columns for the languages list the number of analysis projects for the respective language instead. Their sum does not add up to the number in column *#project* when there are multi-language projects. Overall, the percentage of projects written in two languages is 1.78 % and for three languages it is 0.18 %. There is no project in our corpora written in four languages. That is, 98.04 % are written in only one language. In total, we analyzed 310 MSLOC. Project size is also given in terms of number of tokens. A token is a non-divisible unit of source code, for instance, a keyword, delimiter, literal, or identifier. Tokens are a more suitable measure in our study because we are using a token-based clone detector as explained in the next section. According to Table 3.1, each source line (SLOC) has 6.3 tokens on average.

3.1.2   Clone Detection

To detect clones in our study, we used our own token-based clone detector *cpf*. We prefer *cpf* over our incremental clone detector ICLONES since it is more efficient for single version clone detection—only a single version analysis of the corresponding subject systems is required to investigate our research questions. *cpf* has been used as is and, hence, it is not considered a contribution of this thesis. It runs a lexical analysis to represent the source code of a project as a single token sequence. A clone is then a token subsequence that occurs at least twice.

The comparison of token sequences is based on the token type rather than its textual appearance. The token type classifies a token into the different kinds of keywords, delimiters, literals, operators, identifiers, etc. the programming language consists of. We transform all parameter tokens into one common artificial parameter-token type. In this study, we consider literals, operators, and identifiers as parameters. They are all considered alike and substitutable, e.g., a literal can be replaced by an identifier or vice versa. The syntax of the languages makes it unlikely that operators are replaced by literals or identifiers, although this can actually happen in C++ with user-defined declarations of overloaded operators (e.g., `operator=`). At any rate, treating operators as parameters allows substitutions of `<` by `<=`, for instance.

We note that—unlike other token-based clone detectors [11, 134]—*cpf* does not summarize multiple tokens into one or otherwise transform the original token sequence other than unifying parameter tokens. Thus, we operate on the original code in its exact representation.

To detect repeated token-type subsequences efficiently, the clone detector creates a suffix array for the token sequence in linear time and space [216]. A suffix array is a sorted array of all suffixes of the token sequence. We use the linear-time algorithm by Puglisi et al. [221] to detect all repeating token subsequences in the suffix array with a threshold of minimal length in terms of number of tokens. This approach guarantees that all repeated subsequences with at least the given minimal length will be found. These repeated subsequences are either of type 1 or 2. The distinction of type 1 and 2 can be made in a post-processing step that simply checks whether all parameter tokens in corresponding positions in both sequences have the same textual appearance (e.g., where there is identifier `foo` in one sequence, there is also identifier `foo` in the other one).

Our clone detector does not detect type-3 clones at present, yet a type-3 clone is a token-type subsequence which is in large parts alike to another subsequence and differs only in some gaps. Thus, every type-3 clone is just a set of type-1 and type-2 clones combined into one. When we measure clone rates, we want to measure only the parts that are alike, that is, ignore the gaps of type-3 clones because the gaps are not cloned. For this reason, it is not really needed to detect type-3 clones when it comes only to measuring clone rates. Using our approach, we will find all parts of a type-3 clone that have at least the requested minimal length. It must be noted, however, that shorter parts that are alike in a type-3 clone will be missed. In the study, we used a relatively short minimal length to counter this problem.

Token-based clone detection has many advantages for our study. It is extremely fast, tolerates syntactic errors, is able to analyze preprocessor code without the need to actually run a preprocessor (preprocessor directives are just considered tokens), works at the lowest level of semantic granularity of a programming language—namely, tokens, is insensitive to layout changes, and provides high recall [33]. The downside of token-based clone detection is that its clones may be syntactically incomplete or overlap different syntactic regions. Because we do not intend to refactor clones, but only measure the clone rates, this drawback may be acceptable. That implies that the clone rates derived by token-based clone detection are an upper bound of clones found by a syntactic technique.

Clone candidates as gathered by our automated clone detector are guaranteed to be alike under the constraints described above. Yet, similarity in the representation may not necessarily be considered meaningful in the eye of a human beholder. There are re-occurring structures in programs such as import lists or array initializers spuriously similar. In order to distinguish meaningful and spurious repeated subsequences, the generally used approach is to filter them using code metrics. Our clone detector implements such a filter using the following metrics:

- length L: number of tokens

- number of parameters P

- clone type T: 1 or 2

- diversity D: the number of distinct token types in a sequence

- fraction of non-repetitive tokens FNR

- parameter overlap PO

- parameter consistency PC

- degree of valid references DVR

- fraction of repeated parameters FRP

We describe the details of these metrics in the following. Many spurious clones such as import lists or array initializers are simple, very regular structures. In order to identify such structures one can measure the number of distinct token types, called *diversity* in the following. For instance, in an array initializer {0,0,...0,0} with many repetitions of ,0, the diversity would be four because it contains the four token types: { `literal , }`. A low number indicates that the clone has a very limited vocabulary and, thus, may be trivial. An alternative way to detect such regular structures is to apply clone detection to the clone itself. Every token in a clone sequence S that is not part of a clone within S is considered a *non-repetitive token*. If the fraction of non-repetitive tokens is low, the clone is very regular. For this clone-detection within clones, we use two tokens as the minimal clone length. In the above example of the array initializer, only the tokens } and { would be non-repetitive; the other two sequences ,`literal` and `literal`, are repeating.

The kinds of clones gathered by our clone detector are identical token-type sequences; they can differ only in the textual appearances of tokens considered parameters. To measure their similarity with respect to those parameters, we can simply use the overlap of the parameter vocabularies in both sequences. Let S be a token sequence, then *var(S)* denotes the set of textual appearances of the parameter tokens in S. The parameter overlap of two sequences S_1 and S_2 is defined as $|var(S_1) \cap var(S_2)|/|var(S_1) \cup var(S_2)|$. A type-1 clone must have parameter overlap 1.

Parameter overlap abstracts from the positions where the parameter tokens occur in the sequence. A type-1 clone must not only have parameter overlap 1, but the parameter values must occur at the corresponding positions in both sequences. The metric *parameter consistency* addresses this issue. It is inspired by Baker's parameterized strings [11]. Let S be a token sequence. Let *encode(i)* be a function that assigns a parameter p at position i in S a value as follows: if i is the first occurrence of p from the left, the value is 0; otherwise the value is the distance from p's occurrence at i to the previous occurrence of p. More precisely, let $j < i$ be the position of p in S where there is no k with $j < k < i$ at which p occurs, then the distance is $i - j$; if there is no such j, the value is 0. For instance, in case of the code a = b + a, the encoding would be 0 = 0 + 4. This encoding abstracts from the textual appearance of a parameter but not from its location. In Baker's approach, this encoding is used to detect only consistently parameterized type-2 clones. We will use it here to measure the degree of consistency of possibly inconsistent type-2 clones as follows. Let $par(S) = [p_1, p_2, \ldots, p_n]$ be the sequence of positions at which parameters occur in S in their original order. Then we define $encode(par(S)) = [encode(p_1), \ldots, encode(p_n)]$. Given that, parameter consistency, PC, for two sequences S_1 and S_2 is the fraction of equal corresponding elements in $par(S)$, that is, the location of equal references. A type-1 clone has $PC = 1$.

PC may yield a high value if there are many distinct parameters that occur only once, in which case their references captured by *encode* are all zero. To take into account only real references, we measure the degree of valid references, DVR, analogously to PC but use only those references that are greater than zero. Metric FRP measures the fraction of repeated parameters, that is, FRP is equal to the number of parameters with *encode* greater than zero divided by the number of parameters.

For the clone type of a class, we will use type 1 only if all clone pairs in that class are type-1 clones of each other; otherwise the class is considered a type-2 clone class. The metrics L, P, and D are alike for all fragments of a clone class. All other metrics depend upon a fragment or are relations between two fragments. For the latter, we will use the average over all fragments or pairs, respectively, for aggregating these data from cloned code fragments to clone classes.

The criteria used to filter spurious clones should be complementary. If there are two metrics with a high correlation, one of them is redundant. Figure 3.1 shows a plot of pair-wise mutual Pearson correlations among the metrics at confidence level 0.99. A value of 1 indicates a perfect positive linear correlation, a value of -1 perfect negative linear correlation. The larger the dot, the stronger the correlation. The exact value is shown in the lower part of the matrix. The plot shows a close to perfect correlation among the two size measures L and P and a very strong correlation between DVR and PC, a medium correlation of PO with D, DVR, and PC as well as between D and FRP and a somewhat weaker negative correlation between FNR and FRP.

Our clone detector is state of the art, hence, we do not consider it a novel contribution and consequently a detailed performance evaluation of *cpf* is beyond the scope of this

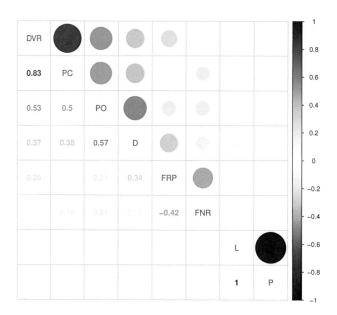

Figure 3.1 – Correlations among metrics

work. Nevertheless to give an idea of its performance, we note that *cpf* needs little more than two minutes to analyze the whole Linux kernel (version 4.4.4) with 13.6 MSLOC, 80.9 million tokens, and 39,490 C source files. It takes 37.5 sec to read and tokenize all files and store the tokens into a token file. The actual clone detection reads this token file (2 sec), creates a suffix array (13.7 sec), and detects, computes metrics, filters, and reports the clones (76 sec). These measures were gathered on a computer with 8 Intel Core i7-4790K CPUs running at 4.00GHz (the application is single threaded and, hence, only one CPU is used), with 16 GB of RAM running Debian 8.

3.1.3   Validity Procedure

The intention of the filters of *cpf* is to improve precision without sacrificing recall. In order to reach that goal, suitable thresholds for these metrics must be determined. Because intuition may err, we calibrate the filters on a set of classified clone candidates empirically. This calibration can be done using automated machine learning to derive a decision tree that works as a classifier for real and spurious clones, respectively. We prefer decision trees (implemented by the package *rpart* of the statistical framework R) over alternative machine learning classifiers (e.g., neural networks) because they are predicates that can be easily interpreted by humans and implemented as a filter in *cpf*.

The oracle upon which this classifier is trained was created manually involving four human raters. Two of the raters are the authors of the original publications [159, 162]. The other two raters are a PhD student of our group experienced in software clones and a graduate student at the master level less familiar with software clones. Both have a degree in computer science and have considerable experience in programming.

The oracle process had multiple stages. In the first stage, all raters validated the same set of clones separately (fully crossed design). All raters used our own clone viewer to look at the clones. It provides syntax highlighting and shows the differences between two fragments. The whole file containing a fragment is shown with the clone region marked through coloring. This way the context of the clone was visible to the rater, too.

The shared guiding principle that was used by the raters was as follows: "Assume you need to modify one fragment of the clone pair, for instance, to correct a defect or make an enhancement. Would you like to see the other fragment of the clone pair to decide whether you need to make the same or a similar change in the other fragment, too?" This principle does not preclude clones that cannot be refactored (because this may depend upon the language features and other factors) and does not enforce that the clones must necessarily be updated if the original code was changed. It is more liberal, yet not arbitrary. There must be a chance that there is a semantic relation between the clones to be worth to be presented to a developer. It represents a maintenance scenario in which a clone detector suggests clones that may require similar updates with high likelihood.

The sample to be validated by the raters was gathered without any filter (except for the minimal clone length of 30 tokens) from the Mockus corpus. The Mockus corpus was chosen just because it was the corpus available to us when we started; the other corpora were collected later (except for the Ubuntu corpus, but that one consists only of C projects). Clones were gathered separately for each language in case there were language-specific characteristics. For each language, the sample consists of 150 clone pairs, which gives us 600 clone pairs—a number that is large enough and still feasible for manual inspection. To make sure that we have a sample covering a large spectrum of the metrics intended to be used as filters, we used a systematic sampling method. Each clone class gives us a vector of the above metrics. For the sample, we want to partition these vectors into clusters of similar vectors and then select only one vector of each cluster. This way we avoid redundant validation of similar vectors and ensure that we are covering the whole spectrum. To obtain these clusters, we used k-means clustering with $k = 150$ (k is the intended size of a sample for each language; 35 iterations where used to converge). K-means clustering partitions the clone-metric vectors into k clusters in which each vector belongs to the cluster with the nearest mean, serving as a prototype of the cluster. We used the Euclidean distance on the vectors normalized by z-score to measure the distance among vectors. The length L and its correlating metric P were not used for this clustering because clone length is a parameter that we vary in the study. Neither did we use the clone type T because this is a nominal categorization derived from PO and PC. The final sample to be validated consists of exactly one representative of each cluster, where we chose the vector of the cluster that is closest to the centroid as representative.

For each language, one sample of 150 clones selected by this process is shown to the raters. For possible answers of the raters we used a Likert scale with *yes* (the candidate is a true clone), *maybe* (the candidate may or may not be a clone), and *no* (the candidate is no true clone).

At the second stage of the oracling process, we looked specifically at two kinds of ratings: (1) those for which a *maybe* could turn an unclear agreement into a clear overall vote and (2) where there is a single rater disagreeing with all other reviewers. In several meetings of all raters discussing these cases, decisive reasons by each rater were brought forward. The goal of this discussion was not to overrule the disagreeing rater, but rather to understand the reasons for the disagreement. All raters, inclusive the disagreeing one, were allowed, but not forced to change their decision in the light of this discussion.

To assess the level of inter-rater reliability (IRR)—that is, how well raters agree— quantitatively, we use two alternative measures. First, Fleiss's exact Kappa measure [241]—implemented in the *R* function *kappam.fleiss*—is used, where we consider only the two decisions *yes* and *no*, that is, two nominal categories. A *maybe* is ignored because the raters are unsure here and their rate is in between *yes* and *no*, which cannot be expressed in a nominal scale. Technically, a *maybe* is treated as *NA* (not available) values in R leading to removal of all clone ratings with at least one *maybe*. The second measure, intra-class correlation (ICC), takes advantage of the ordinal scale of the raters' decisions given as Likert scale. ICC incorporates the magnitude of the disagreement to compute IRR estimates, with larger-magnitude disagreements resulting in lower ICCs than smaller-magnitude disagreements. There are different ICC variants that must be chosen based on the nature of the study and the type of agreement one wishes to capture. Because the clones and raters were chosen by convenience sampling from a larger population and because we used a fully crossed design, we use a two-way model. Second, our IRR should be characterized by consistency in the ratings rather than absolute agreement. That is, it is more important to us that raters provide scores that are similar in rank order and not in the same absolute values. As a consequence, we chose consistency as criterion for ICC. Finally, because all clones are rated by multiple raters and the median of their ratings is used for hypothesis testing in our study, an average-measure ICC is appropriate. We are using function *icc* of the *R* package *irr* to compute the confidence interval of ICC, where we use 0.95 as the confidence level.

Table 3.2 shows the values of the two alternative inter-rater reliability measures for each language and for all clones altogether (*all*) independent of the language. The p-values for all values of Fleiss's Kappa are below 0.01. For ICC, we give the 95 %- confidence intervals. The table shows statistically significant, high degrees of agreement among the raters. According to Landis and Koch [126] Kappa values with values in the range of 0.61 to 0.80 indicate substantial agreement and between 0.81 to 1.0 almost perfect agreement. By the more conservative suggestions of Krippendorff [133] conclusions can tentatively be made for values between 0.67 and 0.80, and definite conclusions be made for values above 0.80. For ICC, Cicchetti [53] provides commonly- cited cutoffs for qualitative ratings of agreement based on ICC values, with IRR being excellent for values between 0.75 and 1.0.

Because of the high agreement among raters, we can use the validated data as a training set for the automated machine learner. The decision tree classifies a clone based on the above metrics into a likely true or likely false clone candidate. The machine learner needs an existing classification of both positive and negative examples from

	Fleiss's Kappa	ICC
C	0.79	[0.87, 0.93]
C++	0.83	[0.89, 0.93]
C#	0.88	[0.93, 0.96]
Java	0.83	[0.91, 0.95]
all	0.84	[0.91, 0.93]

Table 3.2 – Inter-rater reliability

	strict mode				majority mode			
	T	F	R	P	T	F	R	P
C	38	64	0.95	0.90	48	91	0.79	0.83
C#	41	81	0.85	0.90	48	90	0.79	0.86
C++	42	63	0.98	0.98	59	76	0.88	0.85
Java	30	90	0.90	0.90	36	97	0.83	0.86
all	151	298	0.91	0.91	191	354	0.86	0.86

Table 3.3 – T=true clones, F=false clones, R=recall, P=precision

which it can derive the distinguishing criteria. We use the following two ways of merging the different votes of the raters into one to obtain the training set:

- *strict mode*: all four raters must agree on either *yes* or *no* (clones with one ore more *maybe* rating or with no complete agreement are not used for training)

- *majority mode*: the majority vote of raters is used (a *maybe* is ignored in this voting); in case of ties, the clone is not used for training

A decision tree is created for each language individually—both in the strict and majority mode—and one is created where we unite all clones of all languages. Table 3.3 shows the number of true and false clones as well as recall and precision of the learned decision trees. We note that the recall/precision rates are derived from the whole sample and are not representative for recall/precision of *cpf* in general. They are intended only as a measure of the misclassification error of the derived decision tree. Overall, the decision trees describe the samples quite well as the high recalls and precisions indicate.

N-fold cross-validation—which is common for assessing prediction models—is not used here because we use the sample to learn only one definite decision tree which we intend to apply on the whole corpus code. Cross-validation would create multiple decision trees, for which it would not be clear which one to select.

The decision trees for the strict mode of the different languages use all *PO* as their primary decision criterion with very similar thresholds. For C, it is even the only decisive factor. Diversity *D* is the second-most important factor in C# and C++ with the same threshold. For Java, *PC* and *FRP* are used instead of *D*. As Figure 3.1 shows, there is generally a medium correlation among these. For the pooled clones of all languages, *PO*, *D*, and *DVR* are the only relevant factors. *DVR* has a very strong correlation with *PC* according to Figure 3.1.

In the case of majority voting, PO is the most important factor, too, with similar thresholds across languages. Diversity D is used for C and C++, with very similar thresholds (14 versus 16). FRP is used as additional criterion for C and C# whereas C++ has DVR and Java has PC as additional criterion, which are highly correlated. The decision tree for the pooled oracles uses PO, D, PC, FRP, and FNR.

The factors considered in the decision tree are very generic code characteristics and neither the decision trees nor the recall and precision rates indicate a substantial difference among the languages. The observed minor differences are likely due to sample variances rather than actual programming-language differences. Pooling oracles gives the machine learner also a larger and broader training set, which allows us to counter overfitting. For these reasons and for the sake of simplicity, we used the decision trees for the pooled samples for all languages in our study (separated by major and strict mode). The decision trees for the two modes are shown in Figure 3.2. The inner nodes are the filtering criteria. The branch of an inner node to the left leads to cases in which the criterion is true. The leaves are the categories; n for no true clone and y for true clone according to the decision tree. They form a complete partitioning of the clones in the training set. For each leaf (a partition for which a particular combined condition along the path of the tree holds true), the sum of the two values at the bottom of a leaf is the fraction of the overall clone-training set for which the associated criterion is fulfilled. The right number of a leaf labeled by n is the fraction of miss-classified clones (false negatives), that is, clones flagged as false clones by the decision tree, that are actually true clones. Analogously, the left number of a leaf labeled by y are false positives, that is, clones flagged as true clones by the decision tree, that are actually false clones. These numbers indicate the miss-classification error.

3.1.4   Quantitative Analysis

This section reports our quantitative analysis for our research questions. A qualitative analysis follows in the next section. For the clone detection, we use filters learned from summarizing the opinions of the different raters by strict and majority voting. Furthermore, we also use no filter at all as an upper bound and only type-1 clones as a lower bound for clone rates. In summary, we use four different alternative filters denoted by single letters as follows: n for no filter, s for the filter trained in strict mode, m for the filter trained in majority mode, and i for identical clones, that is, type-1 clones only.

We combine these four different filter types with four different values for the minimal clone length: 30, 50, 100, and 200 tokens. Because one SLOC has 6.3 tokens on average according to Table 3.1, these values correspond to roughly 5, 8, 16, and 32 SLOC (ignoring comments and blank lines), respectively, and, hence, favor a high recall. Ducasse et al. [75] used 10 SLOC and Baker [11] 30 SLOC in their studies.

Each combination of a filter and a minimal clone length is called a *configuration* of the clone detector in the following. We will denote these configurations by a pair (F, L), where F is the filter and L is the minimal clone length used.

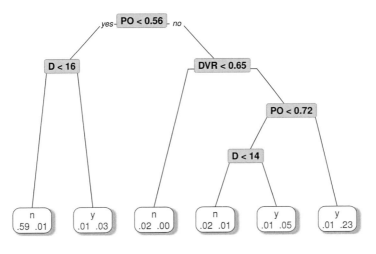

(a) Strict mode

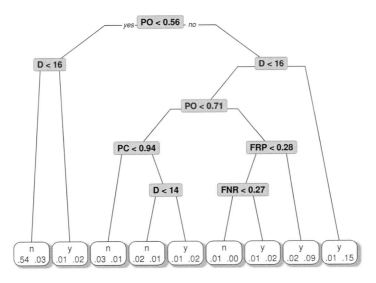

(b) Majority mode

Figure 3.2 – Learned decision trees

Clone Rate

Table 3.4 shows the average clone rates for the different configurations at the level of whole projects (as opposed to file level). The first column lists the type of filter used, the second column the minimal clone length, the third one the percentage of projects with a clone rate above zero (out of 9,666 projects), and the last column the 95 % confidence interval of the average clone rate using a one-sample t-test. We note that we can use the t-test even though the clone rate itself does not follow a normal distribution. By the central limit theorem, means of samples from a population with finite variance approach a normal distribution regardless of the distribution of the population. As a rule of thumb, sample means are basically normally distributed for sample sizes above 30 and ours has 9,666 projects.

As expected, the clone rate varies greatly with the minimal clone length and type of filter. The first row is the upper bound of the clone rate where no filter is used at all and only a very short clone length is required. For that configuration the average clone rate is about 53 %, which is quite high. Because no filter was used, many spurious clones will be included, which highlights the importance of filters and also hints at some "natural" similarity of programs, that is, re-occurring structures such as include/import lists, sequences of assignments, array initializers, and more.

The differences of the filters obtained from strict and majority voting are marginal. Filter s yields consistently slightly higher clone rates than filter m at the same minimal clone length—although only by a very small percentage. For the strictest configuration of type-1 clones with at least 200 tokens, the average clone rate drops below 2 %.

In the following, we will present only five different configurations that are intended to cover the upper and lower bound of the clone rate and the range in between. The configurations used in the following are $(n, 30)$ for the upper bound as well as $(m, 50)$ $(m, 100)$ and $(m, 200)$ for medium configurations with different minimal clone lengths. We use filter m rather than filter s in the remainder of this chapter because the former is slightly more conservative. For a rather conservative estimate, we use $(i, 100)$. That is, clones must be identical and have at least 100 tokens. We use $(i, 100)$ instead of $(i, 200)$ because $(i, 100)$ already requires to have at least circa 16 SLOC of identical code, which can be considered a real clone with high likelihood. Figure 3.3 shows histograms of the relation of clone rates (x axis) to number of projects (y axis) obtained using the different configurations.

We also tried to reproduce Baker's clone rate of 19 % for the X Windows sources [11] to the extent that is possible. Although Baker's tool, *Dup*, as well as our tool, *cpf*, is token-based, the type-2 clones identified by Baker's tool must be consistently renamed, and while Baker used a SLOC-based threshold (30 SLOC) for the minimal clone length, ours is token-based (200 tokens), where the two types of thresholds may not always be equivalent. Baker did not specify which version she analyzed, so we took the version that was the current one in 1995 when she ran her study, namely, version X11R6. Neither did she precisely specify which folders in the source tree and which files she analyzed. We analyzed the folders *lib* and *programs*, summing up to 791 KSLOC. We excluded *include* because it contained only header files and bitmaps. The other folders contained either configuration or build files and were excluded as well. Analyzing the folders *lib* and

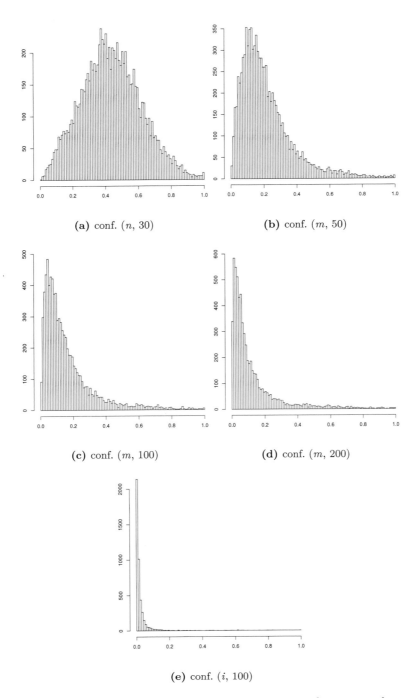

(a) conf. $(n, 30)$

(b) conf. $(m, 50)$

(c) conf. $(m, 100)$

(d) conf. $(m, 200)$

(e) conf. $(i, 100)$

Figure 3.3 – Histograms of clone rates for different configurations; clone-free projects are excluded (x axis: clone rate, y axis: frequency).

filter	min. L	#projects with clones	average clone rate in %
n	30	9614 (97.4 %)	[53.1, 53.2]
n	50	9305 (94.3 %)	[36.8, 36.9]
n	100	8382 (84.9 %)	[20.8, 20.9]
n	200	6627 (67.1 %)	[10.0, 10.0]
s	30	9428 (95.5 %)	[29.7, 29.9]
s	50	9080 (92.0 %)	[25.1, 25.2]
s	100	8097 (82.2 %)	[16.4, 16.5]
s	200	6229 (63.1 %)	[8.6, 8.7]
m	30	9376 (95.0 %)	[28.0, 28.2]
m	50	9047 (91.6 %)	[24.0, 24.1]
m	100	8053 (81.6 %)	[16.0, 16.1]
m	200	6192 (62.7 %)	[8.5, 8.6]
i	30	7831 (79.3 %)	[4.1, 4.2]
i	50	6519 (66.0 %)	[3.3, 3.4]
i	100	4524 (45.8 %)	[2.4, 2.5]
i	200	2702 (27.4 %)	[1.7, 1.7]

Table 3.4 – Clone rates

programs, cpf reports a clone rate of 19.5 % using configuration $(n, 200)$. Baker noted that she excluded 13 files that are essentially tables (containing only declarations of long arrays or lists of #define), but did not mention which files precisely she removed. We looked at the files that had high clone rates and were also large in their number of tokens and excluded 13 files that appeared to be tables. When these table files are excluded, the clone rate reported by *cpf* drops to 16 %. A run of *cpf* with configuration $(m, 200)$ on the same source files including the table files yields a clone rate of 14.4 %, demonstrating that our filter m effectively removed these table files. We note that filter m did not exclude all clones contained in these table files, but instead kept those that were mostly identical. Configuration $(i, 100)$ yields a clone rate of 2.2 %. If we compare all these clone rates to those listed in Tables 3.4 and 3.5 for C, we see that X Window Systems has a higher clone rate than the average and does not appear to be representative.

Regarding our research question 1, we can say that the average clone rate heavily depends upon the configuration. It may range from 53 %—if no filters are used and the minimal clone length is 30 tokens—to only 2 %—if only type-1 clones with at least 200 tokens are considered. These are the two extremes. If we consider the filter configuration $(m, 200)$ that mimics Baker's clone detector, we find lower average clone rates than earlier studies suggested. Yet, the clone rates detected by the medium filter configurations $(m, 100)$ and $(m, 200)$ are still quite substantial (16 % and 8.5 %, respectively). And there are in fact outliers with fairly high clone rates. So cloning is a widely spread bad smell. In Section 3.1.5, we will investigate the outliers.

	config.	C	C++	C#	Java
all	$(n, 30)$	[39.0, 39.9]	[42.6, 45.0]	[50.5, 53.1]	[52.4, 54.4]
	$(m, 50)$	[17.2, 17.9]	[20.0, 22.3]	[29.0, 31.7]	[22.2, 24.1]
	$(m,100)$	[10.9, 11.6]	[12.8, 15.1]	[12.8, 15.1]	[15.1, 16.9]
	$(m,200)$	[6.2, 6.8]	[7.3, 9.3]	[12.7, 15.2]	[8.5, 10.1]
	$(i,100)$	[1.1, 1.3]	[1.5, 2.7]	[3.2, 4.8]	[1.1, 1.7]
Ubuntu	$(n, 30)$	[38.8, 39.7]	n/a	n/a	n/a
	$(m, 50])$	[17.0, 17.7]	n/a	n/a	n/a
	$(m,100)$	[10.8, 11.4]	n/a	n/a	n/a
	$(m,200])$	[6.1, 6.7]	n/a	n/a	n/a
	$(i,100)$	[1.0, 1.2]	n/a	n/a	n/a
Mockus	$(n, 30)$	[42.5, 46.6]	[43.7, 46.5]	[44.7, 51.9]	[50.5, 52.7]
	$(m, 50)$	[19.8, 23.4]	[20.7, 23.4]	[20.8, 27.3]	[20.5, 22.6]
	$(m,100)$	[12.5, 16.0]	[13.2, 15.8]	[13.2, 19.5]	[13.4, 15.4]
	$(m,200)$	[6.9, 10.1]	[7.5, 9.9]	[7.9, 12.5]	[7.1, 8.8]
	$(i,100)$	[1.3, 3.0]	[1.3, 2.9]	[0.1, 3.1]	[0.8, 1.3]
Keinvanloo	$(n, 30)$	[39.2, 48.9]	[39.1, 44.2]	[37.5, 59.8]	[57.3, 60.9]
	$(m, 50)$	[14.8, 25.8]	[17.0, 22.1]	[15.5, 39.6]	[25.6, 29.3]
	$(m,100)$	[8.1, 17.4]	[10.8, 15.7]	[9.2, 31.0]	[18.0, 21.8]
	$(m,200)$	[3.5, 11.6]	[5.6, 10.1]	[3.4, 21.1]	[10.6, 14.2]
	$(i,100)$	[0.0, 6.5]	[1.0, 3.0]	[0.0, 5.3]	[1.1, 2.6]
GitHub	$(n, 30)$	[0.1, 59.5]	[28.2, 43.4]	[50.9, 53.7]	[27.7, 55.3]
	$(m, 50)$	[0.0, 50.5]	[10.3, 20.6]	[29.7, 32.6]	[10.9, 35.6]
	$(m,100)$	[0.0, 46.3]	[5.1, 14.0]	[21.8, 24.7]	[7.5, 29.9]
	$(m,200)$	[0.0, 44.1]	[0.9, 7.6]	[13.1, 15.9]	[3.0, 21.3]
	$(i,100)$	[0.0, 43.2]	[0.4, 3.8]	[3.4, 5.2]	[0.6, 10.1]

Table 3.5 – 95 %-confidence intervals of clone rate in percent per language and corpus

Clone rates versus language

In this section we answer research question 2 about a possible relation of clone rate and language. Beyond that we will also differentiate the clone rates reported in the previous section by corpora. We do that because one could argue that our results may be biased by the use of Ubuntu. Ubuntu is the largest corpus and has only C projects. That is, the clone rates reported in the previous section may be biased by C programs. This would not really matter if all languages showed the same clone rate, but that is something we are questioning in this section.

Table 3.5 lists the 95 %-confidence intervals of clone rates in percent for each language, corpus, and configuration. There are no intervals for C++, C#, and Java in Ubuntu because this corpus has only C projects.

The span of the confidence intervals expresses uncertainty in the data: the wider the span, the more uncertainty. The uncertainty in some of the corpora for particular languages derives from smaller samples. The confidence intervals for Keivanloo's corpus show this high variance found in small samples for C and C#. Likewise, the GitHub corpus shows that phenomenon for C, C++, and Java. As we explained in Section 3.1.1, the purpose of the GitHub corpus was to increase the number of C# projects. The projects in that corpus written in other languages are just a byproduct of some parts written in other languages. They are no original projects of their own. As a consequence, there are only a few of them and they tend to be small for languages other than C#.

The Ubuntu and Mockus corpora show more narrow confidence intervals. When we compare these two for C projects, we notice that the Mockus corpus has higher clone rates than the Ubuntu corpus and also wider confidence intervals, indicating more uncertainty. It is difficult to tell why exactly the Mockus corpus has a higher clone rate for C, but we conjecture it has to do with project sizes to a large extent. As we will see in Section 3.1.4, there is an association between size and clone rate and the Ubuntu corpus has many more smaller and larger projects than the Mockus corpus. Ubuntu also better covers the range of project sizes in terms of SLOC. That is, there are only three larger projects in the Mockus corpus whose size is distinctly different from all other projects (928, 410, and 336 KSLOC). Little can be extrapolated from only three data points at the right extreme.

If we merge all corpora into one (table section "all" in Table 3.5), we can narrow down the clone rate means sufficiently. After having inspected the influence of the corpora, we will now turn to research question 2. The following discussion relates only to the combined corpus including all individually collected corpora.

Figure 3.4 shows the distribution of clone rates separated by languages as boxplots. An ANOVA test on the difference among those means yields a p-value less than 0.001 for all five configurations, that is, there is a statistically significant difference among the languages for each configuration. The ANOVA test compares all languages at once.

To see which pairs of languages are different, one can use Tukey's HSD (Honestly Significant Difference) test [253], which finds pairs of means that are significantly different from each other taking into account all languages. The results of Tukey's test are shown in the tables below the boxplots in Figure 3.4. According to Figure 3.4a, Java and C# seem to have the same degree of "natural redundancy", which is higher than in C and C++, where C has the lowest one. If filter m is turned on, there is always a statistically significant difference among all pairs of languages except for C++ and Java in case of configuration $(m, 200)$. The order of the clone rates from highest to lowest is consistently C#, Java, C++, and then C for filter m. There is no statistically significant difference among type-1 clone rates—gathered through configuration $(i, 100)$—between C and Java, neither for C++ and Java. Yet again C# has the highest clone rate.

Overall, our results indicate that there are statistically significant differences of clone rates among the languages in almost all cases, where C# has always the highest clone rate and C belongs always to the languages with the lowest clone rate. Whether the redundancy of the projects written in those languages is an implication of the language design or whether other factors such as application domain, programmer skills, etc. are causing it, cannot be inferred from our data. To investigate this kind of causality, controlled experiments have to be conducted, where all such factors are controlled.

Clone rate versus size

To answer research question 3, we compare clone rate and project size in terms of number of tokens. Number of tokens is a better measure than lines of code because it is independent of the layout and tokens is the unit at which we detect clones. Figure 3.5 relates clone rate and our size measure.

It is already obvious from the charts that clone rate and size are not linearly dependent. We first use a test suggested by Heller et al. [106]—implemented by the R package *HHG*—checking for consistency against virtually any form of dependence, and not only linear dependence. If both measure were independent in every respect, a cloud of dots filling the whole area of the charts would be expected. This test indicates a statistically significant dependence (p-value < 0.01) between size and clone rate for all configurations. Although HHG shows that there is a relation, it does not tell what the dependence is. Figures 3.5a–3.5d suggests that larger projects tend to have a high clone rate, whereas smaller projects cover the whole range of clone rates. In Figure 3.5a, all but one dots are above a diagonal. This diagonal declines with increasing minimal clone length. The charts suggest a monotonic relation between size and clone rate. Thus, we use the two non-parametric, ordinal rank statistics, namely Spearman's ρ and Kendall's τ, which both test monotonic dependence. Both of these measures are appropriate here, where Kendall's τ tends to yield lower values than Spearman's ρ and is more robust against measurement errors [146]. To validate our findings as well as a point of comparison, we also report Pearson's ρ, which tests for linear dependence, although it is already evident that there is no such relation according to the charts. The different correlations coefficients are shown in Table 3.6. All of them generally yield a value between -1 and 1, where -1 indicates perfect negative correlation and 1 perfect positive correlation. The observed coefficients of Spearman's ρ and Kendall's τ in Table 3.6 indicate a moderate positive monotonic correlation. According to Pearson's ρ, a linear association between clone rate and size for four configurations, on the other hand, is weak, and in case of configuration $(i, 100)$ no such linear relation exists.

All reported correlation coefficients are statistically significant, although we must note that the significance test of Pearson's ρ assumes that the distribution of the

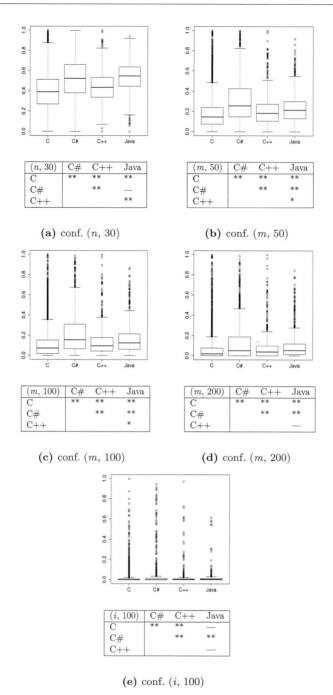

(a) conf. $(n, 30)$

(b) conf. $(m, 50)$

(c) conf. $(m, 100)$

(d) conf. $(m, 200)$

(e) conf. $(i, 100)$

Figure 3.4 – Boxplots of clone rates by language for different configurations; the tables below the boxplots indicate the p-value of Tukey's HSD test as follows: ** $p < 0.01$, * $p < 0.05$, — $p \geq 0.05$.

	$(n, 30)$	$(m, 50)$	$(m, 100)$	$(m, 200)$	$(i, 100)$
Spearman's ρ	0.57	0.46	0.51	0.61	0.59
Kendall's τ	0.41	0.36	0.37	0.44	0.43
Pearson's ρ	0.26	0.19	0.21	0.22	0.07

Table 3.6 – Correlation coefficients for clone rate and size

test variables is normal, for which we have no evidence. Pearson's ρ is used only as a descriptive measure and point of reference for the other two measures; it is not used here for inferential statistics.

Figure 3.5e, showing identical clones, has a different form than the other configurations. The shape of the relation resembles the capitalized letter L. That means that larger projects have generally a lower type-1 clone rate, which is plausible. Otherwise large chunks of identical code were copied in large projects. This might be expected for software variants in a product line where whole programs are copied in an act of ad-hoc re-use [74], but not in ordinary programs. It would be very difficult to maintain such large and highly cloned programs. For smaller programs, we find the whole range of type-1 clone rates instead. Section 3.1.5 will look into projects with high clone rates in more details.

Overall, we can conclude that there is a moderate positive monotonic correlation between clone rate and project size for non-identical clones. The clone rate of identical clones in large projects is rather low.

Locality

In order to assess research question 4 about the locality of clones, we categorize each clone pair into one of mutually exclusive categories based on their proximity in the file system hierarchy as suggested by Kapser and Godfrey [136] and later refined by Roy and Cordy [228]. The file system is chosen as a basis for defining proximity because developers usually follow the practice to put related code into the same file or directory.

The source code of every project is located in a project root directory. Roy and Cordy [228] define a *subsystem* to be a source code directory immediately under the project root directory. Subsystems, in turn, may be further structured into arbitrarily nested directories. Based on the directory hierarchy, Kapser and Godfrey [136] distinguish three cases:

- SF = same file,

- SD = same directory (but different file),

- DD = different directory.

The underlying hypothesis is that the farther the cloned fragments are distributed, the higher the chance that they may be overlooked. Roy and Cordy [228] further refined category DD into SG = same grandparent directory, SS = same subsystem (which is not a grandparent directory), OS = other subsystem, considering the convention to put

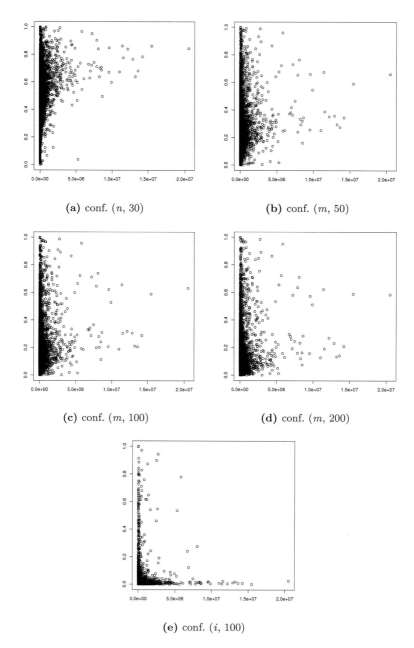

(a) conf. $(n, 30)$

(b) conf. $(m, 50)$

(c) conf. $(m, 100)$

(d) conf. $(m, 200)$

(e) conf. $(i, 100)$

Figure 3.5 – Clone rate (y axis) versus size (x axis) for different configurations

related files into subdirectories with common roots. For shallow directory structures the distinction of SD, SG, and SS vanishes. Then we count the clones only in the most specific category, that is, if SS equals SG, we count them in SG, and if all source files are at top level, we count them only in category SD.

We measure the fractions of clone pairs of these categories for each project. A summary of these data is shown in Figure 3.6. The boxplots show a clear visual distinction for all but SS and OS, which is confirmed by statistical tests. ANOVA yields a statistically significant difference between those categories for each configuration. A closer inspection using Tukey's HSD test [253]—which investigates pairwise differences—shows that neither the difference between OS and SS for configurations $(n, 30)$ and $(m, 200)$ nor between OS and SG for configurations $(m, 50)$ and $(m, 100)$ is statistically significant. All other locality metrics are statistically different at a p-level below 0.01.

The charts in Figure 3.6 show that the majority of clones are in the same file. If they are not, most of them are at least in the same directory. With increasing distance in the file system, the clone rate decreases while the number of outliers increases. That is, except for the outliers most clone pairs occur rather local. Comparing the number of outliers to the overall number of identified clone pairs, it becomes apparent that the number of outliers is still small—otherwise they would affect the boxes or whiskers, respectively.

It is also interesting to see that the averages of SF and SD get closer to each other with increasing strictness of the clone-detector configuration. The looser configurations $(n, 30)$ and $(m, 50)$ are expected to yield a higher false positive rate. Configuration $(n, 30)$—which does not filter at all—may be viewed as a kind of inherent similarity due to re-occurring programming language structures. Figure 3.6a then shows that such similarity occurs mostly within the same file, that is, files tend to be quite regular and self-similar in their choice of language structures. Overall, regarding research question 4, we can confirm the observations made earlier by Roy and Cordy [230] that clones tend to be in close proximity. Roy and Cordy made their observations for a much smaller sample and only for function clones. Our study shows that it holds also for clones at the lowest level of granularity for a huge sample. Moreover, while Roy and Cordy found only few clones within the same file, we found that clones in the same file dominate clones across files. This contradiction can be explained by the different levels of granularity considered in their and our study. Whereas Roy and Cordy investigated only function clones, we looked at copied token sequences.

3.1.5 Qualitative Analysis

Apart from a quantitative analysis of the clone rates we performed a qualitative analysis on projects and files with high clone rates in order to get insights into these statistical outliers. Due to the very large amount of data in our study we were not able to look at all outliers. Therefore, we focused our analysis on projects and files with very high clone rates in two different perspectives: (1) top-ranking of clone rates among all projects and files and (2) large projects with more than 5 million tokens and clone rates of at least

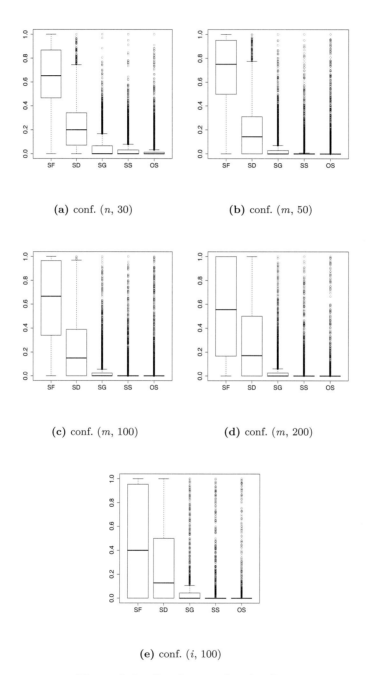

(a) conf. $(n, 30)$ (b) conf. $(m, 50)$

(c) conf. $(m, 100)$ (d) conf. $(m, 200)$

(e) conf. $(i, 100)$

Figure 3.6 – Boxplots on clone locality

15 %. The latter are particularly interesting because we had rather not expected high clone rates for large projects.

For perspective (1), we concentrated on the 25 projects and 25 source files of each corpus with the highest clone rates as detected by configuration $(m,200)$. In total we looked at 100 projects and 100 files more closely. Examining the 25 projects from each corpus that contributed the highest clone rates, ranging from 50 % to almost 100 %, we found three main reasons for the high numbers. First, the high clone rates of many of these 25 projects is due to generated code. Though we used heuristics for recognizing generated code, many projects did not follow the conventions we used to classify code. As we will see again in the discussion about large projects with high clone rates, in many cases one needs to look at the file content to find out whether code has been generated. Second, in some projects developers tend to freeze a certain state of the project by creating a subdirectory and copying the source code into that subdirectory. For instance, an "attic" directory was used to store old versions that just have been kept in case they will be needed some day. These could have been avoided by using the version control system, but apparently there were reasons not to use them (please remember that we derived all the code from version control systems, thus, the developers did use version control systems). Finally, the size of the project was also a factor. Many of the projects with high clone rate we inspected were small and consisted of a few source files only. Under such circumstances, larger clones can have a higher effect on the overall clone rate. Our experimental design has created such projects partly because we separated each multi-language project into its different languages. For instance, if only a small part of a program was implemented in Java and the major part of it in C#, we considered it as two projects: one consisting of the Java sources and one of the C# sources. If only a small fraction is written in another language, that separate logical project becomes small, and then individual files with larger clone rates again get higher weights as above. It could be argued that it makes sense to exclude such smaller parts written in a separate language. Yet, they may contribute interesting code clones that would be missed then. Furthermore such outliers are rare and do not have a real impact on the overall average clone rate reported in Section 3.1.4.

Investigating the 25 source files with the highest clone rates for each corpus, we found that most files with a clone rate higher than 95 % either include generated code or are copies of other files of the same project. In some cases they were slightly modified and adapted to a slightly different context. We further checked whether these copies were old versions similar to the "attic" approach described above. In almost all cases, however, we did not find any clear indications for that, and hence, assume that actually most of the copied files do present real clones. They seem to implement a variation. In addition, high clone rates in files were often due to large sequences of declarations and initializations, respectively. For instance, often very long arrays or strings were initialized at the beginning of a file. We will come back to this issue in our following investigation of large projects with high clone rates.

Regarding perspective (2), we chose 5 million tokens as a lower limit for large projects from the data produced by configuration $(m, 200)$, which is expected to exclude many false positives. The size limit of 5 million tokens is motivated by Figure 3.5d where the tight cloud of dots starts to become a loose set of rather isolated dots. Among the 36 projects above this size, we looked at those 28 projects with a clone rate of at least 15 %, which can be considered above the average clone rate according to Table 3.5. Among these projects, only one was written in C#. As a matter of fact, that C# project, named *Winterleaf*, was even the one with the highest clone rate overall (95 %). *Winterleaf* is a 3D engine. Almost all its clones are located in a directory consisting of five subdirectories which are copies of each other. It seems to us as if these subdirectories are variant demos of the 3D engine. This is a recurring theme that we found in other highly cloned large projects, too—although at a much lower scale. Often whole directories were copied, sometimes to provide variant functionality and sometimes to keep different versions of a subsystem, possibly because all were actually still needed for compatibility reasons or just because the developers might not wanted to retrieve these from the version control system. All programs in our corpora were downloaded from public version control systems, which are meant to free developers from keeping older versions for later use in their file system.

Generated code was another major reason for high clone rates. Although we tried to exclude generated code as described in Section 3.1.1, our heuristics for recognizing generated code are not perfect. Very often one has to look into the file content to detect hints in extremely regular code structures, artificial names, and comments. Neither the filename itself nor the path of the file gave any hints that the code was generated. We did not exclude these generated files from the statistics reported in Section 3.1.4 because then we would have needed to exclude missed generated code in smaller projects, too, and it would have been nearly impossible to inspect them all manually given the amount of projects. Moreover, we do not know whether this code is actually maintained or not. It can well be that developers adjust generated code. Maybe that was a reason to put them under version control in the first place. If the code generators are available, the code should be generated in the build process and does not need to be checked in. If the generators, however, are no longer available or any manual adaptation of the generated code was needed for any reason, the generated code should be checked in.

Large files with long array initializers were another reason for high clone rates. For instance, some programs contained picture or font data in static arrays instead of externalizing them into binary files to be loaded at run-time. We note that our clone detector in configuration $(m, 200)$ excludes such regular structures (cf. Figure 3.2) if they consist of very different identifiers or literals with little parameter-substitution consistency. So these structures must have a substantial degree of similarity to be considered a clone. We have seen cases, in which whole files with large array initializers were copied and modified. Changes in one file might require consistent updates in the other file. Hence, ignoring array initializers altogether may not be a wise decision.

We have found many clones in test code. Test code is often quite simple and regular, which may make the code similar enough (again we note that our filter excludes such regular structures if they do not overlap sufficiently in their vocabulary). Yet, we have also found test code that was rather complicated and nevertheless copied and adjusted. It might be the case that developers disregard the maintainability of test code over fast and simple test case production and, hence, have less hesitations to copy test code than to copy production code.

Another source of higher similarity were variant concepts. For instance, many programs dealing with variant hardware have copies with adaptations to the particular hardware differences (e.g., drivers). Other similar pieces of programs inherit the similarity of the domain concepts they implement. For instance, in Eclipse/JDT we found similar DOM objects implementing AST nodes for similar syntactic Java constructs.

It is difficult for us to find the correct explanations for the high clone rates in these programs because we are not familiar with these projects and their exact circumstances. We believe that many of these clones could be avoided: version control systems are capable of storing old versions and generated code does not necessarily need to be checked in. Hence, these highly cloned large projects may in fact be outliers due to insufficient developer practices or insufficient filtering. Yet, there may also be valid reasons for the developers for their practices. Then a clone detector could help to clean up such redundant code or help to maintain it if the redundant code cannot be avoided, and—as a consequence—these projects should show up in the statistics.

3.1.6 Threats to Validity

Our study is based on four corpora including a very large number of open-source projects from different sources, which gives us some confidence about our observations. Nevertheless, there are some potential threats to validity that we will discuss in this section.

Foremost, our results cannot necessarily be generalized to closed-source projects because all the projects we investigated are open source. Closed source should not be confused with industrial code because many open-source projects are in fact developed by professional developers. For instance, we analyzed sources from Eclipse whose development is heavily supported by industrial organizations and we analyzed code written by Google's developers, too. That is, many projects we analyzed have characteristics of professionalism. Yet, the fact that code is hidden from the general public might influence developer behavior. So, closed source could be different. It is very difficult to get sufficient data about closed-source projects for large-scale studies such as ours. As a preliminary point of reference, we can compare our results to a data set of 34 anonymized closed-source projects listed in Table 3.7, which we obtained from Stefan Bellon sharing it with the public for the first time. Bellon collected this data set in the course of code-quality assessments of various industrial C and C++ projects (most of them from companies based in Germany). In total, he analyzed 13.5 MSLOC. The 95 %-confidence interval of the average clone rate of this data set is [11.1, 18.7]. The data were collected by a syntax-based clone detector where the minimal clone length was 30 SLOC. This clone length compares to our 200-token limit. Because a different clone detector was used, the results cannot easily be related to ours. Syntax-based clone detectors generally have a lower recall and a higher precision [33]. Nevertheless, we ran a t-test to compare the average clone rates of closed and open source. The t-test yields a means of 14.9 % for the closed-source data set and is substantially higher than the means of 7.7 % for our open-source data set with respect to our configuration $(m, 200)$. The p-value is bellow 0.001 and, hence, the difference is statistically significant. That is, we can claim that this closed-source data set is different from our open-source data set. Yet, we also note that we cannot claim that Bellon's data set is representative for closed source in general.

Another threat to validity is the sampling strategy we used to obtain our data set. In the absence of known parameters about the whole population of open-source projects required for a stratified sampling method, we were not able to use a systematic sampling method. Instead we used convenience sampling, which may bias the results. Yet, we analyzed a very large set of projects coming from different sources and application domains, which should mitigate this threat to a large extent.

All projects in our study are written in C, C++, C# or Java only. Consequently, our results may not necessarily hold for other languages.

Our results are partially exposed to our subjective assessment of clones. To mitigate this threat, the manual analysis was performed by four different raters. Differences in the judgment were discussed together. We measured inter-rater reliability and found a high degree of agreement among the raters. Nevertheless, other raters might judge differently.

The accuracy of our results depends on the clone detector used. Our clone detector represents a state-of-the-art tool based on tokens, which is the finest level of program semantics. Moreover, no transformations have been applied. Considering the syntax may help to increase the precision of the results, however. Using only tokens yields the upper bound of what a syntax-based detector would find. Moreover, recall and precision of our results depend on the thresholds used. For this reason, we used different thresholds. A minimum clone length with only 30 tokens is a relatively low threshold, yielding a result leaning toward the upper bound of clone rates whereas a limit of 200 tokens is a relatively strict limit.

Different filters may yield different results [261]. Our filters were trained on a large corpus with majority and strict voting from different raters. As two baselines we did not use any filter (yielding an upper bound) and also limited our search to longer type-1 clones, which are generally quite precise (yielding a lower bound).

To allow other researchers to verify and replicate our study, all data are made available[2]. Researchers can freely use our clone detector *cpf* for research upon request.

3.2   Summary

Given our large-scale study, we can conclude that the partly high numbers on clone rates reported in the literature are not representative—at least for open-source software. We found a lower average of clone rates when we used a configuration of our clone detector that attempts to mimic the settings of earlier researchers who reported higher clone rates. Yet, even for a strict configuration with only type-1 clones of at least 100 tokens, we found that 46 % projects had such clones. That is, cloning is common, although at a lower scale than often reported. We did find outliers, however, with exceptionally high clone rates. Inspecting these qualitatively, we found that copying whole subdirectories,

---

[2]http://www.softwareclones.org/research-data.php

SLOC	cloned SLOC	clone rate in %
9,963	3,179	31.91
12,528	692	5.52
13,522	5,890	43.56
13,666	2,114	15.47
15,160	0	0.00
18,565	2,474	13.33
21,580	2,722	12.61
39,393	3,313	8.41
40,580	3,093	7.62
53,365	5,734	10.74
61,905	3,583	5.79
67,752	11,896	17.56
87,381	12,073	13.82
89,072	10,425	11.70
89,874	15,507	17.25
96,624	17,365	17.97
115,233	30,680	26.62
119,466	7,707	6.45
130,154	8,159	6.27
131,973	8,473	6.42
151,894	30,206	19.89
174,618	34,813	19.94
215,092	31,027	14.42
241,808	4,265	1.76
272,590	11,001	4.04
278,979	9,492	3.40
302,985	29,136	9.62
334,738	48,230	14.41
678,630	101,911	15.02
691,023	102,310	14.81
713,222	69,585	9.76
2,148,391	1,047,122	48.74
2,712,023	689,961	25.44
3,333,109	882,882	26.49

Table 3.7 – Clone rates of industrial closed-source systems

generated code, regular test code, long array initializers representing data in code, and implementing variants at large scale were major drivers for high clone rates.

We found a statistically significant difference of the clone rates among programming languages. C# has always the highest clone rate and C belongs always to the languages with the lowest clone rate. Further research is required to investigate whether the degree of redundancy of the projects written in those languages is an implication of the language design or whether other factors such as application domain, programmer skills, etc. are causing it.

We could confirm earlier research by Roy and Cordy [230] that clones tend to be in close proximity. Our study shows that this observation holds also for clones at the lowest level of granularity and not only at the function level. Contrary to their observation for function clones, however, we found that cloned token sequences are mostly in the same file.

Our results cannot be generalized to closed-source software. Neither do our results imply that clones are harmless just because their rate is lower than previous research claimed or because clones tend to be in the same file. There are studies that indicate that clones may in fact lead to maintenance problems [181, 130, 105]. Our study shows that cloning is common and primarily gives a more realistic estimate of clone rates.

Chapter 4

Evolution of Software Clones

One challenge in clone research is to categorize cloned fragments, detected by clone detection tools, into clones that might be of interest regarding maintenance tasks and those that are of less or no interest in this respect. The evolution of clones provides potential information of different aspects of clones and therefore might help to identify and filter clones that are of interest.

Göde [87, 96] presented a clone tracking technique that maps clones of type 1 to 3 across subsequent versions during an incremental clone detection process (as described in Section 2.5) and implemented it in the tool ICLONES. The model was used to analyze nine open source systems. Based on the data he investigated the amount and the lifetime of clone fragments, the relation between consistent and inconsistent changes and irregularities in clone evolution. However, non-identical clones have not been investigated quantitatively or qualitatively in the case study. Furthermore, the approach introduced by Göde may lead to an ambiguous mapping because clone fragments are mapped without considering their clone class memberships. Example 2.1 illustrates this downside. To overcome this shortcoming in the mapping of non-identical clones, we extend the incremental clone mapping approach in ICLONES by adapting its technique to map non-identical clone fragments between consecutive versions of a system in the context of their clone classes. Thus, preserving the benefits of an incremental approach that integrates the mapping of clones into the detection process.

In this case study, we partially replicate and extend the study of Göde [87] by analyzing the evolution of seven open source systems, considering identical as well as non-identical clones. Based on the mapping, we present quantitative empirical data on the evolution of identical and non-identical clones. By investigating and comparing the evolution of both clone types, we draw conclusions on the relevance of non-identical clones towards clone management techniques. Moreover, we investigate the impact of different parameter settings of the clone detector on the evolution of both clone types. Finally, we will extract and investigate the *Late Propagation* long-term pattern for identical and non-identical clones (clones of type 1 to 3). The *Late Propagation* pattern for non-identical clones has only been targeted by Göde [87, 96]. However, he did not apply his approach to gather empirical data on non-identical clones with respect to the

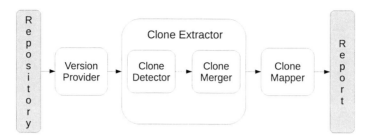

Figure 4.1 – Overview of the framework and its components used to build
the extended clone fragment mapping. The arrows indicate the data flow
between connected components.

Late Propagation pattern. Specifically, the case study answers Questions 5, 6, 7, 8, 9,
and 10.

Figure 4.1 gives an overview of the different components and how they are connected.
Each component is responsible to perform different steps that will be described in
the following sections. The steps are repeated for each version of the software that is
analyzed before the results are reported.

4.1   Repository Mining

The first component is the *Version Provider* which is used to extract all necessary
information from the particular software repository—currently SVN and Git repositories
are supported. The repository log information are used to identify and extract source
files from the repository that are relevant regarding the detection of clones. Only files
are considered that match the programming language of the software system (e.g.
property and documentation files are dismissed). Due to an incremental approach used
in ICLONES, it is not necessary to analyze each version from scratch. Instead, source
code changes of consecutive versions are determined and processed. Therefore, only
files are of interest that are either marked as added, renamed, modified or deleted in
the respective log entry, except for the first version. For the first version the component
handles all files as being added. After analyzing and extracting relevant files the *Version
Provider* passes the fetched information to the *Clone Extractor* component. It is worth
mentioning that source files are kept in memory and are not stored on the filesystem.
Moreover, the approach based on the log entries of a repository can be used to include
additional information of a commit, such as the author name, the actual log message
and the date to further filter files of interest.

4.2   Clone Detection

The clone detection can be separated into two different steps. First all identical clones of
the current version are detected by the *Clone Detector* before they are merged to larger
non-identical clones by the *Clone Merger* if possible. Both steps were implemented by

Göde in the clone detection tool *iClones* [96]. In the following we will briefly describe both steps, due to their technical nature and refer to the original publications for a more detailed description.

First a generalized suffix tree is constructed based on the source code of the first version. Afterwards all identical clones are extracted from the suffix tree. The algorithm of the *Clone Detector* for constructing the suffix tree and extracting the clones is token-based. Based on the information of changed files the generalized suffix tree is updated at the according locations and all identical clones are incrementally detected successively in each version.

Having all identical clones the *Clone Merger* component merges neighboring identical clones to form larger type-2 and type-3 clones if possible. The technique is inspired by previous work by Ueda and colleagues [256] who applied the merging approach on detected type-1 and type-2 clones to form type-3 clones. Göde and colleagues used the merging algorithm on identical clones to form non-identical clones. The length of the corresponding neighboring identical clones is the decisive factor regarding the size of the allowed non-identical parts in between. Identical cloned fragments are not merged if the non-identical token sequences between them is to large. Instead these clone fragments are reported as individual identical clones. Other approaches limit the merging based on a predefined threshold regarding the size of the non-identical parts. ICLONES does not report identical fragments that form a non-identical clone as identical clones anymore because the latter are subsumed by the former. We refer to identical clones that are combined to a non-identical clone as identical blocks of the clone and to the non-identical parts in between as gaps.

Note that the similarity of non-identical clones is not transitive based on the given definition. We already described this fact in Example 2.1 in Section 2.5. In contrast, the definition of identical clones is transitive.

4.3 Fragment Mapping

The mapping is done by the *Clone Mapper* after the merging phase detected all clones and grouped them in clone classes. Our mapping approach replaces the one presented by Göde [87, 93, 96]. Analogously to Göde, we map clone fragments to be able to analyze how they evolve individually instead of tracking clone classes only.

The challenge of mapping non-identical clones compared to identical clones is that in some cases it does not suffice to map cloned fragments exclusively based on their token sequence. Looking once more at Figure 2.5a and 2.5b the fragments f and f' refer to the same token sequence and were both detected in v_i of an arbitrary software system. If the same fragment—referring to the same token sequence as f and f'—is detected during the analysis of v_{i+1} and f', a mapping of f and f' based on their token sequence would be ambiguous. To overcome the ambiguity, we map fragments in the context of their clone classes. The mapping consists of three different steps. First all detected fragments of v_i are put into buckets which are passed to the analysis of v_{i+1}. The fragments within these buckets are updated during the analysis of v_{i+1} according to source code changes introduced from v_i to v_{i+1}. Finally fragments detected in v_{i+1}

are mapped to the updated fragments of v_i. In the following we describe each of these three steps in detail.

4.3.1   Creating Buckets

The creation of buckets is used to accelerate the actual mapping of fragments which is done in the last step. During the analysis of v_i, each existing fragment is put into a bucket based on its hash value. The hashing uses information of the fragment's filename and start-end position of its tokens within the source file—corresponding to line and column numbers. Therefore, fragments that refer to the same token sequence, but belong to different clone classes are put into the same bucket. As described before, this applies to clone fragments that share the same token sequence, but differ in the location of their gaps compared to the other clone fragments of the same clone class. At the end of this step all fragments detected in v_i are attached to a particular bucket.

4.3.2   Updating Fragments

During the analysis of v_{i+1} the fragments of v_i within the buckets need to be updated before a correct mapping can be applied. There are two situations in which fragments need to be updated:

(1) A clone fragment f' of v_i was put into a bucket during the analysis of v_i. f' still exists as a clone fragment f in v_{i+1}, but refers to a token sequence that was modified between v_i to v_{i+1}. To be able to map f to f' the standard UNIX DIFF tool is used to update f' according to the introduced modifications, so that the source code it refers to matches the one of f. By using a diff-based approach changes applied to source code located before f' are considered and the position of f' is updated appropriately. Note, changes to code located after f' do not have any effect on f' nor its position. Every other information (e.g. clone class and type) that goes along with f' remains unchanged.

(2) In the second case, f' is deleted from v_i to v_{i+1}. Therefore, f' is also removed from the corresponding bucket in v_{i+1}.

Having updated the fragments of v_i within the buckets allows a correct mapping of the fragments detected in v_{i+1}.

4.3.3   Mapping Fragments

Each fragment f of v_{i+1} is individually processed and mapped. First the hash value for f is generated based on the same hashing approach used to put fragments into buckets. The hash value is used to identify the bucket containing those fragments of v_i that refer to the same token sequence as f. We refer to that bucket as b. To determine to which fragment f', out of b, the currently processed fragment f needs to be mapped to, we check if the clone class cf of f and the clone class cf' of f' are related. To check whether there exists an ancestor relation between cf and cf', we count how many fragments of both clone classes refer to the same token sequence. Detecting multiple clone fragments in different clone classes that refer to the same token sequence helps to overcome the missing information about the identical blocks and gaps of non-identical clones. Only if at least two arbitrary clone fragments of cf refer to the same token sequences as two clone fragments of cf', these fragments are necessarily formed by the same identical blocks and gaps in both clone classes. Consequently, it does not suffice when only one fragment of a clone class matches a fragment of an other one regarding the token sequence since their identical and non-identical blocks may differ. Based on this property, two scenarios are distinguished to detect an ancestor relation between the clone classes cf and cf' based on the number of matching fragments. The first scenario is denoted as *perfect match* and the second one as *sufficient match*.

In the *perfect match* scenario each clone fragment of cf matches a fragment of cf'. Furthermore, both classes have the same number of clone fragments, which means that there are no unmapped fragments left. In this case it is assured that there will be no other clone class in b that contains more matching fragments regarding the fragments of cf. Consequently, the search is aborted and all fragments from cf are mapped to the corresponding fragments of cf'.

In the *sufficient matches* scenario we search for the clone class cf' in b that has the highest number of matching clone fragments compared to the clone fragments of cf. In this scenario not all fragments of both clone classes match. Therefore, all clone classes of the fragments within b have to be checked, because as long as there is no *perfect match* detected, it might exist a clone class containing more matching fragments related to cf than the one found so far. There are two exceptions to take care of. First, there might be more than one clone class in b that has the same number of matching fragments related to cf. This case is straightforward. We simply map all fragments from cf to the corresponding fragments of the clone classes of b being both *sufficient matches*. In such cases we are not able to fully dissolve a potential ambiguous matching. The second exception applies to a detected clone class of b that contains less matching clone fragments related to cf than the so far detected *sufficient matches*, but even so, all its clone fragments match the fragments of cf. Note that this does not describe a *perfect match* as cf might contain further fragments. Although such a clone class contains less matching fragments compared to the so far detected *sufficient matches*, the fragments of cf are mapped to its fragments, too, as we consider this situation to be a merging of two clone classes from v_i in v_{i+1}. Figure 4.2 illustrates such a merging. It can be seen that the clone fragments of both clone classes are mapped to the fragments of the merged clone class in v_{i+1}. The right clone class of v_i contains less matching fragments than the left one. Nevertheless, the fragments of the clone class in v_{i+1} are mapped to the corresponding fragments of both clone classes in v_i due to their merging in v_{i+1}—both clone classes are regarded as *sufficient matches*. In addition, it can be observed that a merging can also lead to multiple ancestors of a fragment. The fragments r and r' from v_i are both ancestors of the fragment q in v_{i+1}.

Based on the given two scenarios all clone fragments detected in version v_{i+1} are mapped to their ancestors in version v_i and the clone evolution model for identical and non-identical clones is built.

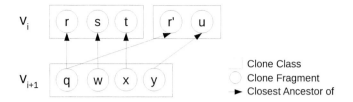

Figure 4.2 – Two clone classes of version v_i are merged in the consecutive version v_{i+1} and the corresponding ancestor relation between the fragments is set accordingly.

4.3.4   Detecting Late Propagation

The definition of the *Late Propagation* regarding identical clones is straightforward: an inconsistent modification to one or more fragments of the same clone class causing the fragments to be non-identical until another inconsistent change to the fragments makes them identical again. The definition is not suitable for near-miss clones as they are already not completely identical and therefore changes between the identical and the non-identical parts have to be differentiated.

One way to define the *Late Propagation* pattern for non-identical clones is to focus exclusively on the identical parts of clone fragments disregarding the gaps, as the gaps are already not common between them. In this case, we consider a non-identical clone to be changed consistently if the identical parts undergo the same modifications and continue to be identical—analogously to the definition of a late propagation of identical clones. To recognize an inconsistent change to a non-identical clone that makes a preceding inconsistent change to the same clone consistent at a later time, all changes to the cloned fragments have to be stored and compared to every new inconsistent change. We implemented a prototype of this approach, but it turned out that it did not scale. Especially detecting late propagations in large non-identical clone genealogies with a high number of inconsistent changes was not feasible because of the costly comparison strategy and the increasing memory consumption to store all inconsistent changes to identical blocks of clone fragments.

Defining the *Late Propagation* pattern for non-identical clones based on clone classes rather than on clone fragments helps to overcome the problem of the cost-ineffective comparison of fragment changes. Instead of focusing on inconsistent changes regarding clone fragments, a clone class is extended by an attribute that provides information about the clone class being consistent or inconsistent. A consistent state is defined as follows: At the time of its creation, a clone class is in a consistent state. In the course of the evolution of its clone fragments, a clone class is in a consistent state if it contains at least all clone fragments that have been part of it the last time it was known to be consistent. The only exception to this rule are clone fragments that were deleted by the deletion of a whole file. This exception is made because we do not consider the deletion of source code by a file deletion to be related to an intended removal of a code fragment. Hence, the deleted fragment does not prevent its former clone class to be consistent. To make sure we do not mistake a moved or renamed file for a deleted

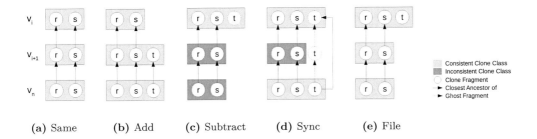

Figure 4.3 – Lineup of the long-term clone class evolution patterns to determine late propagations to non-identical clone fragments. Dotted circles denote changed clone fragments.

one, we use information of the software repositories to enable file mappings between moved and renamed files of two versions. In contrast to a removal of a clone fragment by a file deletion, a deletion of a clone fragment itself is considered to be a conscious decision to remove it. Therefore, a clone class that once contained such a removed clone fragment cannot get in a consistent state again. Note, that the information about deleted fragments is determined by the *Version Provider* component at an earlier stage already.

Based on the above definition of the *Late Propagation* pattern considering clone classes, we derive five long-term change patterns analog to the evolution patterns introduced by Bakota and colleagues [14] (Section 2.6.1) and Kim and colleagues [150] (Section 2.6.2). Figure 4.3 shows an example for each evolution pattern introduced. The described patterns are the following:

- Same: No clone fragment of the clone class was changed between the versions. That is, changes did not affect the clone fragments.

- Add: At least one new clone fragment was added to to the lone class. For instance, due to a newly introduced code fragment in version v_{i+1}. Since the clone class has been in consistent state before the addition, it still remains consistent because all clone fragments are part of the class in version v_{v+1} and any subsequent version v_n that have been part of it in version v_i.

- Subtract: At least one clone fragment disappeared in version v_{i+1} and will not be part of the clone class in any subsequent version v_n anymore. For instance, if a clone fragment was eliminated from v_i to v_{i+1} by a performed refactoring or change such that it is not considered similar to the other clone fragments anymore. This pattern is only valid up to the last version available since the disappeared fragments may occur in a future version again.

- Sync: At least one clone fragment disappeared in version v_{i+1} but is part of the clone class in a subsequent version v_n again. For instance, if the clone fragments are resynchronized after an an inconsistent change. This case denotes a *Late Propagation* pattern according to our definition considering clone classes.

- File: At least one clone fragment disappeared in version v_{i+1} and will not be part of the clone class in any subsequent version v_n anymore. However, the clone fragment disappeared due to a complete file removal which corresponds to the aforementioned exception describing code fragments that were deliberately refactored. This is the case if a source file was deleted between versions v_i and v_{i+1} which contained a clone fragment of a clone class being in consistent state, for instance. Thus, the clone class remains consistent even though not all clone fragments are contained that were part of the class the last time it was in a consistent state.

Analogously to the patterns by Kim and colleagues [150], the presented long-term evolution patterns do not necessarily occur exclusively. Instead, different types of evolution patterns may overlap and implicate each other. For instance, the *Add* and the *Consistent Change* pattern may occur at the same time and the *Inconsistent Change* pattern always implicates a *Subtract* pattern.

4.4   Study Setup

In this section, we describe the study setup including the approach used to select appropriate subject systems and their properties. Based on the described subject systems we evaluated the evolution of identical and non-identical clones using our mapping.

Seven open-source systems have been analyzed to contribute empirical data that supplement previous findings and answer our given research questions. All systems were selected based on the following criteria:

- The systems are open source and represent different programming languages to investigate the impact of a programming language on clone evolution.

- Each system is maintained using a software repository and is publicly available.

- The average size of each system is above 50 KSLOC to provide a sufficient amount of data.

- The systems were already analyzed by Göde in his study [87] on the evolution of identical clones to allow for comparisons on the results.

The systems selected are ARGOUML, HTTPD, ANT, NAUTILUS, FILEZILLA, UMBRELLO and JABREF. We investigated four years of each system's history starting from June 2005 to April 2009. The time period has also been used by Göde in his study [87] and is supposed to be long enough to ensure a sufficient amount of changes to each subject system. Snapshots have been analyzed on an interval of one day. Dates that did not contain any commits including relevant changes to the source code were skipped. Details of the subject systems are given in Table 4.1.

System	Language	KSLOC	#Versions
ARGoUML	Java	167 – 189	1212
HTTPD	C	188 – 182	1222
ANT	Java	162 – 168	1181
NAUTILUS	C	85 – 137	986
FILEZILLA	C++	22 – 106	936
UMBRELLO	C++	74 – 93	1401
JABREF	Java	38 – 81	660

Table 4.1 – Subject systems used for studying clone evolution.

Each system was analyzed four times using different parameters regarding the minimum clone length (MCL) and the minimum identical block length ($MIBL$) of non-identical clones in tokens. We have configured ICLONES by combining an MCL of 50 or 100 tokens with an $MIBL$ of 10 or 20 tokens, respectively, regarding non-identical clones. The different length settings were used to measure their impact on the clone evolution of identical and non-identical clones. Note that the $MIBL$ setting exclusively affects the detection of non-identical clones and is not related to the detection of identical clones.

The reported output of each analysis gives information of all detected clones in the corresponding system. On the one hand, the results are clone fragments of each version, organized in clone classes. On the other hand, the ancestor relation for clone fragments of consecutive versions is built. Based on these data different aspects of the evolution of identical and non-identical clones for each system have been evaluated and our research questions have been answered.

4.5 Findings

This section describes the findings obtained from analyzing the data extracted from the subject systems.

4.5.1 Clone Rate

To check how frequent identical and non-identical clones occur, we investigated the clone rate of each system. By looking at the bars of Figure 4.4, which shows the mean clone rate for identical and non-identical clones using an MCL of 50 tokens and 10 and 20 tokens for the $MIBL$, an interesting attribute of the $MIBL$ parameter can be seen. A less tolerant setting regarding the block parameter causes the amount of non-identical clones to decrease in each system, whereas at the same time the amount of identical clones increases. Due to a smaller number of identical clones that can be merged during the clone detection, because of the stricter block setting, more identical clones and less non-identical clones are reported. As expected the same behavior could be observed using 100 tokens for the MCL and 10 or 20 tokens, respectively, for the $MIBL$. Figure 4.5 shows the result using these more strict parameter settings. According to this observation the gap between the number of identical and non-identical clones becomes smaller using a

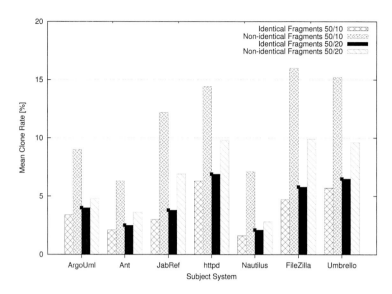

Figure 4.4 – Mean clone rate (among all analyzed versions) of each subject system by identical and non-identical clones using settings of 50 tokens *MCL* and 10 and 20 tokens *MIBL*.

stricter *MIBL* setting. The results show that for each setting the number of detected non-identical clones was higher than for identical clones. We used the non-parametric Mann-Whitney U-test (since we cannot assume a normal distribution of the data set) to check for statistical significance of this observation. We performed the one-tailed paired variant of the U-test obtaining a p-value of 0.000002 verifying that the rate of non-identical clones is significantly higher compared to the rate for identical clones for all parameter settings applied. Moreover, it was found that the number of both types of clones decreases using a larger *MCL* setting, which is straightforward. Using the same approach to test for statistical significance, we compared the results obtained using an *MCL* of 50 against an *MCL* of 100. Again, statistical significance could be verified with a p-value of 0.000002.

To further investigate how the clone rate of identical and non-identical clones changes over time, we compared the change of the system's size to the change in the amount of identical and non-identical fragments from the very first to the very last version for each system. Table 4.2 shows the results for an *MCL* of 50 tokens and an *MIBL* of 10 tokens.

In NAUTILUS, FILEZILLA, UMBRELLO and JABREF the increase in system size was not as large as in the number of cloned fragments, which means that the rate of clones increased in these systems. The rate of identical clone fragments increased in these systems more compared to the rate of non-identical clone fragments except for FILEZILLA. For ARGOUML and ANT the rate of non-identical clones increased whereas the rate of identical clone fragments decreased despite the fact that the system grew in size. HTTPD is the only system where the system size and the amount of identical as well

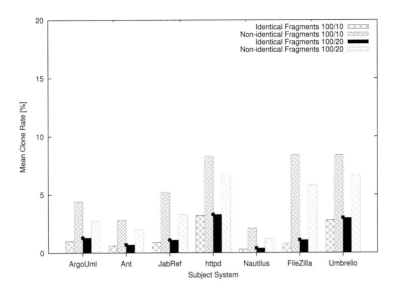

Figure 4.5 – Mean clone rate (among all analyzed versions) of each subject system by identical and non-identical clones using settings of 100 tokens *MCL* and 10 and 20 tokens *MIBL*.

System	ΔSLOC	ΔIdentical Fragment	ΔNon-Identical Fragment
ARGoUML	13.4	-4.5	10.7
HTTPD	-3.0	-34.7	-9.2
ANT	4.0	-9.9	2.3
NAUTILUS	60.2	142.4	129.6
FILEZILLA	388.9	467.5	703.9
UMBRELLO	25.8	51.0	37.2
JABREF	112.4	322.1	229.1
Mean	**28.8**	**26.3**	**48.6**

Table 4.2 – Increase (positive numbers) and decrease (negative numbers) of system size and number of fragments given in % using 50 tokens for the *MCL* and 10 tokens for the *MIBL*

	50 / 10			50 / 20			100 / 10			100 / 20		
	Java	C	C++	Java	C	C++	Java	C	C++	Java	C	C++
Increased Identical	1	1	2	1	1	2	1	1	2	1	0	2
Decreased Identical	2	1	0	2	1	0	2	1	0	2	2	0
Increased Non-Identical	3	1	2	1	1	2	2	1	2	1	1	2
Decreased Non-Identical	0	1	0	2	1	0	1	1	0	2	1	0

Table 4.3 – Growth trend of the clone rate of identical and non-identical clones distinguished by different parameter settings (*MCL* / *MIBL*) and programming language.

as non-identical clones decreased over time. Still, the rate of the identical clone fragments decreased more than three times more than the rate of non-identical fragments. Based on the results it cannot generally be observed that the rate of non-identical clones grew more than the one of identical clones or vice-versa. Nevertheless, taking the average of all systems, the code size increased by 28.8% and therefore grew just slightly more than the number of identical clones. In contrast, the number of non-identical clones grew almost twice as much as the system size.

Investigating the results regarding the different parameter settings of the *MCL* and the *MIBL*, we could not identify patterns that allow for general conclusions on their impact on the evolution of clones. The same applies to the programming languages. A quantitative summary of the results is provided by Table 4.3. It can be observed that independent from the parameter setting, the clone rate of non-identical clones increased for the majority of the analyzed systems—we already validated this observation by statistical significance testing.

Towards Question 7 it was found that regarding the clone rate the rate of non-identical fragments was significantly higher than the one of identical fragments. We could also observe a trend that the number of non-identical clones grew faster, although the rate depends on the particular system that was analyzed.

4.5.2 Fragment's Lifetime

Separating clones that are more interesting to a programmer from those that are of less interest is an important task regarding clone management. The lifetime of clone fragments is considered to be one indicator for their relevance. Cloned fragments that are long-lived are usually claimed to be more relevant regarding maintenance tasks like refactorings. For instance, it might not pay off to remove clones proactively if they exist only for a short period in a system. To investigate the lifetime of clones in the subject systems and answer Question 8, we calculated the lifetime, which is in our case the number of consecutive versions a fragment exists in, of each clone fragment by traversing the clone genealogies based on their ancestor relation. The mean of the resulting lifetimes is given in Table 4.4. It should be taken into account, that all values represent just an extract of the actual lifetime of the fragments within the systems, because only a certain period of each system's history has been analyzed. For this reason we cannot make any assertions regarding the clones that already existed before the first analyzed version as well as those that continue to exist beyond the last version

System	50 / 10		50 / 20		100 / 10		100 / 20	
	Identical	Non-Identical	Identical	Non-Identical	Identical	Non-Identical	Identical.	Non-Identical
ARGoUML	46.3	164.7	106.3	112.7	27.5	163.9	62.3	148.2
HTTPD	176.0	524.4	335.8	377.4	133.	528.7	217.2	469.4
ANT	137.0	518.6	254.7	374.1	75.6	566.5	125.5	475.1
NAUTILUS	59.6	302.2	148.3	188.8	28.7	275.2	64.5	262.7
FILEZILLA	51.9	227.2	115.1	172.3	12.8	224.3	32.9	219.0
UMBRELLO	111.2	294.8	201.3	206.6	95.2	297.9	133.4	259.5
JABREF	35.9	172.4	96.1	147.5	18.4	162.8	157.2	475.1

Table 4.4 – Mean lifetime of identical and non-identical clone fragments in versions using different parameter settings (*MCL* / *MIBL*)

analyzed in this study. Therefore, results are considered a minimum bound of the actual lifetime of fragments.

Again four different parameter settings for the *MCL* and the *MIBL* of clones have been applied. Values of identical clones range from 12.8 versions average lifetime for FILEZILLA using an *MCL* of 100 tokens and an *MIBL* of 10 tokens to 335.8 versions average lifetime for HTTPD using a parameter setting of 50 tokens *MCL* and 20 tokens *MIBL*. We considered type changes from identical to non-identical fragments and vice versa as well and present results in the upcoming Section 4.5.3. Looking at non-identical clones we observed a trough of 112.7 versions for ARGoUML using an *MCL* of 50 tokens and an *MIBL* of 20 tokens and a peak of 566.5 versions for ANT using a parameter setting of 100 tokens *MCL* and 10 tokens *MIBL*. As every version represents at least one day (days without relevant check-ins have been skipped), identical clones in HTTPD and non-identical clones in ANT have the highest minimum life expectancy of nearly one year or more than one and a half year, respectively.

Table 4.4 shows that independent from the parameter setting non-identical clones are more long-lived than identical clones. Analogously to the clone rate, we used the non-parametric Mann-Whitney U-test to check for statistical significance of our observation. Based on the one-tailed paired variant of the U-test, a p-value nearly 0.0 ($3.725e^{-09}$) was obtained verifying statistical significance.

Comparing different parameter settings for the *MIBL*, using the same *MCL*, it was found that the lifetime of identical clones grew remarkably for all systems with a stricter configuration of 20 tokens *MIBL*. At the same time the lifetime of non-identical clones decreased slightly. Accordingly the gap between the lifetime of identical and non-identical clones scales down.

Another interesting finding is that identical clones have a slightly shorter life expectancy using 100 tokens for the *MCL* compared to 50 tokens if 10 tokens are used for the *MIBL*. In contrast the lifetime of non-identical clones remains stable. This causes the gap between identical and non-identical clones to grow. The gap also grows using the same *MCL* parameter but a stricter *MIBL* setting of 20 tokens. In this case the lifetime of identical clones decreases again but the lifetime of non-identical clones even increases slightly.

Answering Question 8, we generally observed that non-identical clones were more persistent than identical clones on a statistically significant level.

4.5.3   Clone Type Changes

The next research question that we tackle is how often identical clones change into non-identical clones and vice versa. Detecting type-changes of fragments enables to map clones with different clone types to each other and to continue to keep track of their evolution. For instance, an identical clone of v_n will not be tracked in v_{n+1} in consequence of a type change, if type changes of clones are not considered. The aforementioned situation would lead to a new non-identical clone in v_{n+1} that is actually the same clone as in v_n. To prevent these situations we track clone fragments and consider type changes between different versions. Based on our mapping approach we measured how many identical clones changed per version to non-identical ones and vice versa. After a type change of a clone fragment, we assign occurrences of the fragment in subsequent versions to its new clone type.

We found a couple of clones that changed their types but they are quite rare. The maximum values for changes of identical clones to non-identical clones per version range from 4 in NAUTILUS up to 29 in HTTPD using 50 token for the *MCL* and 10 tokens for the *MIBL*. For changes in the opposite direction the maximum values range from 2 in NAUTILUS to 44 in ARGOUML using the same setting. ARGOUML is the only system including a version, in which more non-identical clones have been changed to identical clones than the other way round. Stricter parameter settings result in a continuously decreasing number of detected type changes, approaching zero for both directions using an *MCL* of 100 tokens and an *MIBL* of 20 tokens. Nevertheless, the ratio for both directions of changes remains stable.

Regarding question 9, we observed that the type of clone fragments changed very infrequent, but still more identical clones changed to non-identical clones for the majority of analyzed systems and settings. However, a p-value of 0.9979 was obtained using the U-test indicating that the observation is not statistically significant. We assume that the rare number of overall type changes is the main reason for the rather high p-value.

4.5.4   Change Consistency

To investigate whether identical or non-identical clones change more frequently, we investigated consistent and inconsistent changes to clone fragments. We determined whether a change is consistent or inconsistent by comparing a change to a fragment to changes that were made to the other fragments of the same clone class. There are two main interests in analyzing the frequency of changes to clones and whether they are consistent or inconsistent. On the one hand, based on the frequency one can decide whether a clone is relevant with respect to maintenance costs. For instance, a programmer is most likely more interested in tracking and managing clones that are frequently changed and therefore cause more maintenance effort than other clones. On the other hand, inconsistent changes to clones are assumed to be a potential indicator for defects.

Figures 4.6, 4.7, 4.8, and 4.9 show the mean number of changes to fragments for each system using each parameter setting. The results of analyzing our subject systems using

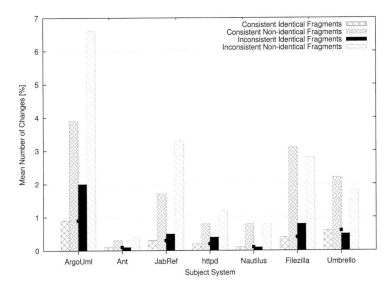

Figure 4.6 – Mean number of changes to consistent identical and consistent non-identical fragments, as well as inconsistent identical and inconsistent non-identical fragments using 50 tokens for the *MCL* and 10 tokens for the *MIBL*.

the different parameter settings for the *MCL* and the *MIBL* show that non-identical clones are more frequently changed than identical clones are. Using the U-test to test for significance, a p-value of 0.0 is obtained comparing the amount of all changes to identical clones to the amount of changes to non-identical clones. Accordingly, non-identical clones are changed significantly more often—answering Question 10. Furthermore, results indicate that inconsistent changes are also more frequent than consistent ones. A p-value of 0.0061 was obtained using the U-test for statistical significance—comparing the amount of all consistent changes to all inconsistent changes applied overall (not separating changes to identical from changes to non-identical clones).

4.5.5 Late Propagation

The last aspect we focused on in our study is the late propagation pattern applying our approach introduced in Section 4.3.4. Based on our definition of the *Late Propagation* pattern considering clone class relations, we evaluated the subject systems to check how many clone classes are in a consistent and how many are in an inconsistent state throughout the evolution of identical and non-identical clones. In addition, we measured how often an inconsistent clone class changed to a consistent one, which corresponds to our definition of late propagations.

Using an *MCL* of 50 tokens and an *MIBL* of 10 tokens, it was found that much more clone classes were detected that are in a consistent state than clone classes that are in an inconsistent state. Figure 4.10 shows the results for identical as well as non-

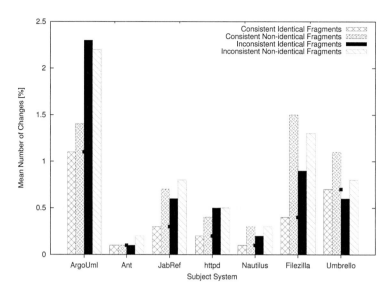

Figure 4.7 – Mean number of changes to consistent identical and consistent non-identical fragments, as well as inconsistent identical and inconsistent non-identical fragments using 50 tokens for the *MCL* and 20 tokens for the *MIBL*.

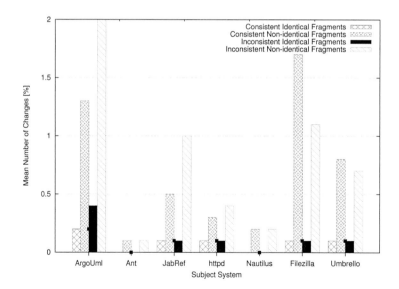

Figure 4.8 – Mean number of changes to consistent identical and consistent non-identical fragments, as well as inconsistent identical and inconsistent non-identical fragments using 100 tokens for the *MCL* and 10 tokens for the *MIBL*.

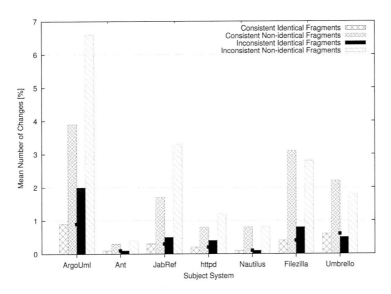

Figure 4.9 – Mean number of changes to consistent identical and consistent non-identical fragments, as well as inconsistent identical and inconsistent non-identical fragments using 100 tokens for the *MCL* and 20 tokens for the *MIBL*.

identical clones. We found the same pattern using the stricter parameter settings for *MCL* and *MIBL*, observing continuously decreasing numbers of detected clones. Thus, the majority of clone fragments remain within the same clone class once they were added to it independent from the parameter thresholds used. This observation is confirmed to be statistically significant (p-value of $2.2e^{-16}$) by comparing the numbers of identical and non-identical clone classes in consistent state against the numbers of identical and non-identical classes in inconsistent state using the U-test again. Results of all parameter settings were included in the significance test showing that the strictness of the thresholds does not have an effect on the ration of consistent and inconsistent clone classes detected.

Based on the results of consistent and inconsistent clone classes, very few late propagations have been detected of which slightly more refer to non-identical clone classes. Using 50 tokens for the *MCL* and 10 tokens for the *MIBL* ANT is the only system with no late propagation found at all. Changing the *MIBL* to 20 tokens results in NAUTILUS and FILEZILLA containing no late propagation as well. Using 100 tokens for the *MCL*, this also holds for JABREF. Therefore, for three out of four parameter settings no late propagations were detected in more than half of the subject systems.

Concerning Question 10, we observed that the majority of detected clone classes were in a consistent state for both, identical and non-identical clones. Accordingly, a very small number of late propagations were detected overall. Although a slight trend could be observed that late propagations occur more frequently for non-identical clones, no clear conclusions could be made due to the small number of identified late propagations.

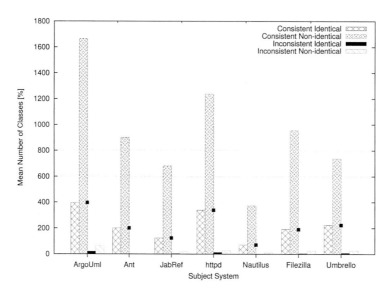

Figure 4.10 – Mean number of classes containing identical and non-identical clone fragments, respectively, that are in consistent and inconsistent state using 50 tokens for the *MCL* and 10 tokens for the *MIBL*.

4.6 Threats to Validity

Construct Validity. The accuracy of our results depends on iCLONES including the new mapping approach introduced in this thesis. We did not conduct a manual inspection of the results provided by iCLONES due to the huge amount of clone data, and hence, recall and precision are potential threads.

Internal Validity. We based our study on seven open source systems from different domains that are implemented in three different languages, only a cutout of their history has been analyzed. It might affect the findings using a different period of time or analyzing snapshots at a different interval. It was also not evaluated if all systems are comparable regarding the analyzed aspects—comparing a long-lived system to a short-lived one might bias the results.

External Validity. The UNIX-DIFF tool is used in iCLONES to identify the differences of two consecutive files and therefore has a strong effect on the mapping results. Unfortunately there are some limitations in handling ambiguities that can cause false mappings in our model.

4.7 Summary

Based on the mapping technique presented, we tracked individual clones of seven open-source systems over a period of four years. Investigating the results from these systems, we answered four research questions regarding different aspects of code clones.

Comparing identical clones to non-identical clones it was found that the majority of detected clones were non-identical clone fragments and that the number of non-identical clones also tended to grow faster over time.

Regarding the lifetime of identical and non-identical clones we observed that non-identical clone fragments were generally more persistent than identical ones. During the lifetime of both types there were only few type changes, but still more identical clones changed to non-identical clones than vice versa.

We investigated the amount of consistent and inconsistent changes to identical and non-identical clones and found that overall non-identical clones underwent more changes than identical clones and that most changes were inconsistent. Finally, late propagations were investigated using the definition introduced in this thesis which suites not only identical but also non-identical clones. Overall too few late propagations were detected to allow for clear conclusions.

Our observations suggest that non-identical clones tend to be the dominating clone type regarding the analyzed aspects and, therefore, clone management tools might pay higher attention to them. Moreover, we observed that different parameter settings regarding the *MCL* and the *MIBL* in ICLONES have influenced the results but conserved the relations.

Chapter 5

Clone Removals and their Return on Investment

To support project managers to make decisions and developers to take actions plenty of clone detection and management tools have been introduced [157, 226, 231]. The efficiency of such tools has been successively improved over the years so that they scale even for very large systems. Still, clone management has not yet become an integral part of the daily work of developers. A major hindrance to the use of clone management tools is a missing relevance ranking of clones. Because results provided by state-of-the-art clone tools are based on structural similarity in the source code only, users are exposed to a vast amount of clone information. The amount of data increases the effort or makes it impractical to filter useful clones just manually. Therefore, clones that have been automatically detected need to be ranked by the relevance to a specific maintenance task. Analyzing the evolution of clone fragments provides important insights into the phenomenon of cloning, however, it is substantial to understand a clone's evolution from its creation to its removal for a complete picture. Studying clones that were actually removed by developers may give indicators to introduce and improve a relevance ranking of the results provided by a clone detector.

A reason for widely neglecting the detection of clone removals may be that the identification of such refactorings is rather time consuming as there is no technique to accomplish the task automatically. To contribute to a comprehensive understanding of how developers deal with clones, we believe that techniques are needed supporting the detection and analysis of clone removals.

Apart from the challenge of building an appropriate relevance ranking of detected clones, a still blurry understanding of economic costs and benefits exists when it comes to the question whether cloned code is a big issue to software maintenance. If it cannot be shown that cloned code causes higher maintenance costs than an abstraction which is appropriate to replace the clone there is no obvious gain in removing code redundancies. Knowing how and how much effort is spent to refactor duplicated code and, afterwards, maintain code fragments that have been introduced in consequence of a deliberate clone removal will provide useful information in this respect. By identifying clone refactorings and tracking code fragments over time that were introduced in the course of these refactorings various characteristics can be investigated, e.g., the frequency of removals but also the frequency of changes to the introduced abstractions, to provide valuable insights regarding the return on investment of clone removals.

In a previous study Göde [89] investigated deliberate clone removals in the evolution of four open-source systems to campaign for more observance of a maintainer's view. Göde found a large discrepancy between clones detected by a state-of-the-art clone detector and code clones removed by developers as the scopes of the clones hardly ever matched. His results suggest that value can be added to clone management tools by considering knowledge about duplicated code that has been selected for refactoring by a programmer. Previous studies on clone removals and the differences to ours are described in detail in Section 2.8.3.

To provide further insights and answer Questions 11, 14, and 15, we replicate and extend the work by Göde [89] in this case study because he considered only a small number of subject systems and investigated exclusively those clones that were deliberately removed. To overcome these shortcomings in our study, we analyze the evolution of eleven subject systems over a two year time period. Moreover, we extend the study by also considering accidental clone removals and collect additional metrics that might indicate good candidates for clone removal through refactoring. To validate results in a more comprehensive way, we added two software systems that we are experts of as we actively contributed to them—one of them being a closed-source system. Finally, for three systems under study, we analyzed the first two years of their development to gather data representing snapshots of software systems in early development stages. Thus, allowing to compare results obtained by analyzing mature systems to results obtained by analyzing immature systems.

This chapter describes the semi-automated detection of clone refatorings and the tracking of introduced abstractions to remove clones in the evolution of a software system. We will perform two main steps: First, we detect refactorings that removed code clones either deliberately or accidentally. In the second step, we use the information gained in the previous step to track code fragments that have been introduced in the course of the identified refactorings. Each of the two steps can in turn be separated into different phases that are repeated for each version in the evolution of the systems. We extend our framework presented in the previous Chapter 4 in Figure 4.1 accordingly. An overview of the extended framework is given in Figure 5.1. We will describe our approach in detail in the following sections.

5.1 Identification of Clone Refactorings

Detecting clone removals is quite difficult and time consuming as there is no method to do the task completely automated. Accordingly, we are not aware of a formal way to describe the process. Manual decisions we take are critical to our study and exposed to subjective judgment. Therefore, we describe the criteria we apply as good as possible to make our decisions comprehensible. Göde [89] presented an approach

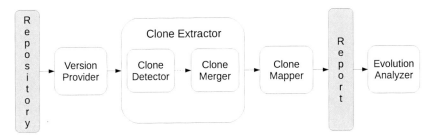

Figure 5.1 – Overview of the extended framework and its components used to analyze clone refactorings.

that is intended to help detecting duplicated code that has been removed between two consecutive versions v_i and v_{i+1} of a software system. We adapted this method to detect deliberate and accidental clone removals and integrated the approach into our clone extraction framework presented in Chapter 4. The identification of removals consists of four steps using the information provided by our framework. The first two steps are automated and concerned with detecting all clones in a system and, afterwards, filtering clone fragments from the result set that cannot be part of any removal—this is performed by the *Evolution Analyzer* component of our extended framework. The third step is to manually decide which of the left-over clones are in fact affected by removals of duplication. We denote the set of all clones detected by our framework as *All*—no matter whether they are related to a removal or not. The set *All* is reported as output after the *Clone Mapper* component mapped clone fragments between subsequent versions. Finally, we build a classification scheme to categorize and group detected clone removing refactorings. In the following we describe the steps to identify clone removals in the evolution model.

5.1.1 Clone Detection

A clone detector is used to analyze all versions of the software systems under study. Our proposed framework uses an enhanced version of the clone detector presented by Göde [96], namely ICLONES, as described in Chapter 4. We configured ICLONES such that the *Clone Merger* component merges identical code fragments that are at least 10 tokens in size and the number of different tokens between two fragments needs to be smaller in size than the shorter of the two neighboring fragments. In addition, ICLONES has been configured to report only identical and non-identical clones with a minimum total length of 50 tokens. The values of 10 and 50 tokens for the minimum length thresholds are chosen rather conservative and based on our experience from former studies using ICLONES [26, 29, 31, 87, 89, 96, 104]. Figure 5.2 illustrates these bounds for identical (a) and non-identical (b) clone fragments.

After detecting clone fragments in every version of a system ICLONES writes the clone data into an output file in the *Rich Clone Format* (*RCF*)—corrsponding the *Report* component of our framework. *RCF* is a data format to store and analyze code clone information and defines an extensible schema which makes it flexible for different

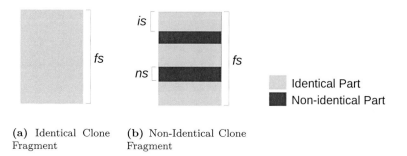

(a) Identical Clone Fragment   (b) Non-Identical Clone Fragment

Figure 5.2 – Identical and non-identical clone fragments need to be at least 50 tokens in size in total to be reported by ICLONES. The total length is depicted by the *fs* measure. In addition, each identical part of a non-identical clone fragment needs to have at least 10 tokens (exemplary depicted by the measure *is*) and the gaps need to have at least the same size as the shortest neighboring identical part (exemplary depicted by the measure *ns*).

kinds of information [103]. The *RCF* file is used by the *Evolution Analyzer* component to detect clone removals in the next step. We use and extend the clone visualization tool CYCLONE by Harder and Goede [103] described in Section 2.8.2.

5.1.2   Filtering Clone Fragments

The data generated by ICLONES contains all relevant data including the required information to build the evolution model, that is, it encompasses all components of our framework up to the *Report*. Accordingly, CYCLONE is solely used to inspect the huge amount of data computed by ICLONES and has no impact on the detection of cloned code, and hence, on precision and recall of the results. The *Evolution Analyzer* which works on the reported clone data represents the use of CYCLONE in our framework. It is particularly used to visualize the evolution model and helps the user to inspect different aspects of cloned code over time. To identify the removal of cloned code, the first objective is to determine the set of clone fragments that have been either modified or deleted out of the set *All*. Clone fragments that have not been changed can be ignored. In addition, fragments are filtered that have only been marginally changed between two versions of a system and, therefore, can most probably be neglected from further considerations. CYCLONE offers a threshold that specifies the minimum bound of modified and deleted tokens in a clone fragment. In this study, we used the same bound of 15 tokens as Göde did [87]. His study showed that this is an appropriate bound to filter many uninteresting changes with only a small risk to miss true removals. Let *Marginal Change* be the resulting set of clones that have not been changed sufficiently and *Sufficient Change* the set of clone fragments that have been. That is, less than 15 tokens of each fragment in set *Marginal Change* and equal to or more than 15 tokens of each fragment in set *Sufficient Change* changed across two subsequent versions. Note, it is not sufficient to consider only clone fragments that have been completely removed from v_i to v_{i+1} as the scope of a refactoring hardly ever matches the scope of the detected clone fragments precisely.

The set *Sufficient Change* for each system is automatically detected based on source-code changes between consecutive versions determined using the diff algorithm[1]. Every clone fragment that is part of *Sufficient Change* is marked in the evolution model by CYCLONE and the user is able to navigate through the whole set.

5.1.3 Manual Inspection

The decision from which fragments out of set *Sufficient Change* clones have been removed either deliberately or accidentally and if possible refactorings were missed by developers must be done manually. For each clone of set *Sufficient Change* we checked the commit messages and reviewed the source code before and after the corresponding changes to judge whether code duplication has been removed or not. To assist the manual examination of commit messages CYCLONE marks versions in the evolution graph whose commit messages include indicating keywords, e.g., removal, refactoring or duplication. Depending on the commit messages we sometimes had clear indications that code duplication was removed and where these changes took place exactly. However, from our experience commit messages are often imprecise or inaccurate so we used them only to get a first impression of what was done and not as decisive criterion. This means that we always analyzed the source code changes even if the commit message already gave a clear hint.

Afterwards, we analyzed the source code changes between two versions to get more reliable information. The code review was done on different levels. First, we used the integrated source-code view of CYCLONE, which focuses on the cloned fragments. It gives us the files, the exact positions of the cloned fragments and for non-identical clones the identical and non-identical parts at a glance. Especially, the non-identical parts of non-identical clones have to be kept in mind further on to separate changes to them from changes to the actual cloned parts. Due to the fact that our evolution model is based on clone classes, detected clone fragments might appear in more than one clone class of the same version. For instance, if fragments of different clone classes partially overlap the same code segments. Therefore, we used information about the fragments' file paths and source locations for grouping overlapping fragments of different clone classes to save us from analyzing changes to the same code multiple times.

For a detailed code review we used either diff information provided by the repository system or the visual diff tool MELD[2]. If necessary, we also imported the projects into ECLIPSE[3] IDE for further information. Based on the information collected using CYCLONE we used the stated tools to extract and review all modifications that might have led to a removal of code duplication. In some cases we were not able to decide whether or not cloned code has been removed based on the change information provided by these tools. In such cases it was necessary to review more general project attributes

---

[1] http://code.google.com/p/google-diff-match-patch/
[2] http://meldmerge.org/
[3] http://www.eclipse.org/

in addition to the diff, for instance, library and API updates. We used ECLIPSE to review the corresponding project attributes before and after the changes happened.

If we were able to detect the elimination of code clones by a refactoring, we exported the information of the corresponding clone fragments using CYCLONE. The export is done automatically and collects different kinds of data. Among others we have exported basic information such as the version in which the refactoring took place, the file paths and source locations of the affected fragments, and the date of change. In addition, we also exported different metrics, for instance, *LOC*, the number of consistent and inconsistent changes to the clone fragments before the refactoring and the *Cyclomatic Complexity* of the fragments. We compute *Cyclomatic Complexity* using the definition by McCabe [194] which is basically the number of conditions plus one for any arbitrary code fragment. These metrics are used in our case study to investigate whether or not a ranking of clones can be based on these metrics. Such a ranking is needed to reduce the amount of clone data delivered to the users by clone management tools. If, for example, the number of changes to a certain clone fragment was high before it was removed, it might be an indication that the developers wanted to avoid the extra effort of continuously changing the cloned code and decided to refactor it.

5.1.4   Categorization and grouping

Based on the above decision process, we manually identified refactorings that removed code duplication and categorized the observed code removals. A schematic illustration of the resulting categories is shown in Figure 5.3. We started our categorization based on the initial set *All* of all clone fragments identified by our clone detector. Using CYCLONE the set *Sufficient Change* of potential clone removals was extracted from *All* and manually inspected. Set *Marginal Change* contains only clone fragments that have not been changed sufficiently to be considered a removal of duplication and was neglected from further analysis. Then we split set *Sufficient Change* (which is the complement to *Marginal Change*) in the sets *NotRemoved* and *Removed*. Set *NotRemoved* denotes clones that did change but were not subject to removals of duplication and, therefore, were dismissed from further consideration. Set *Removed* contains all clone fragments related to clone removing activities.

During the manual inspection we identified clone fragments related to refactorings that removed code duplication but missed some clones of the clone class that could have been removed by the refactoring, too. We considered these removals incomplete and assigned them in a separate set *Missed*. All complete removals were assigned to the complementary set *Complete*. Lastly, we split the set *Complete* into the two subsets *Deliberate* and *Accidental*. *Deliberate* includes clone fragments that were deliberately removed using appropriate refactorings. In contrast, *Accidental* contains clones removed accidentally as a side effect of a change with different intention.

Figure 5.4 provides an example taken from JETTY to illustrate our decisions on deliberate clone removals—details of the subject systems and our selection process are given in Chapter 5. Besides refactorings that were mainly performed to remove code clones, we also identified refactorings that removed code duplication accidentally as a

Figure 5.3 – Schematic illustration of the categorization of clones.

side effect. This means that we found clear indications that the goal of the corresponding changes was actually not to remove clones.

Example 5.1 – Two clone fragments f_a and f_b are refactored into a new method m using an *Exttract Method* refactoring. At the same time new functionality has been implemented in m that was neither provided by f_a nor f_b. There is no direct relation between the added functionality in m and the former clone fragments f_a and f_b. □

The above refactoring is rated to be accidental since there is no relation between the eliminated clone fragments and the new functionality of the new method, for instance, to adapt and merge differences between the fragments. Clone fragments involved in such refactoring activities are assigned to the set *Accidental*. We encountered different types of refactorings removing duplication as side effect, for instance, the removal of deprecated or dead code and updates of external libraries and APIs. However, our decision process was directed to decide if a refactoring was performed to remove cloned code only and we have been very restrictive regarding this decision to assure high confidence. We did not investigate intentions that lead to accidental removals in detail since they are not in the scope of our work.

Note that clone fragments related to a refactoring that missed suitable clones are assigned to the set *Missed* independent from the fact whether the refactoring was meant to remove duplication or not. The number of missed clones in this set is a helpful indicator when it comes to the question how much developers can benefit from using clone management tools that could pinpoint to similar code during code editing. Figure 5.5 shows an example of a missed clone removal taken from ARGOUML—slightly adapted to improve readability.

Finally, we grouped clone fragments within the sets *Deliberate*, *Accidental* and *Missed* further. Clone fragments within the same set that are part of the same refactoring activity were counted as a ROD (Removal of Duplication) unit. The term ROD is adapted from Göde [89] and denotes a set of changes to remove duplication

```
1   public void sendMessage(byte frame, String content) throws
2   IOException
3   {
4
5   _generator.addFrame(WebSocket.SENTINEL_FRAME,content,
6   _maxIdleTimeMs);
7       _generator.flush();
8       if (!_generator.isBufferEmpty() && _endp instanceof
9   AsyncEndPoint)
10          ((AsyncEndPoint)_endp).scheduleWrite();
11      _idle.access(_endp);
12  }
```

(a) Prior to the change

```
1   public void sendMessage(byte frame, String content) throws
2   IOException
3   {
4       _generator.addFrame(frame,content,_maxIdleTimeMs);
5       _generator.flush();
6       checkWriteable();
7       _idle.access(_endp);
8   }
9
10  private void checkWriteable()
11  {
12      if (!_generator.isBufferEmpty() && _endp instanceof
13  AsyncEndPoint)
14          ((AsyncEndPoint)_endp).scheduleWrite();
15  }
```

(b) Subsequent to the change

Figure 5.4 – Deliberate removal of duplicated code in the system JETTY. An *Extract Method* refactoring has been applied on the if statement of the method *sendMessage* that was used by two code segments located in the same file. After the refactoring the newly created method *checkWriteable* is called at the corresponding positions instead.

```
1    ...
2      super(owner, settings);
3      middleGroup = new FigTextGroup(owner, settings);
4
5      if (getNameFig() != null) {
6        middleGroup.addFig(getNameFig());
7      }
8      middleGroup.addFig(getStereotypeFig());
9      addPathItem(middleGroup,
10         new PathItemPlacement(this, middleGroup, 50, 25));
11     ArgoFigUtil.markPosition(this, 50, 0, 90, 25,
12         Color.yellow);
13
14     Object[] ends = // UML objects of AssociationEnd type
15         Model.getFacade().getConnections(owner).toArray();
16   ...
```

(a) Prior to the change

```
1    ...
2      super(owner, settings);
3      createNameLabel(owner, settings);
4
5      Object[] ends = // UML objects of AssociationEnd type
6          Model.getFacade().getConnections(owner).toArray();
7    ...
8
9    protected void createNameLabel(Object owner, DiagramSettings
10   settings) {
11     middleGroup = new FigTextGroup(owner, settings);
12
13     // let's use groups to construct the different text
14     // sections at the association
15     if (getNameFig() != null) {
16       middleGroup.addFig(getNameFig());
17     }
18     middleGroup.addFig(getStereotypeFig());
19     addPathItem(middleGroup,
20         new PathItemPlacement(this, middleGroup, 50, 25));
21     ArgoFigUtil.markPosition(this, 50, 0, 90, 25,
22         Color.yellow);
23   }
```

(b) Subsequent to the change

Figure 5.5 – The routine to create a label in (a) (line 4 - 13) is a clone of another code fragment located in the same file with the only difference being the last parameter passed to the method *ArgoFigUtil* (line 13) which determines the color. The code fragment presented in (a) has been refactored in the next version and the routine to create a label has been extracted into a new method as shown in (b). However, the corresponding clone fragment to (a) has been missed in the course of the refactoring performed.

in which all clone fragments affected by one or more refactorings originated from a common intention, for instance, extracting equal functionality of a class into a method. RODs are manually identified and may contain fragments affected by refactorings that have been performed in different versions—corresponding to different commits—of a system as long as all of them have been carried out for the same reason.

Example 5.2 – Three clone fragments f_a, f_b, and f_c are affected by the removal of code duplication. Fragments f_a and f_b were eliminated in version v_i whereas fragment f_c was eliminated in version $v_i + 1$. In addition, new utility class c was introduced in $v_i + 1$ as well. The utility class c includes a method m providing the same functionality as the deleted fragments f_a, f_b, and f_c and the former code of the three fragments has been replaced by a method call to method m. □

In the above example we count the three removed fragments as one ROD, though, they were not replaced by the method call in the same version. Note that RODs can even have only one clone fragment assigned.

Example 5.3 – Two statement sequences S_a and S_b are clones of each other with S_b being the body of a method m. Sequence S_a is replaced by a call to m. □

Replacing a clone by a call to an existing method, it is sufficient that only one clone fragment changes to remove code duplication. Accordingly, such a ROD encompasses only one removed clone fragment.

5.2   Tracking Refactored Code Fragments

Having identified refactorings that have been performed to remove code duplications, we are able to investigate code fragments that have been introduced in the course of these removals. In this step, we focus on deliberate clone removals, set *Deliberate*, only since these refactorings have been performed to achieve a benefit in the long term by eliminating clones. In contrast, the set *Accidental* includes clones that have been removed by chance due to a refactoring actually performed for some other reason. These refactorings cannot be consulted to investigate costs and benefits of clone refactorings, because other cost and benefit factors of the refactoring which are not related to clone removals are unknown. Thus, their costs and benefits could most probably not be separated from costs and benefits related to clone removals in a meaningful way.

Compared to the identification of clone removing refactorings in which basically all variants of refactorings have been taken into consideration, only certain refactorings are well suited for an ongoing tracking of their resulting source code. With ongoing tracking we refer to the tracking of source code in the history of a system after the code has been initially introduced in consequence of a clone removal. In this respect, it is advantageous to focus only on those refactorings that result in a contiguous code fragment after a clone removal, for instance, *Extract Method* and *Pull Up Method*. We denote *Deliberate*$_{track}$ as a subset of *Deliberate* containing refactorings that are well suited for an ongoing tracking.

To track and analyze code fragments from set *Deliberate*$_{track}$ that have been introduced by refactorings, we extended CYCLONE such that it allows to track not only cloned code but also user determined code fragments over time. To track a code

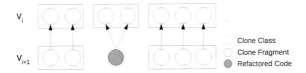

Figure 5.6 – The dark grey circle in v_{i+1} represents the code fragment introduced by a clone removing refactoring which is also the successor of the corresponding clone fragments in v_i.

fragment, the user selects a file and marks the desired code within the file using an integrated source code view in CYCLONE. Afterwards, the selected code segment is tracked and added to the evolution model of the software system under study. Figure 5.6 illustrates the integration in the evolution model of CYCLONE. The tracking approach uses information of source code modifications provided by the repository of the software system. Based on the information of the repository again a diff is used to update the position of the code fragment between two consecutive versions v_i and v_{i+1} and, hereby, tracked over time.

In addition to the tracking, CYCLONE also provides functionality to support the user analyzing the tracked code fragments and export various information directed towards changes. First, it uses repository information of changes hitting tracked code fragments to highlight these fragments in the evolution graph. This enables the user to easily navigate between changed fragments. Selecting a code fragment in the evolution graph allows to open a source code view in split screen mode. The split screen lines up the selected fragment in the current and previous or in the current and next version, respectively. Highlighting is used in that view to visualize source code changes that were applied between two subsequent versions. We use these features to manually inspect changes to source code that has been introduced due to a clone removal. We use the same approach as described in Section 5.1.3 to analyze changes manually and gather further metrics automatically, e.g., position and size of each fragment.

The information collected by this approach is used in Section 5.7 to investigate certain characteristics of changes to code fragments introduced by a clone removing refactoring, such as frequency, complexity, and committer. This will help us to answer Question 15 as, for instance, whether a high frequency of changes to an introduced code fragment indicates that developers decreased maintenance effort by eliminating clones and saving themselves from applying the same changes to different locations in the source code—which means tracking all clone fragments, deciding whether or not a change has to be applied to all of them, performing the actual modifications and testing every change.

5.3 Study Setup

In this section, we present the setup of our evaluation. We analyzed 15 realistic open-source and one closed-source system to gather empirical data that supplement previous findings and answer our research questions. The approach to detect and track clone removing refactorings was used to investigate different characteristics of the subject systems. Each system was required to satisfy the following criteria to be considered for our analysis:

- The systems are maintained using either a SUBVERSION or a GIT repository.

- Each system has a reasonably long history to provide a sufficient amount of data to obtain meaningful results, but is still manageable for manual inspection.

- We included systems that have already been analyzed by Göde [89] to allow for comparisons to his results.

In contrast to our last study focusing on clone removals in the evolution of mature software systems [29] only, we considered immature subject systems this time as well. That is, systems were considered mature if they possessed several releases or years of development before the version we used as starting point for our analysis. In contrast, we denote a system immature when performing our analysis starting from its very first version such that we are able to observe the development of a system during its early stages. By analyzing mature as well as immature systems, we investigate our research questions considering differences regarding clone removing activities and a system's maturity, if any exist. Moreover, we also selected two subject systems, one in the mature and the other one in the immature category, for which we are experts of as we actively contributed to them. By choosing to analyze these systems, we ensured a high accuracy in our assessment regarding code changes and refactorings. Thus, we were able to further rule out possible design flaws in our manual inspection approach. For instance, we were able to compare clone refactorings detected during the manual inspection to our knowledge concerning such activity and verify that the manual process resulted in correct findings.

The mature systems we analyzed are ADEMPIERE-CLIENT, ANT, ARGOUML, BAUHAUS, FILEZILLA, FINDBUGS, FREECOL, Apache's HTTPD, JABREF, JETTY, NAUTILUS, TORTOISESVN and UMBRELLO. ADEMPIERE-CLIENT, ARGOUML and TORTOISESVN were analyzed in Göde's study [89] as well. Göde also analyzed KDE-UTILS, which we did not because KDE-UTILS is a collection of different tools. Removing code duplication within one software system compared to the removal of clones between different systems is a different use case and brings in other aspects that need to be considered. The tools of KDE-UTILS are related but though have their own source code and, therefore, present a combination of intra-system and inter-system clone detection use case. Finally, the subject systems for which we analyzed their source code starting from the first version available are AIDE, HIBISCUS and POOKA. The systems we are experts of are AIDE and BAUHAUS. The subject systems together with their specification details are listed in Table 5.1—mature systems above and immature systems below the dashed line.

We investigated two years of each mature system's history, starting from January 2009 to December 2010. We chose a time period that subsumes the time period investigated by Göde [89], which was from January 7 to October 29, 2009 to make the results comparable as good as possible. Nonetheless, we decided to increase the time

System	Language	KSLOC	Clone Classes	Clone Fragments
ADEMPIERE	Java	68 – 63	1,908,109	5,010,007
ANT	Java	175 – 160	696,446	1,813,720
ARGOUML	C++	181 – 259	873,485	2,249,690
BAUHAUS	Ada	1,000 – 1,100	5,579,366	17,494,520
FILEZILLA	C++	103 – 113	513,912	1,150,498
FINDBUGS	Java	160 – 216	260,678	628,940
FREECOL	Java	94 – 108	614,193	1,605,787
HTTPD	C	187 – 200	747,684	1,734,741
JABREF	Java	80 – 103	347,460	888,642
JETTY	Java	87 – 177	1,074,288	2,890,580
NAUTILUS	C	136 – 115	330,957	807,891
TORTOISESVN	C++	150 – 260	1,054,250	2,438,919
UMBRELLO	C++	200 – 202	734,862	1,774,858
AIDE	Java	1 – 92	253,096	618,855
HIBISCUS	Java	<1 – 23	79,826	206,757
POOKA	C	4 – 30	103,340	261,556

Table 5.1 – Subject systems used for studying clone removals.

period under study, because Göde reported that he had to dismiss different software systems from investigation as he was not able to find indications of clone removals. To lessen the risk of having the same problem and to check the impact the time period under study has on the results, we analyzed a longer period of the evolution of the subject systems. In contrast to the time period analyzed for the mature systems, we chose to increase it to about three years for the three systems for which we investigated the evolution starting from their first version available. Looking at a larger time period for these systems helped to gather more relevant refactorings, since the code base of the early versions was rather small for each system, but increased sufficiently in the time period of three years. We analyzed the time period from January 2011 to September 2013 for AIDE, from February 2004 to February 2007 for HIBISCUS and from January 2000 to January 2003 for POOKA. Snapshots have been analyzed on an interval of one day for the mature as well as immature systems under study. Dates that did not contain any commits including changes to the source code were skipped though.

We configured ICLONES to analyze the subject systems and report clone fragments with an overall minimum length of 50 tokens and a minimum length of 10 tokens for identical parts regarding non-identical clones as described in Section 5.1.1. The reported output of each analysis was analyzed using CYCLONE. In total, we inspected 6,505 clone fragments in 3,961 clone classes (spread over 650 snapshots) that have been assigned to the set *Sufficient Change* of clone fragments, using our manual inspection approach. From these, we assigned 1,606 fragments to the set *Removed* of clones that are directly related to either deliberate, accidental, or missed removals of code duplications. Unifying fragments that were related to the same refactoring task we identified 357 RODs.

To ensure the accuracy of the manual inspection and lessen the impact of subjectivity of the oracle, the two authors as well as a third assessor performed the manual inspection separately from each other. The first author did the manual analysis as described in Section 5.1.3, before the second author checked 20 % of the results for each subject system under study in a sampling process using the same approach as the first one did—not knowing the decision of the first author. The result of the sampled cross-check uncovered disagreements regarding the assessment of the authors in 15 cases. Differences occurred assessing the scope of refactorings compared to the scope of detected clone fragments, for instance. The disagreements were all minor, often originated from mistakes by one of the two authors.

To accurately resolve the disagreements, cases that were assessed differently have been investigated by a third oracle[4] who is an expert for software clones. Instead of playing the role of a judge, the third oracle assessed the cases independently from the results of the first two oracles and all results have been discussed in a joint session afterwards. By discussing the results rather than making majority decisions, we rule out possible mistakes (oversights). Note that the joint discussion is not meant to convince any of the oracles of a certain assessment. Out of the 15 cases for which the first two oracles disagreed, the assessment performed by the third oracle did not lead to a different judgment in nine of these cases. In these cases the third oracle judged either equal to the joint decision of the authors or followed that decision after the discussion phase—in most cases due to an oversight by himself. For the other six cases, the third oracle judged different and the decisions were changed after the discussion phase compared to the joint decision of the first two authors. Thus, in six out of 15 cases of disagreement the final decision differed from the original judgment of the authors. However, the 15 cases assessed by a third oracle have to be considered the most difficult ones to decide since they represent the only cases for which no agreement was achieved by the first two authors from the beginning. The reason for changing decisions was mainly that the third oracle gave hints important for the assessment that were not identified by the first two authors.

Example 5.4 – A method in version v_i named *foo* is renamed to *bar* in version v_{i+1}. Simultaneously, the location of the method changed in the source code. An other change replaced two clone fragments f_a and f_b from version v_i to v_{i+1} by a call to method *bar* each. □

The following example is adapted from one of the assessments for which the third oracle disagreed the assessment of the first two oracles. It describes a case in which the first two oracles did not recognize the method renaming and, therefore, rated the refactoring an *Extract Method*—assuming the method to be newly introduced. Indeed, a *Call Existing Method* refactoring was applied since the method existed already and was just renamed across the subject versions.

Finally, we validated our results as far as possible using the study from Göde [89]. For those systems that have been covered and for those aspects that have been investigated by both studies we also found a general agreement regarding our results—details on the differences and their explanation are given in Section 5.4.

---

[4]The third oracle is Marcel Steinbeck who is an employee in our working group for several years with one of his research focus' being software clones and bad smells in general.

5.4   Refactoring Frequency

Table 5.2 summarizes the quantitative results of our manual inspection of clone removals and answers our research questions 11 and 12. The first column lists the subject systems. The second and third columns show the number of clone classes and clone fragments detected by ICLONES that were related to clone removal activities (RODs) in the inspection process. The overall number of resulting RODs is given in column four and the relative number of RODs per each KSLOC in column five (system sizes are shown in Table 5.1). Finally, the last three columns give numbers for removals rated deliberate, accidental, and missed. It can be seen that the numbers vary for each system with TORTOISESVN contributing the largest and UMBRELLO the smallest number of RODs in absolute terms. Correlating the number of detected RODs to the size of the subject systems column five shows clones were removed in UMBRELLO the least as indicated by the absolute numbers as well. However, by far the most clone removing refactorings were identified for HIBISCUS in relative terms with more than 1.5 RODs every KSLOC. Comparing the numbers obtained analyzing the mature systems to those obtained for the immature, it can be observed that for all immature systems notably more RODs were detected in relative terms. While 1.67 RODs every KSLOC were found for HIBISCUS and slightly more than 0.70 RODs for AIDE and POOKA, TORTOISESVN contributes the highest number of RODs with 0.43 per each KSLOC among the mature systems. On average the mature systems show an average of 0.14 RODs every KSLOC. The relative numbers of RODs compared to the size of the subject systems show that clearly more clones were removed in the immature systems than in the mature ones.

The last three columns present the absolute numbers of detected RODs within the corresponding set of clone fragments as described in Section 5.1 in paragraph "Categorization and grouping". The overall number of RODs generally correlate with the numbers of affected clone classes and fragments. Comparing deliberate and accidental removals, it can be observed that they are relatively balanced over all systems no matter whether mature or immature. The only striking gap was found for NAUTILUS for which no deliberate, but 22 accidental RODs were detected. Moreover, for the systems JABREF, JETTY and UMBRELLO we did not discover any removal in some change categories. These results answer our research question 11 suggesting that for the systems under study systematic clone management has been performed by the developers, but clones have also been removed unknowingly as a side effect of other refactoring activities. Regarding our research question 12 directed towards code clones that have been missed by suitable refactorings, we were able to detect only a few, except for TORTOISESVN. The results show that there is an opportunity for clone detectors to reduce the likelihood of missed refactorings, though, numbers the potential seems rather small.

Overall, we can confirm the results of Göde's study on deliberate clone removals for the software systems he analyzed [89] too—considering the shorter time frame used in his study. Göde reported for ARGOUML one and for TORTOISESVN four more deliberate removals for the time period shared by both studies. The reason for the differences is that we classified these RODs as accidental removals. We assume that our more differentiated categorization compared to Göde's contributed to this divergent

System	Classes	Fragments	RODs	RODs/KSLOC	$|Deliberate|$	$|Accidental|$	$|Missed|$
ADEMPIERE	30	57	13	0.20	5	5	3
ANT	26	42	6	0.04	1	3	2
ARGOUML	165	368	36	0.16	14	16	6
BAUHAUS	30	79	29	0.03	12	16	1
FILEZILLA	32	55	11	0.10	8	2	1
FINDBUGS	17	30	8	0.04	4	3	1
FREECOL	64	133	31	0.31	10	18	3
HTTPD	17	37	7	0.04	3	3	1
JABREF	2	5	2	0.02	1	1	0
JETTY	36	85	36	0.27	19	17	0
NAUTILUS	38	75	23	0.18	0	22	1
TORTOISESVN	270	482	88	0.43	42	28	18
UMBRELLO	4	8	1	0.01	0	1	0
AIDE	33	68	33	0.71	17	14	2
HIBISCUS	22	50	20	1.67	6	13	1
POOKA	13	32	13	0.76	6	6	1
Total	**799**	**1606**	**357**	**0.31**	**146**	**170**	**41**

Table 5.2 – Removal of Duplication

judgment. Göde did not further classify RODs. Our differentiation may have led us to judge more strictly on deliberate removals.

5.5   Refactoring Types

To investigate how clones are removed by developers and answer our research question 13, we investigated the refactorings related to the detected RODs presented in Section 5.4. A better understanding of which clones attract the attention of developers might help to improve existing detection and management tools to produce more useful results by ranking them. Our case study setup suits the use case of removing code duplication. Therefore, we inspected what type of refactorings developers used to remove clones and how well the scope of these refactorings fit the scope of the clones reported by our clone detector. Göde inspected refactorings and their scope in his study [89] also. He stated that a good matching with high recall is the basis for the use of clone management tools. On the contrary, a bad matching indicates either automated clone detection is not accurate enough or developers are not aware of the duplication's extent. He found that there is a remarkable discrepancy between clones detected by a state of the art clone detection tool and duplications removed by developers—the scope of the refactorings hardly matched the scope of the detected clone fragments. deliberate removals.

We adapted the approach to categorize RODs from Göde [89] to our results. The taxonomy we used to classify refactorings is an extended version of his taxonomy and emerged as a result of our manual inspection process to detect refactorings that removed

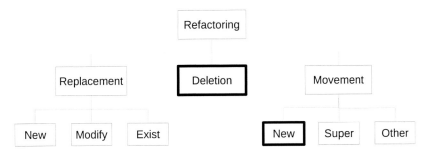

Figure 5.7 – Classification of clone removing refactorings identified by our manual detection approach.

code clones. That is, we identified the type of refactorings used to remove clones within the set *Removed* as introduced in paragraph "Categorization and grouping" of Section 5.1. Our classification is based on refactorings commonly quoted as suitable to remove duplications, for instance, *Extract Method* and *Pull Up Method*. Figure 5.7 shows the resulting classification. The bold rectangles depict which parts have been added to our classification compared to the one presented by Göde.

We detected three categories of refactorings that were applied to remove clones. In contrast to Göde, we do not separate unifications (gathering code that provides equal functionality in a single place) into a category on its own, because it is based on the movement of the corresponding code. Instead we count such unifications in the *Movement* category.

Replacement We distinguish two cases in this category. The first one is that a sequence of statements has been replaced by a single method call either to a newly introduced method (*New*) or to a method that already existed before the refactoring took place (*Exist*). The second one refers to modifications in terms of replacing a sequence of statements by another sequence of statements (*Modify*). In most cases we detected that the nesting within methods has been reduced due to high complexity—which also led to the removal of clones.

Movement This category includes refactorings—such as pull-up field or method—that gather two or more field declarations or methods providing equal functionality in a single class. We differentiate between three types of movements. First, the code is moved to a new class that did not exist before (*New*). Second, the code of the affected classes is moved to a superclass (*Super*) of them. Last, the code is moved to an existing class that provides functionality used by a range of classes, e.g., a utility class, but that class is not a superclass of the classes from which the code is moved (*Other*).

Deletion Field declarations or methods are removed. This category includes deletions of dead or deprecated code. Though, deletions commonly go hand in hand with other modifications of the code base which make the deleted code fragments dead or deprecated, we focus only on the actual removal of duplication rather than what introduced it. We will describe our decision based on the following example in more detail.

Example 5.5 – A method m_{new} is introduced and evolves over several versions of a system. In version v_i method m_{new} provides at least the same functionality as an other method m_{old} that existed in the code base already before m_{new} was introduced. Afterwards, all uses of m_{old} were replaced by using m_{new} instead until m_{old} is dead or deprecated in version v_j with $j > i$. However, m_{old} was not removed in version v_j but kept existing in the code base. Finally, m_{old} was removed in version v_k with $k > j$. □

In the above example a dead or deprecated method existed for some period of time until a developer removed it finally. In this use case, the removal of the duplicated method is separated from its replacement or other related actions that were applied before and, therefore, is considered a conscious removal of cloned code by us. Note, that we count deletions of dead or deprecated code that is removed in version v_i when its functionality is redundant for the first time in the *Movement* or *Replacement* category, respectively, depending on the refactoring type performed.

In addition to the taxonomy, we adapted the approach of comparing the scope of refactorings to the scope of clone fragments reported by our clone detector from Göde [89]. For each ROD the scope of its clone fragments is manually compared to the related refactoring performed. An advantage of the manual comparison is that we can tolerate various artifacts of token-based clone detection at the beginning and end of fragments, for instance, brackets. The comparison results in each fragment being classified to either:

- *Match*: if all statements of the clone fragment are part of the refactoring and vice versa

- *Containing*[5]: if the changes refer only to statements within the bounds of a clone fragment

- *Contained*[5] if the scope of the refactoring (the statements changed by the refactoring) subsumes the clones either completely or partially, that is, just overlaps with the clone fragment

We found that for all clone fragments in the same ROD the comparison of scopes led to the same classification because of which we report the resulting numbers based on RODs rather than on clone fragments. Table 5.3 presents the results of deliberate RODs classified as either *Match*, *Containing* and *Contained* based on our taxonomy shown in Figure 5.7. It shows the number of RODs related to the different types of modifications and how well these RODs and modifications, respectively, actually matched the scope of detected clones. The results give indications whether specific refactoring, for instance, a certain type of replacement, is more often used when cloned code is removed. Moreover, the data also shows whether certain refactoring types match the scope of detected clones better than others. Although we have analyzed accidental and missed RODs and their corresponding scope as well, we leave out the exact numbers, because these RODs were not meant to remove code duplication in the first place. It is arguable whether the scope

---

[5]Göde used the term Superior instead of Containing and Inferior instead of Contained—we considered the terms Superior and Inferior mistakable

Refactoring	RODs	Match	Containing	Contained
Replacement	**91**	**28**	**38**	**25**
New	70	21	30	19
Modify	3	2	0	1
Exist	18	5	8	5
Movement	**53**	**8**	**13**	**32**
New	13	1	2	10
Super	37	7	10	20
Other	3	0	1	2
Deletion	**4**	**3**	**1**	**0**
Total	**148**	**39**	**52**	**57**

Table 5.3 – Scope of clone removing refactorings compared to clone fragments

of such refactorings need to match the scope of the clone fragments at all. However, analyzing the results for accidental and missed RODs, we generally found the same trend as presented for deliberate RODs.

To answer our research question 13, we quantitatively investigated how often clones were removed by certain kinds of refactorings. Table 5.3 shows that most clones were removed by replacing the duplicated code that has been mainly replaced by a new method. Also, we found that clones are more often replaced by already existing code than code that needed modifications beforehand. In contrast to the *Replacement* category, clones were more often replaced by moving instances to a super class rather than to a new class implemented to allow for a removal. Movements to other classes, such as utility classes, as well as deletions as described before were quite rare.

Furthermore, our results confirm the large discrepancy between the scope of detected refactorings and the scope of detected clone fragments stated by Göde [89]. Overall only about 25 % of all refactorings have been categorized to match the scope of the detected clone fragments. Göde found 16 % of his analyzed refactorings to match the scope of clone fragments. There is also no remarkable difference observable across the different refactoring types of our taxonomy in this respect—the overall trend is similar for all. The only exception is the category of deletions, but since we identified only a small number of such refactorings results cannot be considered representative. Focusing on refactorings that did not match the scope of detected fragments, we found that for the category *Movement* clearly more refactorings go beyond the scope of clone fragments. In contrast, there is no clear trend for refactorings that replaced source code regarding how well their scope fits the scope of detected clones. However, summing up the numbers for refactorings that replaced code and those which moved code an almost balanced distribution between the categories *Containing* and *Contained* is obtained. That is, overall we found 52 removals in the *Containing* and 57 removals in the *Contained* category.

Finally, we analyzed how many of the clone classes that included clone fragments affected by deliberate or accidental removals of duplication disappeared in the version after the corresponding refactoring was applied. The disappearance in such cases is either due to the fact that the fragments have been removed completely or reduced in size such that they got smaller than the configured minimum length of clones detected by the clone detector. We found that about 90 % of the clone classes affected by deliberate clone removals and about 79 % of the clone classes affected by accidental removals disappeared in the following version. This could be assumed to prove a high success rate in reducing clones regarding the refactorings chosen by developers. However, it should be kept in mind that the amount of clone classes and fragments related to the reduction of duplications is quite small compared to the overall number of clone classes and fragments detected by our clone detector.

5.6   Ranking Clones

To investigate whether and what measurable characteristics may help in ranking clone candidates for removal and answer our research question 14, we collected different clone metrics based on our retrospective analysis. Göde investigated different aspects of clone removals to contribute to the ranking of clones regarding the use case under study [89]. He limited his study to the following attributes: length, similarity, distance in the source tree, and number of source code files that contain the fragments of a ROD. Overall his results did not yield clear findings, only for the distance attribute there was a trend that developers mostly removed duplicated code located in the same source code file. Göde assumed that other attributes may help in ranking clones for removal. To contribute and extend Göde's preliminary analysis we collected and evaluated additional clone characteristics based on the clone classes and clone fragments related to our identified RODs.

5.6.1   Clone Types

The first aspect we investigated is whether developers tend to perform more refactorings on code clones that are identical or just similar. We analyzed how often RODs were related to identical clone fragments (type-1), clone fragments with parameter renamings (type-2), and clone fragments with further differences (type-3) based on detected clone classes as well as on individual clone fragments. Though, each fragment of a clone class is of the same type, it is not sufficient to consider clone classes only, because they may consist of a different number of fragments. That is, the number of clone classes is just an indicator regarding the extent of cloning, but not as exact as the number of individual clone fragments.

   Example 5.6 – A clone class cc of type 1 consists of three clone fragments while an other clone class cc' of type 2 consist of two clone fragments. Due to refactorings between versions v_i and v_{i+1} the fragments of both classes were removed. □

   In the above example each clone class increments the counting of type-1 and type-2 clone classes by one, respectively. However, considering the fragments of the two classes, less clone fragments of type-2 were removed. Tables 5.4 and 5.5 show the results considering clones out of set *All* and *Sufficient Change*, respectively. The first column

System	#Classes	Classes [%]			#Fragments	Fragments [%]		
		Type-1	Type-2	Type-3		Type-1	Type-2	Type-3
ADEMPIERE	1,908,109	7,09	48,51	44,40	5,010,007	7,26	50,09	42,66
ANT	696,446	24,50	22,84	52,66	1,813,720	26,78	22,76	50,46
ARGOUML	873,485	29,01	27,67	43,32	2,249,690	29,58	28,92	41,50
BAUHAUS	5,579,366	17,94	21,50	60,56	17,494,520	17,07	18,58	64,35
FILEZILLA	513,912	21,76	22,11	56,13	1,150,498	23,60	22,45	53,95
FINDBUGS	260,678	24,22	28,90	46,88	628,940	24,78	32,24	42,97
FREECOL	614,193	28,60	19,88	51,52	1,605,787	30,76	19,17	50,08
HTTPD	747,684	26,11	19,06	54,83	1,734,741	27,18	19,04	53,78
JABREF	347,460	41,98	19,21	38,81	888,642	39,30	19,80	40,90
JETTY	1,074,288	29,42	18,81	51,77	2,890,580	32,61	18,19	49,20
NAUTILUS	330,957	16,25	28,70	55,05	807,891	16,77	32,59	50,64
TORTOISESVN	1,054,250	25,74	19,96	54,29	2,438,919	28,99	19,86	51,16
UMBRELLO	734,862	22,42	25,45	52,13	1,774,858	24,34	26,17	49,49
AIDE	253,096	33,76	25,78	40,46	618,855	34,67	25,56	39,78
HIBISCUS	79,826	18,14	28,64	53,22	206,757	18,47	28,20	53,33
POOKA	103,340	36,43	18,62	44,95	261,556	36,90	16,63	46,47
Total	15,171,952	21,06	25,36	53,57	41,575,961	21,19	24,28	54,53

Table 5.4 – Types of clones in set *All*

lists the subject systems followed by four columns related to clone classes of which the first gives the total number of detected classes and the letter three the relative amount related to each clone type expressed as a percentage. Analogously, the last four columns give numbers and percentages of involved clone fragments distinguished by type. It can be seen that the general trend is similar for both sets, *All* and *Sufficient Change*, showing that most clones involved are of type 3—around 50%. The amount of detected type-1 and type-2 clones is rather balanced with values around roughly 25%. This trend can also be observed for the main share of individual subject systems with few exceptions only. Finally, comparing the mature to the immature systems generally the same trends are found except for AIDE for which more type-1 and less type-3 clones where detected.

To investigate whether a certain clone type has been attracted developers attention with respect to refactorings than the other, we gathered the same information for the clones assigned to the set *Removed*. We distinguished refactorings according to the set *Deliberate*, *Accidental*, and *Missed*. Tables 5.6, 5.7, and 5.8 show the resulting numbers in the same way as described for the tables 5.4 and 5.5. Looking at the absolute numbers, type 3 is the dominating clone type for deliberately removed clones as shown in Table 5.6. Table 5.8 shows that only few clones were found that were missed by an appropriate refactoring, that is, few clones were assigned to the set *Missed*. The only exceptions are ANT, ARGOUML, and TORTOISESVN. However, for these type 3 was identified to be the dominating clone type also.

System	#Classes	Classes [%]			#Fragments	Fragments [%]		
		Type-1	Type-2	Type-3		Type-1	Type-2	Type-3
ADEMPIERE	290	22,76	17,93	59,31	398	23,87	19,85	56,28
ANT	28	25,00	17,86	57,14	39	25,64	20,51	53,85
ARGOUML	779	40,95	17,07	41,98	1312	37,12	20,73	42,15
BAUHAUS	1775	15,15	18,42	66,42	2604	16,21	20,16	63,63
FILEZILLA	311	19,94	24,76	55,31	599	24,87	22,04	53,09
FINDBUGS	81	33,33	12,35	54,32	118	29,66	14,41	55,93
FREECOL	1259	22,88	18,43	58,70	2010	25,87	20,50	53,63
HTTPD	140	22,86	7,14	70,00	257	28,40	8,56	63,04
JABREF	43	46,51	13,95	39,53	55	49,09	18,18	32,73
JETTY	904	34,51	15,15	50,33	1559	36,56	15,39	48,04
NAUTILUS	114	13,16	29,82	57,02	194	15,98	28,87	55,15
TORTOISESVN	685	37,81	19,27	65,69	1061	25,64	74,36	0,09
UMBRELLO	11	27,27	45,45	27,27	23	26,09	52,17	21,74
AIDE	711	47,68	18,28	34,04	1067	44,61	21,37	34,02
HIBISCUS	327	17,74	32,72	49,54	526	18,44	35,36	46,20
POOKA	250	34,00	17,60	48,40	385	32,99	17,40	49,61
Total	**7,708**	**28,04**	**18,69**	**55,29**	**12,207**	**27,83**	**25,03**	**47,15**

Table 5.5 – Types of clones in set *Sufficient Change*

In contrast to the rather large gap of type-3 clones compared to type-1 or type-2 clones, the gap is considerably smaller for clones in the set *Accidental* as shown in Table 5.7. Particularly, the gap to type-1 clones is quite small. Comparing type-1 and type-2 clones there is no general trend observable. Numbers of these two types are quite balanced for accidentally removed clones. On the other hand, clearly more type-1 clones are related to deliberate clone removals than type-2 clones whereas it is the other way round for the category of missed clones. Comparing trends of detected clone types between mature and immature system, we did not found distinct differences between them. Numbers mainly follow the general trend of type 3 being the most frequent clone type with the only exception being that slightly more deliberately removed type-1 than type-3 clones were detected for AIDE.

Results for the individual subject systems mainly follow these trends with minor exceptions. For instance, no clones were detected for NAUTILUS and UMBRELLO in the set *Deliberate* and for JABREF, JETTY, and UMBRELLO in the set *Missed*. There are also a few systems for which all clones were assigned to one of the three clone types, for example, all clones were of type-1 for FINDBUGS in the set *Missed*. However, in these cases just very few clones were identified in the corresponding subject system and set at all. Therefore, it was not surprising as chances are good that if very few clones are identified they may all fall into the same type.

While the absolute numbers indicate that type-3 clones are more frequently subject to removing refactorings, the relative numbers with respect to the results obtained for the set *Sufficient Change* (Table 5.5) do not support that trend. Since the set *Sufficient*

System	#Classes	Classes [%]			#Fragments	Fragments [%]		
		Type-1	Type-2	Type-3		Type-1	Type-2	Type-3
ADEMPIERE	13	23,08	23,08	53,85	20	20,00	25,00	55,00
ANT	2	50,00	0,00	50,00	2	100,00	0,00	0,00
ARGOUML	87	42,53	19,54	37,93	185	42,70	18,38	38,92
BAUHAUS	13	30,77	23,08	46,15	31	29,03	19,35	51,61
FILEZILLA	24	20,83	25,00	54,17	43	23,26	23,26	53,49
FINDBUGS	6	66,67	16,67	16,67	11	63,64	18,18	18,18
FREECOL	16	50,00	25,00	25,00	36	44,44	16,67	38,89
HTTPD	8	50,00	25,00	25,00	17	47,06	23,53	29,41
JABREF	1	0,00	100,00	0,00	2	0,00	100,00	0,00
JETTY	19	36,84	26,32	36,84	45	33,33	22,22	44,44
NAUTILUS	0	-	-	-	0	-	-	-
TORTOISESVN	174	29,89	17,82	52,30	293	30,03	18,09	51,88
UMBRELLO	0	-	-	-	0	-	-	-
AIDE	14	35,29	29,41	35,29	36	38,89	27,78	33,33
HIBISCUS	8	37,50	12,50	50,00	21	23,81	14,29	61,90
POOKA	6	33,33	33,33	33,33	14	28,57	28,57	42,86
Total	**391**	**36,20**	**26,91**	**36,90**	**756**	**34,52**	**19,71**	**45,77**

Table 5.6 – Types of deliberately removed clones in set *Removed*

System	#Classes	Classes [%]			#Fragments	Fragments [%]		
		Type-1	Type-2	Type-3		Type-1	Type-2	Type-3
ADEMPIERE	11	45,45	27,27	27,27	24	33,33	37,50	29,17
ANT	13	23,08	23,08	53,85	17	23,53	29,41	47,06
ARGOUML	46	34,78	23,91	41,30	97	32,99	36,08	30,93
BAUHAUS	16	31,25	37,50	31,25	46	34,78	43,48	21,74
FILEZILLA	5	20,00	20,00	60,00	9	22,22	22,22	55,56
FINDBUGS	10	40,00	20,00	40,00	17	47,06	17,65	35,29
FREECOL	45	40,00	17,78	42,22	96	37,50	23,96	38,54
HTTPD	8	50,00	12,50	37,50	18	55,56	11,11	33,33
JABREF	1	0,00	100,00	0,00	3	0,00	100,00	0,00
JETTY	17	52,94	11,76	35,29	40	60,00	10,00	30,00
NAUTILUS	37	16,22	35,14	48,65	70	14,29	37,14	48,57
TORTOISESVN	67	23,88	25,37	50,75	115	23,48	24,35	52,17
UMBRELLO	4	25,00	50,00	25,00	8	25,00	50,00	25,00
AIDE	14	35,71	14,29	50,00	28	35,71	14,29	50,00
HIBISCUS	13	30,77	46,15	23,08	27	33,33	44,44	22,22
POOKA	6	50,00	16,67	33,33	16	43,75	31,25	25,00
Total	**313**	**32,44**	**30,09**	**37,47**	**631**	**32,49**	**29,32**	**38,19**

Table 5.7 – Types of accidentally removed clones in set *Removed*

System	#Classes	Classes [%]			#Fragments	Fragments [%]		
		Type-1	Type-2	Type-3		Type-1	Type-2	Type-3
ADEMPIERE	6	0,00	33,33	66,67	13	0,00	30,77	69,23
ANT	11	18,18	18,18	63,64	21	19,05	14,29	66,67
ARGOUML	32	21,88	28,12	50,00	79	18,99	27,85	53,16
BAUHAUS	1	100,00	0,00	0,00	2	100,00	0,00	0,00
FILEZILLA	3	33,33	33,33	33,33	3	33,33	33,33	33,33
FINDBUGS	1	100,00	0,00	0,00	2	100,00	0,00	0,00
FREECOL	3	0,00	33,33	66,67	11	0,00	18,18	81,82
HTTPD	1	100,00	0,00	0,00	2	100,00	0,00	0,00
JABREF	0	-	-	-	0	-	-	-
JETTY	0	-	-	-	0	-	-	-
NAUTILUS	1	0,00	100,00	0,00	5	0,00	100,00	0,00
TORTOISESVN	29	17,24	20,69	62,07	74	20,27	21,62	58,11
UMBRELLO	0	-	-	-	0	-	-	-
AIDE	2	0,00	0,00	100,00	4	0,00	0,00	100,00
HIBISCUS	1	0,00	100,00	0,00	2	0,00	100,00	0,00
POOKA	1	0,00	0,00	100,00	2	0,00	0,00	100,00
Total	92	30,05	28,23	41,72	220	18,64	25,00	56,36

Table 5.8 – Types of missed removed clones in set *Removed*

Change includes the clones manually assessed by the oracles, the amount of clones from each type in that set is an important factor. That is, the initial set *Sufficient Change* encompasses more type-3 clones than type-1 or type-2 clones already. Comparing the relation of identified type-1, type-2, and type-3 clones in that set to their relation in set *Removed*, it was found that there is no real tendency towards one of the analyzed clone types. Each clone type assigned to sets *Deliberate*, *Accidental*, and *Missed* (Table 5.6 to 5.8) roughly occurs with the same frequency as they contribute to the set *Sufficient Change*. This finding is a bit surprising as we expected a more distinct trend towards deliberate removals of identical clones, because a semantic preserving refactoring of non-identical clones is assumed to require more effort. Moreover, often there is no automated tool support that can be used to perform such refactorings. On the other hand, we assume differences of type-2 clones to be rather moderate what makes them close to identical and, hence, easier to refactor. If this assumption is true, our results match the expected result as summing up the numbers for type-1 and type-2 clone refactorings result in a higher refactoring frequency of these types than clone of type 3.

5.6.2   Clone Metrics

Apart from the clone type, we collected data regarding the length of fragments and how many fragments affected by RODs decreased in size. Regarding changes to clone fragments we have analyzed how often detected clone fragments have been changed consistently or inconsistently, respectively, over time until they have been refactored

Refactoring	Token [∅]	-Tokens [∅]	Con. Changes	Incon. Changes	Complexity [∅]
Deliberate	103.8	61.0	3	2	4.5
Accidental	106.4	72.0	3	3	4.3
Missed	74.4	45.4	3	1	2.8

Table 5.9 – Metrics of removed clones

by developers. The change frequency of clone fragments may indicate which clones might be good candidates for a removal. Assuming that a high change frequency of cloned code causes additional effort to keep the clones synchronized, a high change frequency is costly for developers and a refactoring probably pays off in the long term as changes have to be done at only one single place afterwards. The last characteristic of clone fragments we looked into is the *Cyclomatic Complexity*. A high *Cyclomatic* complexity is an indicator for source code that has a more involved control flow. As a consequence changes need more effort to be performed and tested. Based on this assumption the *Cyclomatic Complexity* may be useful to identify clone fragments that are good candidates for refactorings, too.

Table 5.9 summarizes the results for the collected metrics. The first column specifies whether a deliberate, accidental, or missed clone removal has been performed. The second column gives the average size of the affected clone fragments in number of tokens. By how many tokens the clone fragments have been decreased on average is given in the third column. The next two columns depict the maximum numbers of consistent and inconsistent changes to clone fragments related to RODs before they have been refactored. The last column gives the average *Cyclomatic Complexity* of clone fragments related to RODs.

The results show that the clone fragments related to RODs are clearly reduced in size by the performed refactorings. For all categories (deliberate, accidental and missed) of clone removals we measured an average decrease roughly around 60 % of the fragment's size. To investigate the size metric in more detail we used box plots. Figure 5.8 shows the length of clone fragments of set *Deliberate* in tokens before they have been refactored. We can see that the mean values are just marginally influenced by a few outliers for some systems. Note, that there have not been any deliberate removals for NAUTILUS. To compare the fragment's length before and after the refactorings have been applied, we show the same data for clone fragments after they have been affected by a refactoring in Figure 5.9. It shows mainly a similar picture as Figure 5.8 but with smaller fragment sizes. Again, mean values are hardly influenced by outliers. We leave out box plots for clone fragments of set *Accidental*, however, they show the same trends—a reduction of size after refactorings were applied and relatively few outliers with negligible effect on the mean values. Finally, statistical significance testing was used to verify the reduction of clone fragments after being refactored. That is, the size of clone fragments before a corresponding refactorings was compared to the size of the same fragments after the refactoring has been performed. We used the non-parametric Mann-Whitney U-test since we cannot assume a normal distribution of the data set. We tested clone fragments from set *Removed* and *Accidental* using the one-tailed paired variant of the U-test. For

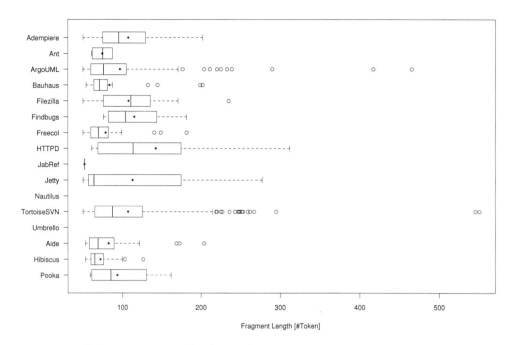

Figure 5.8 – Length of clone fragments before being refactored.

both data sets we got a p-value of nearly 0.0000 ($2.2e^{-16}$) verifying that clone fragments decreased in size significantly.

Analyzing how frequent the affected clone fragments have been changed before the removals took place, we detected very few changes at all. Looking at the maximum number of consistent and inconsistent changes to the clone fragments, we see that they range from 1 to 3. Figures 5.10 and 5.11 show that on average less than 1 % of the clone fragments of set *Deliberate* changed before the detected refactorings—no matter whether consistent or inconsistent. Outliers are very rare as well. Trends for fragments out of set *Accidental* are similar again and plots are left out. The numbers of changes to clone fragments are rather small and, therefore, we cannot draw any conclusion from these spare data regarding maintenance effort—actually results indicate that the change frequency of cloned code is so low that it hardly has an effect on software maintenance at all.

Figure 5.12 shows the results obtained analyzing the *Cyclomatic Complexity* of fragments from set *Deliberate*. We detected a diverse distribution between fragments with absolute numbers ranging from 1 to more than 70 (an outlier for FREECOL). On average the *Cyclomatic Complexity* ranges from 2.8 up to 4.5 per fragment as shown in Table 5.9. Because of the large diversity among clone fragments, we could not identify any pattern to rank clones using the *Cyclomatic Complexity*. However, the boxes of the box plot indicate that the complexity of most fragments is up to ten. Again, trends were very similar for clone fragments of set *Accidental*.

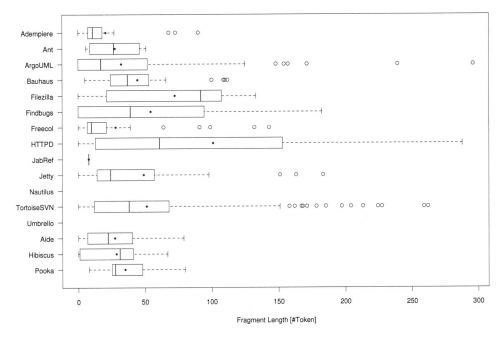

Figure 5.9 – Length of clone fragments after being refactored.

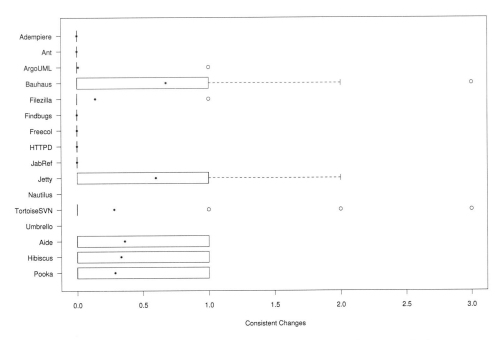

Figure 5.10 – Number of consistent changes to clone fragments before being refactored.

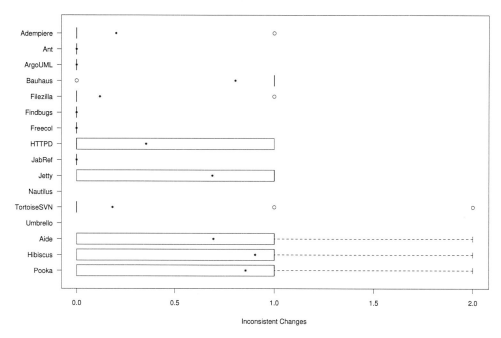

Figure 5.11 – Number of inconsistent changes to clone fragments before being refactored.

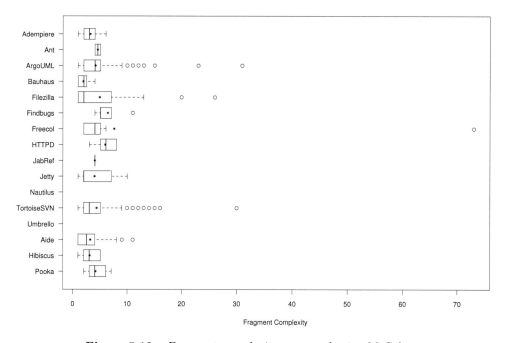

Figure 5.12 – Fragment complexity measured using McCabe.

5.7   Return on Investment

Based on the identified refactorings that deliberately removed clones in the source code of the subject systems, we analyzed if, with what frequency and by what type of changes developers modified source code introduced in the course of a preceding clone removal. By analyzing changes to source code that was introduced to remove redundancies we will gather information related to long-term consequences and answer our research question 15.

An important aspect and also the basis for further investigation regarding our research question 15 is whether source code that has been introduced to apply a clone removing refactoring does change over time at all. In total, we tracked 179 code fragments introduced in the course of deliberate clone removals—set $Deliberate_t$—throughout the evolution of the subject systems using our clone investigation tool CYCLONE as described in Section 5.2. Out of these 179 fragments of set $Deliberate_t$ 84 fragments were identified to be modified at least once within the time period under study and 96 did not change at all. This result indicates that more than half of the code fragments introduced to replace code duplications do not change anymore and, therefore, most probably do not decrease maintenance effort in terms of changing existing source code compared to the preceding version that contained the corresponding clones. Nonetheless, it must be considered that such refactorings are still beneficial if they improve the readability of the source code and by that support developers to understand the semantic more easily. However, in this study we focus on a cost and benefit analysis of the half of fragments that did change over time. We denote the set of these fragments out of $Deliberate_t$ as subset $Deliberate_{tc}$.

5.7.1   Refactoring Types

Based on the detection of clone removing refactorings as described in Section 5.1, we analyzed by what type of specific refactoring code fragments of the set $Deliberate_{tc}$ have been introduced. Five refactorings from literature were identified that were applied to remove cloned code: *Extract Method, Pull Up Method, Pull Up Class, Call Existing Method* and *Unify Methods*. Figure 5.13 shows how many fragments of set $Deliberate_{tc}$ were introduced by which type of refactoring. *Extract Method* is the refactoring identified to be applied the most to remove clones contributing 42 of the 84 fragments of set $Deliberate_{tc}$—almost 50% of all fragments introduced by a clone removing refactoring that have changed subsequently. This is not surprising since the *Extract Method* refactoring is well suited to remove clones located in the same file and is also a rather common and simple refactoring for which accurate automated tool support exists when performing the actual refactoring. Overall, all refactorings considered in our case study to be applied to remove code clones are of reasonable complexity once all clone fragments of the same clone class have been detected, e.g., using a clone detection tool.

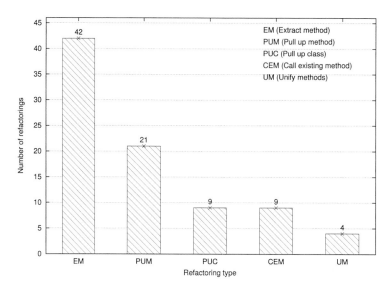

Figure 5.13 – Number of code fragments removed by certain types of refactorings.

5.7.2   Committer Know-how

Next, we focused on changes applied to the code fragments of $Deliberate_{tc}$ after they have been introduced. As described, set $Deliberate_{tc}$ contains fragments that have been changed at least once. We analyzed whether the same committer who applied the clone removing refactoring has also been the one who performed the first change to the resulting code fragments in $Deliberate_{tc}$. The information about authors in this relationship is of interest assuming that an author is able to understand and change source code that he introduced himself faster and probably even more accurate than others. Analyzing the committer information provided by the software repository system, we found that 40 code fragments out of 84 from set $Deliberate_{tc}$ were modified by the same author, and hence, 44 by an author who did not perform the preceding refactoring. That is, slightly more than half of the fragments under study were changed by someone else.

The performance of a developer on understanding and changing the code fragments of $Deliberate_{tc}$ depends heavily on the time factor as well. Assuming that a code fragment is changed by the same developer who introduced the fragment, it is important that the developer is able to retain his knowledge related to the corresponding source code at the moment when he is doing the actual change. Obviously, human beings forget things over time. The larger the time period between the moment of learning and the moment trying to retain knowledge the more information will be forgotten. This fact has been studied and shown by different researchers. Ebbinghaus introduced the so called *Forgetting Curve* which is still valid today [76]. The *Forgetting Curve* describes how many (in percent) of the learned can be retained after how much time has been passed

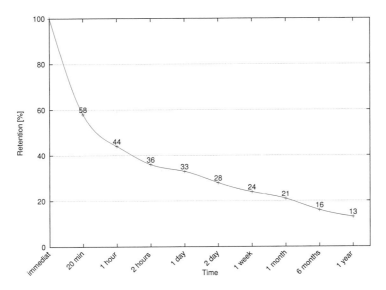

Figure 5.14 – Ebbinghaus' *Forgetting Curve* for the time period of one year.

without refreshing the information in the meantime. Figure 5.14 shows the relation of the capability to retain specific information and time for a one-year period.

Considering that an author forgets information over time, we investigated how much time has passed from the introduction of a code fragment of $Deliberate_{tc}$ till its first modification. Each fragment of $Deliberate_{tc}$ has been assigned to a time frame corresponding to the time frames of the *Forgetting Curve* as shown in Figure 5.14. That is, we measured the time passed between the introduction of a code fragment due to a clone removal and its first subsequent change and arranged them in groups inferred from the *Forgetting Curve*. Results indicate how much a developer might be able to retain from what was learned while performing the refactoring to remove cloned code. Figure 5.15 shows the number of fragments assigned to one of the time frames presented in Figure 5.14. Code fragments that have been changed between one and six months after their introduction present the largest group using the time periods suggested by Ebbinghaus. Consequently, an author forgets between 79% and 84% of the information related to that code fragment learned during his last modification performed before he modifies the same fragment again. Even if the time period is much smaller, e.g., one or two days, about 30% of the knowledge is recallable only. Just two changes have been detected to be performed within the same day of the clone removing refactoring, thus, enabling a developer to retain between 50% and 100% of information learned. This indicates that removing a clone decreases maintenance costs related to an upcoming change only in a limited way. That is, a committer is able to retain only a small share of information collected during the refactoring after a short period of time. Note, that with forgetting we do not (necessarily) refer to forgetting a clone fragment per se but

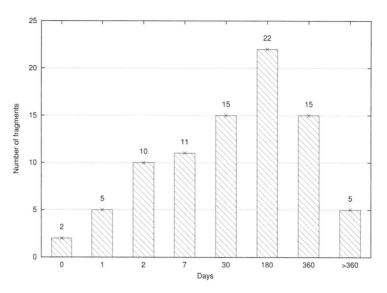

Figure 5.15 – Number of fragments of set $Deliberate_{tc}$ assigned to time frames based on the *Forgetting Curve* by Ebbinghaus.

primarily to its context, e.g., its functionality or dependencies. Nonetheless, the effect of forgetting information would be even larger for cloned code as developers would forget information to multiple code fragments (at different locations in the source code) that need to be restored when changes are supposed to be applied to the clones. The sum of information lost related to various clone fragments is most probably higher—though not linear to the number of clone fragments involved—compared to information needed to retain for only one code fragment that does replace various clone fragments.

5.7.3 Quantitative Analysis

Finally, we analyzed all changes to the code fragments of set $Deliberate_{tc}$ quantitatively and qualitatively within the time period under study. The frequency of changes and the changes itself, e. g., type and complexity, are very useful indicators regarding possible decrease of maintenance costs due to the removal of clones. The number of changes to each fragment of $Deliberate_{tc}$ is interesting since the assumption is that removing clones decreases maintenance effort in the long term because certain activities related to clones get eliminated, for instance, changes have to be applied at a single location only. In contrast, each change applied to a fragment in $Deliberate_{tc}$ must had been applied multiple times, depending on the number of clone fragments in the same clone class, if the clones would still exist in the software. Figure 5.16 shows how many fragments of the set $Deliberate_{tc}$ have been modified how many times after being introduced. In total, we found 218 changes applied to the tracked code fragments with 52 fragments being changed only once. Thus, less than 40% of the overall fragments changed at least twice. Large numbers of changes to the code fragments are rather rare, for instance, only five

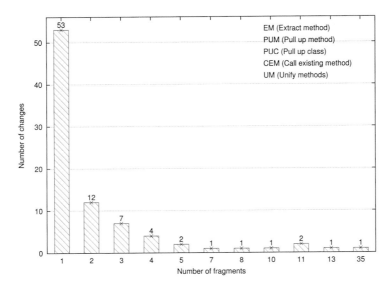

Figure 5.16 – Number of changes applied to fragments of set $Deliberate_{tc}$ over time.

fragments changed ten times or more frequently with 35 changes to one fragment being the highest value in this respect. In our qualitative inspection of changes which will be described in detail below, we did not find any specific characteristic of the code fragment that have been changed 35 times over time as this is clearly an outlier. In fact, it seems that the code fragment was part of the system's functionality being actively worked on at the time period under study. A wide range of changes have been applied to the fragment, e.g., exception handling and conditional statements, but nothing prominent that would explain the large number of performed changes, for instance, many small and trivial changes like formatting that have been spread over several commits.

The results indicate that the benefit of clone removals might be rather small considering that the frequency of changes to the clone fragments of the preceding version (still containing the clone) would have been small accordingly. However, two more aspects need to be considered in this respect to shed more light on possible cost savings: The number and size of clone fragments that have been eliminated by each code fragment in set $Deliberate_{tc}$ and the complexity of these. Regarding the number of clone fragments we measured an average of 2.6 fragments that have been eliminated by the refactorings over all software systems under study. The largest clone class found to be refactored contained six clone fragments. Since each refactoring considered in this study introduced exactly one code fragment to remove cloned code an average saving of about one and a half fragments have been achieved. In Section 5.6 (Table 5.9) we showed already that the deliberately removed clone fragments had an average size of 103.8 tokens. The average size of code fragments in set $Deliberate_{tc}$ is 152.7 tokens. Although, the introduced fragments are larger in size compared to the clone fragments before, overall the size has been reduced subtracting the size of the eliminated clone fragments. Considering that our set $Deliberate_{tc}$ consists of 84 code fragments that replaced 218 (84×2.6) clone fragments on average, the average decrease in terms of tokens is as follows:

$$218 \times 103.8 - 84 \times 152.7 = 9,801.6$$

Overall, the refactorings to remove cloned code decreased the source code size by 9,801.6 tokens which is 55,6 tokens each refactoring considering the total number of 179 refactorings analyzed in this study. To investigate the complexity of the clone fragments prior to the refactorings we measured the *Cyclomatic Complexity* of each clone fragment. We found an average of 4.5 regarding *Cyclomatic Complexity* before removing the clone fragments and an average of 7.1 afterwards. Analog to the size of fragments, it can be observed that the average complexity of the introduced code fragments is higher compared to the clone fragments they replaced. In return, the overall number of code fragments is less than half as much as clone fragments in the preceding version. Based on the same calculation strategy as for the size metric a total reduction of 384.6 is achieved regarding *Cyclomatic Complexity*:

$$218 \times 4.5 - 84 \times 7.1 = 384.6$$

5.7.4   Qualitative Analysis

In addition to the quantitative analysis based on metrics, we also performed a qualitative analysis of the changes applied to the code fragments of set $Deliberate_{tc}$. To do so, we manually analyzed all modifications between two consecutive versions that affected code fragments within set $Deliberate_{tc}$ and build a classification based on the type of changes performed. Figure 5.17 shows our taxonomy used for classification which is a result of the manual reviewing process, because there are no other previous studies on changes to code fragment introduced in the course of clone removing refactorings. Each modification is either assigned to the class *Minor* or *Major*. *Minor* contains modifications of the fragments that have only little or no semantic effect, e.g., renaming of local variables, and are mainly rather simple, for instance, removing deprecated or dead code segments. The *Major* group contains more complex modifications related to changing the semantic of the system. We divide such modifications in the following types:

- *Parameter*: The class *Parameter* denotes semantic changes made to a code fragment that are related to the introduction of new or the change or removal of existing parameters or class and local variables. For instance, if the type of a local variable needs to be changed from a basic type, e.g., a string, to a custom object type, e.g., holding a reference in addition to the string, due to a more complex computation performed.

- *Movement*: In case a modification extracts and moves parts of the code fragment to some other location or moves some other code to the subject fragment, we

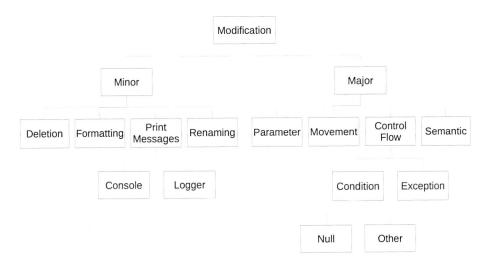

Figure 5.17 – Classification of modifications to code fragments of set *Deliberate_{tc}*.

assign this change to the class *Movement*. For example, if a specific computation of a code fragment is extracted to a new method that is called from the fragment in the following.

- *Flow*: All modifications affecting the control flow of the source code are assigned to the class *Flow*. We further distinguish this class in the groups *Condition* and *Exception*. The letter involves exception handling in form of throw or try-catch clauses. The group *Condition* subsumes all conditional statements to control the program flow, for instance, simple if-else clauses or conditions of loop signatures. Often we found that developers added null checks to conditional statements that have most probably been missing before to avoid *NullPointerExceptions*. Therefore, we separate such conditional statements from other types of conditionals as we are quite confident that they indicate necessary bug fixes—either in retrospect or in advance.

- *Semantic*: The last class contains all other modifications that could not be assigned to one of the previous classes. The majority of such modifications were rather complicated in terms of affecting larger parts of the code fragment but also of other source code locations. For that reason, we have not been able to accurately determine the exact purpose and related consequences caused by such changes. In general, modifications in the class *Semantic* can be considered to be more complex changes affecting the system's semantic.

Figure 5.18 shows the evaluation of the manual classification process. It can be observed that clearly most changes have been assigned to the class of *Major* changes. This result indicates that rather complex changes were more frequently applied compared to trivial ones. Within the class *Major* most changes either moved source code

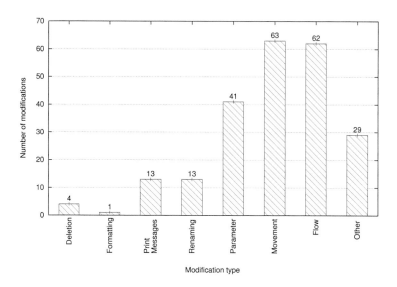

Figure 5.18 – Number of changes related to the classification of applied changes.

or affected the control flow of the program. Analyzing the subset *Condition* we detected 9 changes regarding null-check modifications out of 62 changes within this group in total. These are potential bug fixes. We also found many conditional statements related to equality comparisons which might also indicate possible bug fixing scenarios. With 29 changes the *Semantic* group of modifications is the smallest within the class of *Major* modifications. However, considering that the changes were too large and opaque to grasp details in our manual inspection, the effect of the preceding clone refactorings on the maintenance is probably rather high—assuming that the removal of clone fragments saved the authors of these changes from applying them to different code fragments at different locations but also from understanding the contexts related to each of the clone fragments. Overall, changes in the *Major* class may be considered relatively costly. Thus, removing cloned fragments decreased maintenance costs in that respect. That is, instead of performing the *Major* changes multiple times at different locations, they need to be applied only once at a single location. In this respect, the results indicate that removing cloned code does potentially decrease costs of maintenance tasks in the long term.

5.8   Threats to Validity

There are certain threats to the validity of our study, which we describe in this section.

Internal Validity The accuracy of our results depends on recall and precision of ICLONES and its parameter settings defining what is regarded as a clone. ICLONES uses a token-based detection technique and token-based techniques are considered to provide high recall and reasonable precision [33]. To mitigate the threat of an improper parameter setting, we used settings from former studies of ours that turned out to be suitable for our use case. Another threat related to the clone detector used in this study, is the standard diff algorithm used in the mapping of code fragments between consecutive versions. The diff algorithm cannot detect movements of code and may produce artifacts resulting from ambiguous situations. However, the manual inspection of the data reported by our clone detector reduced the threat of low precision strongly.

External Validity We based our study on 16 software systems from different domains covering mature as well as immature systems. 15 of them being licensed open-source and one closed-source software. Moreover, the systems under study covered four different programming languages: Java, C, C++ and Ada. Yet, this sample may still not be representative. Only a part of their history has been analyzed. Using a different period of time or analyzing snapshots at a different interval might affect the findings. Obviously, the more data is collected and investigated the higher are chances that findings are representative. However, due to the manual analysis process we used to identify and confirm refactorings it is not feasible to extent the cutout of the subject system's history arbitrarily. A fully automated technique may help to overcome this issue, but can hardly be achieved. In addition, the development strategy may effect the results of our clone detector, for instance, if commits to the repository include clones that were meant to be changed and evolve independently in the future. That is, an intermediate version of the source code may be committed containing temporal clones.

Construct Validity Our results are partially exposed to our subjective assessment of clones and refactorings. To mitigate the threat, the manual analysis was first performed by one of the authors and, afterwards, the second author independently checked a sample of 20 % of the findings to verify the results. Finally, a third independent oracle was used to assess cases in which the authors disagreed at first. In addition, we added software systems that were subject to related studies performed by other authors concluding that there is a general agreement related to the assessment of clone removals for these systems. Finally, we analyzed two subject systems which we are experts of and results show that our approach to manually detect and classify refactorings and code modifications is well suited.

5.9   Summary

In this paper, we extended our case study on refactorings that have been performed to remove code duplications. We applied a semi-automated approach to detect clone removals and to track code fragments that have been introduced in the course of these removals. Integrating this approach into our clone inspection tool CYCLONE we analyzed 16 software systems over a period of two years to answer our five research questions.

Investigating deliberate clone removals it was found that the applied refactorings mainly replaced existing code by calls to newly introduced methods and gathered common code of specialized classes in their superclass. Compared to deliberate removals, accidental ones occurred slightly more often in the time period under study. Nonetheless, the refactorings used are basically the same for both. Based on the overall similarity in the frequency and type of the applied refactorings regarding deliberate and accidental removals, we conjecture that an integration contributes to the acceptance of clone management tools as integral part of the development. That is, there is a high chance that existing refactoring support can be used for clone management, too. In addition, we detected situations in which refactorings missed some clone fragments that could have been removed as well. This observation suggests that further research should investigate whether developers aided by automated clone detection during refactoring remove clones more completely.

To enable automated ranking of clone candidates for removals, we gathered different characteristics of cloned code that have actually been removed. Interestingly, more non-identical clones were removed in the systems than identical clones. At least for identical clones we expected to detect more deliberate removals, because removing non-identical clones normally needs more sophisticated refactorings. Analyzing the change frequency in the evolution of clone fragments revealed that the removed clone fragments rarely changed before, contrary to our expectations. Our results did also not show any relation between control flow complexity measured as *Cyclomatic Complexity* and clone removal.

Finally, we tracked and analyzed code fragments that have been introduced to remove cloned code in terms of costs and benefits. Half of the code fragments analyzed did not change after being introduced at all indicating that the clone removals may not decrease maintenance costs over time. In contrast, we were able to show that the complexity of the refactorings was rather small and those which introduced code fragments that have been changed afterwards most probably decreased maintenance costs considering a reduction of the system's size and control flow complexity measured as *Cyclomatic Complexity*.

Based on the results of our study, we suggest to reinforce the analysis of evolutionary clone data including source code that has been introduced to remove code redundancies. Potential costs and benefits of clones have not conclusively been investigated—especially considering non-cloned code that is related to or removed cloned code. To improve the understanding of effects of cloning on software maintenance it is necessary to focus on non-cloned code since only such data allows to compare characteristics of clones and their implications to characteristics of non-cloned code—in particular of appropriate abstractions—and their implications. In this context our study provides first insights in that direction.

Chapter 6

Developers Fixing Cloned Bugs

The majority of empirical studies on the effect of duplicated code is commonly based on retrospective analysis using source code repositories or defect tracker databases. Although such data may provide valuable insights towards the relation of clones and maintainability, other important factors are left out since retrospective analysis considers only the result of a possibly more complex sequence of actions. For instance, a bug fix with preceding tedious localization effort may appear as a simple and small change in the source code. To observe and investigate the benefits of clone-management tools and human interaction in dealing with clones within maintenance activities such as defect reproduction, program comprehension, code changes, and testing, other approaches are necessary [45]. Controlled experiments are appropriate to bridge the gap and help to investigate such aspects in a controllable manner.

Human-based studies on the effect of clones in defect localizing and repairing tasks are very rare in clone research [49, 50, 105]. None of the existing studies has sufficiently evaluated the support clone-management tools can offer in such tasks yet (a more detailed review of these works was described in Section 2.9). Either the developers were not supported by any kind of clone management tool in these studies or the level of tool support was minimal, that is, only a simple clone report as a textual list of clones without any further integration in an integrated development environment (IDE) was provided. So these studies did not investigate the full potential clone management tools can offer.

We conducted a controlled experiment that evaluates how a programmer's performance—in terms of time and correctness—is affected when clone information is provided while dealing with a common bug-fixing task involving a cloned defect. Specifically, we investigate how the removal of a cloned defect is affected by the fact that clone information is provided in the IDE and how missing clone information is compensated by developers. To overcome the shortcomings of pure textual information, we offer a more realistic tool support in our experiment that provides *contextual* clone

	Null hypothesis	Alternative hypothesis
Question 1	H_0^{time}: The time needed to remove a cloned defect without clone information is *shorter or equal* compared to the time needed to remove a cloned defect using clone information.	H_1^{time}: The time needed to remove a cloned defect without clone information is *longer* compared to the time needed to remove a cloned defect using clone information.
Question 2	H_0^{corr}: The probability of a correct removal of a cloned defect without clone information is *higher or equal* compared to the probability of a correct removal of a cloned defect using clone information	H_1^{corr}: The probability of a correct removal of a cloned defect without clone information is *lower* compared to the probability of a correct removal of a cloned defect using clone information.

Table **6.1** – Null and alternative hypothesis of our human-based experiment.

information integrated in the IDE (i.e., only the clones of the currently inspected file are shown) and enables the user to easily browse through existing clones and to identify the location of each clone fragment. This kind of tool support is more realistic for assessing the effect of clone management tools that try to compensate for risks imposed by clones and leverages the user's experience with his or her familiar IDE.

Insights gained by our human-based experiment will help in complementing findings of our previous case studies described in Chapter 4 and Chapter 5 assessing the relevance of clone information.

6.1   Experimental Design

This section describes the experimental design of our controlled experiment. Based on the hypotheses and variables as well as on the selection of appropriate subjects and objects we investigate Question 16 and Question 17. Finally, we also describe the instrumentation of the experiment in this section.

6.1.1   Hypotheses and Variables

Our hypotheses are directly derived from our two research questions. The alternative hypotheses are both one-tailed. Table 6.1 shows the relation of the hypotheses to our research questions.

Since we want to investigate the impact of clone information on the performance of programmers solving bug-fixing tasks, the sole independent variable of our experiment is whether clone information is provided or not. The dependent variables are based on our research questions and used in similar experiments [49, 105]: (1) the *time* needed to complete a given task and (2) the *correctness* of the solution. The *correctness* of a solution is further distinguished in the following two factors:

	A	B
Task 1	tFB_c	tFB_{nc}
Task 2	tPM_{nc}	tPM_c

Table 6.2 – Assignment of Groups to tasks.

(1) *Addressed.* The performed actions corrected one out of two defects that are part of the given task. The defects are located in two differnt fragments that are clones of each other, thus, the defects are alike.

(2) *Complete.* The performed actions correct both defects that are part of the given task.

This distinction implies that every *complete* solution is also *addressed*, but only *complete* solutions are regarded as correct results. That is, fixing just one of two defects in cloned code—*addressed* solutions—does not suffice in terms of correctness. Nonetheless, we will provide and evaluate data of both *addressed* and *complete* solutions in the results section.

6.1.2 Design

For the execution of our experiment we use two existing small open-source Java games, namely, FROZENBUBBLE[1] and *Pacman*[2]. Both have been used in previous similar experiments [49, 105]. Harder and Tiarks [105] developed a laboratory package including the source code of the games, defective versions of the source code with and without cloned bugs and corresponding bug reports. We used that package which is freely available[3] and derived our maintenance tasks from it. For each game, we defined one maintenance task that requires the developers to fix a cloned defect. The tasks are denoted as tFB for FROZENBUBBLE and tPM for *Pacman* in the following. For each of these tasks, we either provided information regarding existing clones in the systems or not. The different variants of provision of information constitute two levels of the sole independent variable in our experimental design, which is whether clone information is available for the programmers or not. Task tFB_c is the variant of FROZENBUBBLE for which clone information is provided, while the variant without any clone information is denoted as tFB_{nc}. Likewise, we will refer to the task variants for *Pacman* as tPM_c and tPM_{nc}.

The subjects were separated into two groups A and B. The participants of each group have been either randomly assigned to the task variant tFB_c and tPM_{nc} or to the contrariwise variant tFB_{nc} and tPM_c. This division of subjects results in a 2×2 factorial design [264] and allows for comparison of the results. Table 6.2 shows the assignment of groups to the corresponding tasks.

---

[1]http://www.frozen-bubble.org/
[2]http://code.google.com/p/pacman-rkant/
[3]http://www.softwareclones.org/experiment

Subject	1	2	3	4	5	6	7	8	9	10	11	12	13	14	15	16	17	18	19	20	21	22	23	24	25	26	27	28	29
Skill	56	52	67	70	80	60	50	57	87	78	44	74	0	68	69	83	40	71	72	74	80	80	79	80	45	70	60	53	77

Table 6.3 – Self-assessment of subjects regarding Java skills

Group	Subject														
A	1	2	3	4	5	6	7	8	9	10	11	12	13	14	15
B 16	17	18	19	20	21	22	23	24	25	26	27	28	29		

Table 6.4 – Assignment of subjects to the groups A and B

6.1.3 Subjects

The participants of our experiment were all computer science students from the University of Bremen in their third or fourth term. We selected the participants based on two main requirements:

(1) Basic Java knowledge was needed because both software systems under study are written in Java. As a basic principle of the University of Bremen, all computer science students learn Java as primary programming language in their first two terms. Beyond that we did not ask students to participate who were in their early terms, that is, students who have not taken part in any software engineering, software architecture or software quality courses yet. Finally, by asking the subjects to self-assess their Java skills on a scale from 1 to 100 with 100 being perfect, we did find some small differences regarding their skills. Table 6.3 shows the result of the self-assessment for each subject (subject M will be dismissed from further consideration later). The assessed skills range from less than 50 up to more than 80. We believe that some subjects assessed their skills rather conservative while others were quite optimistic. Nonetheless, since all subjects were selected such that they all took part in the same Java engineering courses, we consider their skills comparable with respect to the tasks and good enough to solve each task of the experiment.

(2) Participants needed basic knowledge in using the Eclipse IDE for Java development because we wanted everybody to use the same setup during the execution. This makes it easier to prepare a standardized programming environment in which unexpected actions by the participants are minimized and relevant data can be reliably collected. Asking the subjects whether they use the Eclipse IDE for development, all approved of using it regularly. Analogously, we were confident that the subjects have sufficient Eclipse knowledge since it is the primarily IDE used in our engineering courses from the second term on.

In total, 29 students participated in the experiment of which all were randomly assigned to the groups A and B with no further mechanism of blocking. Blocking was not applied because not all participants were known at the time we started the experiment. The assignment of subjects to the groups A and B is shown in Table 6.4.

6.1.4 Objects

We already described that we prepared different task variations upon two small open-source Java games. By using existing software systems that have not been artificially created by us we wanted to provide a maintenance scenario that is as close and thoroughly as possible to real-world problems. The given tasks demanded the participants not only to fix the defects but also perform various steps that usually belong to such a maintenance task, such as reading a defect report and getting familiar with related features and the corresponding source code, locating and correcting the defects by applying appropriate changes to the code and testing whether the applied changes cause the desired correcting effect. If not, correcting and testing are repeated until success is achieved.

By covering all necessary activities of a common bug-fixing approach it is possible to measure the time needed to complete a whole maintenance task, and moreover, to accurately verify the correctness of the solution. If we required the subjects to perform only certain activities, for instance, to locate the defects without fixing and testing, they would not be able to check whether they overlooked a defect or its clone. By asking the subjects to also fix and test their solutions we avoided this problem. Note, that in contrast to the studies of Harder and Tiarks and Chatterji and colleagues we excluded the time participants spent on reading the bug reports from the data evaluation [49, 105]. The reading speed of subjects is very different as far as we experienced and is not an activity that is directly related to locating or changing clones.

To emulate a whole maintenance task of a real world scenario as well as possible the selected objects needed to meet two essential requirements. As a result of the limited time of an experiment like this and the variables that are to be analyzed the selected software systems must not be too small and not too big and the game idea simple enough to be understood by the subjects—also allowing to reproduce the defects—but still be realistic.

Both systems FROZENBUBBLE as well as *Pacman* meet the requirements regarding the size of the source code with 3,000 and 2,400 SLOC, respectively. In addition, the defect reports contain some hints that allows to limit the search space. The second constraint is approached by the fact that we used simple and intuitive games—that are also widely known—which allows to verify their correctness by playing them for just a few seconds. For that reason, the tasks were designed such that the defects cause wrong program behavior, but not an entire crash. We deliberately chose rather small and localized defects, because Harder and Tiarks [105] found that participants require too much time to solve more complex defect scenarios.

Another important requirement for the design of our experiment was that each task includes two defects that need to be fixed and that one defect is a clone of the other one. This scenario corresponds to a reactive clone management, that is, clones are handled only when they need to be modified. Proactive clone management, on the other hand, would try to eliminate clones when they are detected even if it is not clear whether they need to be modified in the future. Reactive clone management is a more realistic setting especially for large systems with many clones.

To provide the subjects visible symptoms for both defects of each task we designed the tasks such that each defect of one task has its own visual symptom it is causing. Only when both occurrences were fixed, all symptoms would disappear. This way, we enabled the participants to check whether they fixed all existing defects. If the subjects did not remove both symptoms, the solution is considered incomplete, hence, only if the defect and its clone for each task have been located and fixed, the outcome is considered a correct solution.

Both systems contained different clones already that could be used instead of introducing artificial clones to the existing code. That is, for both variants of the given tasks, code fragments that existed multiple times were used. We inserted the defects at appropriate clone fragments. In the following we describe the two tasks and the defects in more detail.

Task *tFB*

The goal of the game FROZENBUBBLE is to eliminate colored bubbles that are arranged at the top of the game screen. This is done by shooting likewise colored bubbles from a launcher at the bottom of the screen at the bubbles on top. If a group of at least two equally colored bubbles is hit by a newly shot bubble of the same color, these are eliminated. If a newly shot bubble does not hit a group of equally colored bubbles, it sticks to these. Besides the bubble placed on the launcher, a preview of the upcoming bubble to be shot is shown below the launcher. Figure 6.1 shows a screenshot of the game. The different colors of the bubbles are implemented by loading stored image files. The loading of the images is implemented in the classes *FrozenGame* and *LaunchBubbleSprite*. *FrozenGame* implements the loading of the bubbles at the top and the preview of the upcoming bubble. The bubble in the launcher is loaded by almost the same routine located in *LaunchBubbleSprite*. Figure 6.2 shows the code snippet from *FrozenGame* in pseudo code to improve readability. The same code except for the third array and consistent parameter renaming is located in *LaunchBubbleSprite*. Therefore, the code segments are type-3 clones of each other.

Harder and Tiarks [105] inserted the same defect in these clone fragments by changing the $i + 1$ to 1 in lines 6–8. As a consequence, only the bubble is loaded whose image corresponds to the index 1—a gray colored bubble. Therefore, only gray bubbles appeared, thus, all bubbles at the top, the one on the launcher and the one from the preview. Since there is no distinction between bubbles and their visual representation in the data structures of the program, the defects cause that all bubbles are eliminated by the first shot, because a gray bubble is shot on a group of also gray bubbles at the top.

To emulate a real-world maintenance task we provided the following defect report to the subjects: *There are eight differently colored bubbles in the game. When a level starts, only gray bubbles appear on top. The launcher at the bottom will also fire only gray bubbles. Obviously not all available bubbles are loaded.* Since, Harder and Tiarks [105] found in their experiment (as well as in a pilot test to it) that subjects may spend a long time seeking the defect in wrong classes, the defect report provided some additional hints where not to look. For instance, the following hint was used similarly

Figure 6.1 – Screenshot of FROZEN BUBBLE.

```
1   bubbles  = Image[8]
2   bBubbles = Image[8]
3   fBubbles = Image[8]
4
5   for i in 0 .. 8 do
6     bubbles[i]  = load("b-"  + toString(i+1) + ".gif")
7     bBubbles[i] = load("bb-" + toString(i+1) + ".gif")
8     fBubbles[i] = load("fb-" + toString(i+1) + ".gif")
9   end for
```

Figure 6.2 – Pseudo code for Task *tFB*.

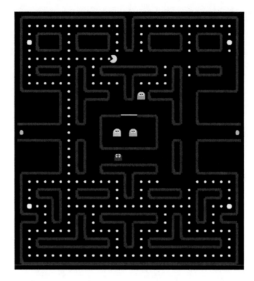

Figure 6.3 – Screenshot of PACMAN.

for both tasks: *The bug is located in the default package. You do not have to modify the packages lib, manager, or screens.*. We intended to exclude libraries and packages drawing the game scenes from possible defect locations. This information has been given because of the time constraints in such an experiment.

Task *tPM*

Pacman is a very well known arcade game in which the player navigates the main character Pacman through a right-angled maze. The goal is to collect different items while fleeing from four ghosts that kill Pacman on collision. Figure 6.3 shows a screenshot of PACMAN. Based on this scenario two characters of different kinds are involved: the Pacman and the ghosts. Both characters are implemented as classes, each extending a generic class called *Actor*. Although, the character classes inherit from the same generic class, the movement routines are implemented independently in the classes *Player* and *Ghost* and form clones of each other. In contrast to the previous task, the two clones are now linked in the code through the inheritance hierarchy. Based on this link we can investigate whether programmers may be guided by semantic code relations in their search for duplicated defects if clone information is not provided by a tool.

For the movement of both characters two coordinates are used. The first one is the position of a character on a coarse-grained invisible grid. This coordinate is used to check for actor collisions and possible movement directions (gridX and gridY) from the current position. The second coordinate is a movement delta, relative to the center of the current grid cell (deltaX and deltaY). Based on two loops all characters are successively moved on the screen pixel by pixel in their current direction. As soon as a character reaches the center of the next grid cell, it is assigned to this cell. The original movement routine of the Pacman character without the inserted defect is shown in Figure 6.4 as pseudo code. The same code can be found in the *Ghost* class except for the check whether a movement is possible—lines 3, 13, 23, and 33—because the ghosts move on precomputed paths and cannot get stuck. Therefore, the defective code segments are type-3 clones of each other. For *tPM* we inserted the defect in both characters by changing the subtractions in lines 8 and 38 to additions.

The following defect report was presented to the subjects for task *tPM*: *For all game characters, the movement up and left does not work correctly. Instead of moving up or left the characters move in the opposite direction in a flickering motion. Moving down and right works fine for all characters.* As with *FrozenBubble*, the bug report provided hints where not to look for the defects. In addition, a rough overview on how the movement is implemented by describing the two coordinate systems and how they relate was given in the report.

6.1.5   Instrumentation

We provided all subjects a standardized development environment including all tools to execute the experiment and to analyze the outcome afterwards. The use of tools other than those provided by us was not allowed to ensure equal prerequisites for all participants and simultaneously avoid bias based on different levels of experience with other tools. For this reason, the Eclipse IDE was used as development environment and all subjects were required to have basic knowledge in programming with Eclipse. For our purpose we extended the Eclipse IDE by two plugins. The first plugin was particularly developed to support the execution of such experiments and collect relevant data for later analysis. It was successfully used in previous experiments [49, 105, 222] already. In detail the plugin provides functionality to:

- guide the participants through the whole experiment by step-by-step instructions, for instance, displaying the task descriptions and defect reports,

- automatically log user actions, e.g., record the usage of various Eclipse features like searches and debugging as well as to display surveys and collect answers,

- record the time needed to complete each task.

We used this plugin for two main reasons: First, it allows the subjects to work autonomously on the tasks which avoids bias by potential feedback from us and minimizes the extent to which the performance of the participants is influenced caused by the awareness that they are monitored by us. Second, the automated collection of relevant data to evaluate the results is more accurate than a manual approach, for instance, by taking our own notes or ask the subjects to protocol their proceeding and the time required to complete the tasks.

The second plugin we integrated in the Eclipse IDE allows to navigate through code clones of a software system. It is based on the results of our clone detector ɪCʟᴏɴᴇs. We pre-configured ɪCʟᴏɴᴇs to detect clones of type 1, 2, and 3 with a minimum total length of 50 tokens consistently to our former studies [26, 29, 87, 89, 104]. However, we provided

```
1   switch currentDirection
2     case up
3       if canMoveTo(gridX, gridY − 1) then
4         deltaX = 0
5         deltaY = deltaY − speed
6         if |deltaY| >= CELL_SIZE then
7           deltaY = 0
8           moveTo(gridX, gridY − 1)
9         end
10      end
11      break;
12    case right
13      if canMoveTo(gridX + 1, gridY) then
14        deltaX = deltaX + speed
15        deltaY = 0
16        if |deltaX| >= CELL_SIZE then
17          deltaX = 0
18          moveTo(gridX + 1, gridY)
19        end
20      end
21      break
22    case down
23      if canMoveTo(gridX, gridY + 1) then
24        deltaX = 0
25        deltaY = deltaY + speed
26        if |deltaY| >= CELL_SIZE then
27          deltaY = 0
28          moveTo(gridX, gridY + 1)
29        end
30      end
31      break
32    case left
33      if canMoveTo(gridX − 1, gridY) then
34        deltaX = deltaX − speed
35        deltaY = 0
36        if |deltaX| >= CELL_SIZE then
37          deltaX = 0
38          moveTo(gridX − 1, gridY)
39        end
40      end
41      break
42  end
```

Figure 6.4 – Pseudo code for Task tPM

the resulting clone information for both games such that the subjects needed to know neither anything about the configuration nor the detection of clones itself. Therefore, our experimental design does not depend on ICLONES, hence, any other tool providing clone information can basically be used. Certainly, it is required that the defective clone fragments are detected at least. The plugin provided the subjects a simple user interface with a list of existing clones grouped in clone classes (a clone class contains fragments that are clones of each other) as a table in a split-screen window below the source code. Figure 6.5 shows a screenshot of the plugin integrated in the Eclipse IDE. The table presents each fragment together with basic information: a unique id, the path of its source file, its start and end line within the file, and, the level of similarity (type 1, 2, or 3). We implemented two main mechanisms in the plugin to provide the user with context-related clone information only. First, the list of clones covers only clone classes which contain at least one fragment that is located in the currently opened source file in the IDE. All irrelevant clones with respect to this file are invisible, which makes it much easier to overview the clone information. Moreover, we use markers next to the source code—at the left edge where usually line numbers are displayed in editors— to indicate that the code segment the user currently inspects is a clone, similarly to the familiar error indicators in Eclipse. The markers can be used by clicking to jump to the corresponding clone in the clone table to identify the other clone fragments of the same clone class. Finally, by clicking fragments in the table, it is possible to jump directly to their location. The corresponding source file is opened in the editor (if not yet opened), the focus is set to the position of the selected fragment, and the cloned code is highlighted. By providing such context-related clone information we increase the usability of clone data which usually suffers from a large amount of detected clones and potential false positives.

6.2   Experiment Execution

We executed the experiment several times, each time different subjects participated because various time constraints did not allow us to bring all participants together at one time. Each time the experiment was executed with small groups of participants or in individual appointments together with at least one supervisor. To establish the same conditions for subjects of different runs, a repeatable workflow was used. Mainly, this workflow consists of the four different phases: *Introduction, Installation, Execution,* and *Data Collection.* In the following we describe each phase in detail.

Introduction. We started by introducing the subjects using a slide presentation together with a scripted talk. Information was given on the course of the experiment, time constraints, how to use the delivered materials and what the subjects are supposed to do. Describing the tasks, no information on code clones was provided in any way, hence, the subjects were not aware that the experiment focused on clones. Finally, we gave an introduction to the integrated plugin which allows to navigate through existing clones. Again, we did not use the term clone here. We presented the plugin as an extension to the search feature of the Eclipse IDE that enables the user to locate similar or identical code fragments. We chose to avoid the term clone and presented

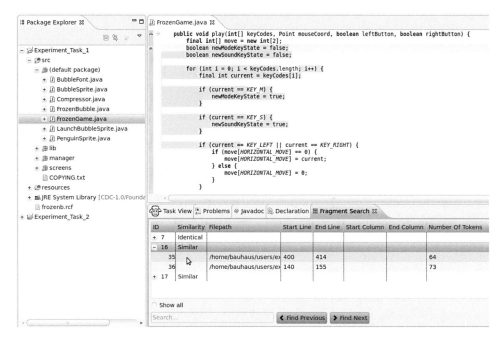

Figure 6.5 – Screenshot of the plugin used in the experiment.

the plugin as an advanced version of an already existing feature to avoid bias—talking about clones or a clone-management tool may affected the expectations of the subjects. The plugin was developed such that it can be used very similar compared to other features in Eclipse to foster an intuitive usage of the tool based on existing experience and further mitigate possible bias. The subjects were informed that the tool will only be available for one of the two tasks and that there is no dictate to use it. Therefore, all the standard features of Eclipse could be applied without further constraints.

Installation. The participants used their own notebooks for the experiment. For an easy and fast installation each participant received a pre-configured Eclipse IDE including the additional plugins for the experiment and an Eclipse workspace including the two tasks. Based on our dependent variable, the participants got a workspace including clone information either for task tFB or task tPM. Since Eclipse is written in Java, no additional installation or configuration was needed—everything was prepared to work out of the box. Moreover, a handout with a short summary of the *Introduction* was provided.

Execution. In the *Introduction* and the handout, all relevant information was presented to the participants to start the experiment and then to continue by following the step-by-step guide of our Eclipse plugin. All activities of the participants to complete the experiment were set, except for the time spent on the two tasks. That is, the duration the participants worked on each task was not limited to avoid incomplete or incorrect results due to lack of time. Such results could not be compared to the timing and correctness of those that have been produced within a given time limit. Harder and

Correctness	tFB_c		tFB_{nc}	tPM_c		tPM_{nc}
addressed	747.67	$<$	2,039.00	637.00	$<$	1,036.67
complete	1,016.89	$<$	1,580.18	600.82	$>$	545.11

Table 6.5 – Collected average times for each task in seconds.

Tiarks [105] observed in pilot studies to their experiment that a time limit was a major mortality threat to obviate if the number of available subjects is rather small. However, subjects were allowed to skip a task if they were not able to locate or fix the bugs.

Data Collection. As soon as a participant finished the tasks, his or her workspace including all relevant data for our analysis was automatically archived. By automatically packing the workspace the possibility of flaws during a manual copying process have been bypassed.

6.3   Evaluation

From the 29 subjects that participated in our experiment we analyzed only the data of solutions complying with our requirements. Therefore, we excluded the result from one student who stated missing Java skills in the self-assessment—subject *13* from Table 6.2. Furthermore, three participants who gave up on both tasks were excluded from our analysis. Solutions of participants who did not finish the whole experiment cannot be compared to the other solutions in a meaningful way regarding timing and correctness. In total, we analyzed 25 results of subjects who fulfilled the requirements and stated that they finished both tasks.

Based on the recording of user interactions by our Eclipse plugin, we found several participants that did not use the provided clone information, which resulted in an uneven distribution of participants to the given tasks. For instance, if a subject with the task combination tFB_c and tPM_{nc} chose not to use the clone information to locate the defects, but instead searched them manually or used other Eclipse features such as the debugger, we counted their results to the tasks tFB_{nc} and tPM_{nc}. As mentioned before, the participants were free to choose how to approach the given tasks to avoid bias, and therefore, it was not compulsory to use the clone plugin even if it was available. Comparing the performance of those participants to the other ones and also considering their self-assessment towards programming experience, we did not find any indication that they chose to do the tasks without the clone information based on superior skills or experience as their results have neither been remarkably better nor worse. We will discuss the reasons for doing the tasks without the tool support in Section 6.4.

6.3.1   Descriptive Statistics

We use statistical tests to investigate the performance of the subjects and pursue our first research question. Table 6.5 shows the average times needed by the participants to solve the tasks. Figure 6.6 visualizes the distribution of the timing data.

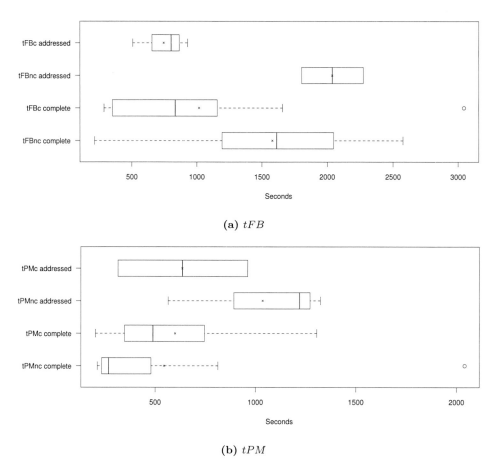

(a) tFB

(b) tPM

Figure 6.6 – Performance of the participants in seconds.

First, we investigate whether a learning effect can be observed or not. Based on our experimental design as shown in Figure 6.2 (described in Section 6.1.2), group A started with task tFB_c and proceeded with task tPM_{nc}. Group B dealt first with tFB_{nc} and then with tPM_C. Table 6.5 as well as Figure 6.6 show that participants of group B needed less time to solve task 2 than task 1 considering *addressed* as well as *complete* solutions. There is no clear trend for group A. Although participants of this group were faster on solving task 2 when considering *complete* solutions only, they have been slower considering *addressed* solutions. However, the gathered data suggest that participants managed the tasks related to PACMAN more successfully and efficiently in general—that was also stated by the participants after the experiment. In addition, we believe that a learning effect with respect to the tasks should be very small if there is one at all, because all participants started with a task related to FROZENBUBBLE and then had to switch to an entirely different program (PACMAN). Except of a learning effect regarding the software systems under study, the participants may perform differently among both tasks due to a bias caused by the clone information. That is, group A got clone information for the first task while group B for the second task. Thus, participants of group A may be more sensitized to clones when starting with the second task than group B. As a result, times needed for tPM_{nc} should be shorter compared to tPM_c. However, results do not confirm such a bias. Though, participants were faster considering *complete* solutions of task tPM_{nc}, the gap is rather small and participants were even slower for *addressed* solutions of task tPM_{nc}.

Comparing the performance of the participants with and without clone information, they were faster on average for both tasks when clone information was provided. The difference is most distinctive for tFB, where the group without access to clone data needed clearly more time to finish the task. The average time for tFB_c and tFB_{nc} differs by 563 seconds—more than 9 minutes—regarding *complete* solutions. In relative proportion, the average time increased by 55.39 %. The respective box-and-whisker plots in Figure 6.6a indicate that the difference in the mean (denoted by the $*$ symbol) is effected by one outlier only. A shift of the distributions can clearly be observed. The variance of the time measures for *addressed* and *complete* results is rather small. That is, the results indicate that *addressed* solutions were neither achieved much faster nor much slower.

The time difference measured for the tPM task is much less distinctive than for tFB, even though the results again show that the subjects required less time on average to solve the task using clone information. The average time for tPM_c and tPM_{nc} differs only by 55.71 seconds for *complete* solutions. In relative proportion, the average time decreased by 9.3 %. Figure 6.6b shows that the mean values are affected by an outlier in tPM_{nc} (denoted by the $\circ$ symbol). Comparing the timings of only *addressed* solutions to *complete* ones, we observe a rather small difference between *addressed* and *complete* solutions for tPM_c and a more distinct difference for tPM_{nc}.

The investigation of our second research question is based on the numbers for correct and incorrect solutions provided. To assess correctness, we manually inspected the changes to the source code of each subject using the Unix *diff* tool. Furthermore, we executed the programs to assure they are running properly. For each task we analyzed whether any of the defect occurrences were corrected. If not, the subject was eliminated

Correctness	tFB_c	tFB_{nc}	tPM_c	tPM_{nc}
addressed	0 (0 %)	4 (25 %)	1 (16.7 %)	1 (5.6 %)
complete	9 (100 %)	12 (75 %)	5 (83.3 %)	18 (94.4 %)

Table 6.6 – Solutions for each task in absolute numbers and percent.

Correctness	Student's T-test		Mann-Whitney U-test	
	tFB	tPM	tFB	tPM
addressed	**0.0006**	0.3871	**0.0022**	0.5819
complete	**0.0002**	0.3467	**0.0002**	0.5407

Table 6.7 – Results of significance tests for times (p-values).

from the data evaluation because these were submissions on which the subjects gave up and did not perform any changes at all. There is no meaningful way to compare such results to *addressed* or *complete* ones. Accordingly, we checked for each task whether both defect occurrences were corrected to distinguish between *addressed* and *complete* results. Table 6.6 shows the results of our manual inspection.

Generally, most participants were able to locate and fix both defects inserted in the software systems. In tFB, all participants who used the available clone information corrected both defects. If no clone information was given or was not used, 25% of the subjects fixed only one of the two defects. Similarly, the solutions for the tPM task were predominantly correct. The relative success rate for the task tPM_{nc} is with 94.4% very high—surprisingly even higher than the success rate for tPM_c.

6.3.2 Hypothesis Testing

To test our hypothesis we use statistical tests to evaluate the recorded data. To support our first hypothesis H_1^{time} regarding the time needed to fix both defects, the null hypothesis H_0^{time} has to be rejected based on the results of the statistical test. We use the parametric Student's T-test as well as the non-parametric Mann-Whitney U-test for independent samples on the time data. Since, we cannot assume a normal distribution and our sample is relatively small the U-test is the more adequate significance tests in our case, although it does not take into account the degree of the time differences but only their ranking. For both statistical tests we use the one-tailed variant, because the alternative hypothesis H_1^{time} postulates that the time needed to correct a cloned defect is larger if no clone information is provided. The results are shown in Table 6.7. Values below the commonly used threshold for statistical significance $p < 0.05$ rejecting the null hypothesis H_0^{time} are printed bold.

Statistical significance is reached for tFB based on the T-test as well as the U-test. In contrast to tFB, no statistical significance has been reached for the task tPM using both tests. The p-values of tPM are rather high. Based on the different results of the two tasks regarding statistical significance H_0^{time} cannot be rejected.

Test	tFB	tPM
Fisher	0.1439	0.9500
Barnard	0.0854	0.3200

Table 6.8 – Results of significance tests for correctness (p-values).

To test the statistical significance regarding our second hypothesis towards correctness, the null hypothesis H_0^{corr} has to be rejected to support H_1^{corr}. We use Fisher's and Barnard's exact tests to test statistical significance of the correctness since both tests are appropriate but differ in the way they handle nuisance. Both tests can be used to test significance of categorical data in the form of contingency tables. Moreover, both tests support small sample sizes like ours. Similar to the timing, H_1^{corr} is a one-tailed hypothesis, because it postulates that the probability of a correct removal of a cloned defect is higher when clone information is used. The one-tailed variants of the two statistical tests are used accordingly. Table 6.8 shows the results.

Statistical significance is reached neither for task tFB nor task tPM. Based on the results the null hypothesis H_0^{corr} cannot be rejected for any of the two tasks. The p-value for tFB is relatively low, especially using the Barnard's test, but do not suffice to reject H_0^{corr}. Therefore, H_1^{corr} cannot be supported.

6.4 Discussion

In this section we discuss the results and interpret peculiarities. Apart from the recorded data of our Eclipse plugin, we asked every participant to write down his or her solving strategy and also talked to them in a feedback session subsequent to the experiment. Furthermore, we remark on observations that may help to gain important insights towards further research.

The results of our experiment did not show a statistically significant benefit of the clone information on correctness, but that was expected. The participants were allowed to execute and test their modified version, so testing was able to compensate for missing clone information. That is, the participants were able to continue their search for the cloned defect in case they fixed only one of the two defect occurrences.

We expected the participants to find cloned defects faster if clone information was available. We found this to be true for both programs as the means of the time needed to fix the defect is smaller for the experimental group with clone information. Yet, the difference is statistically significant only for time tFB of FROZENBUBBLE. The difference in tPM of PACMAN is marginal. We assume the inheritance hierarchy reduced the time needed to locate the cloned defect when there was no clone information—which we expected to observe when preparing the defect scenarios. Both tasks have in common that the cloned instances of the bugs are located in different classes, however, the inheritance hierarchy of PACMAN seems to have helped the participants to identify the corresponding class just by looking at the file tree or type inheritance tree. The cloned defects in PACMAN were in two sibling classes (ghost and player character) as opposed to FROZENBUBBLE where the defects were in a cloned loading sequence of images in the otherwise semantically unrelated classes *FrozenGame* and *LaunchBubbleSprite*. So the inheritance hierarchy gave hints on where to look for the defects only in PACMAN. This explanation was also stated in several strategy reports of the participants. This is probably the reason why nearly 50 % of the participants who were offered the clone tool decided to do without it for the task *tPM* compared to only 25 % for *tFB*.

Apart from the complexity of the two tasks, participants who decided to do without using the tool quoted that they preferred to use other features of Eclipse. The feature that was referred to the most is the keyword search functionality of Eclipse—which was also commonly used to locate the defects when no clone information was provided. Besides being familiar with it, the participants stated that after they located the first defect it has been obvious to them what to search for. Regarding task *tFB* keywords that were mainly used are "bubble" and "color" or a combination of both. The keywords mainly used for task *tPM* are "move" and "delta". Hence, there was no need to use another feature. This feedback shows two things: (1) the subjects preferred to search the source code of the games by specifying their own patterns based on the information they gained by browsing through the code before, (2) the advantage of clone information was recognized based on the degree of complexity regarding the given task.

Some of the participants who did not use the clone information also reported that a substantial training or a more eye-catching presentation of the clone tool may increase the probability of being used. We deliberately chose a rather short introduction to the plugin and a presentation that is characteristic to Eclipse features to avoid bias in the expectations of the subjects and support an intuitive usage. Giving a more detailed training probably improves the performance of the subjects, but the challenge is to find the right balance to minimize bias in such human-based studies as much as possible.

Another factor which may have contributed not to use the clone tool and, moreover, which may explain the high number of correct solutions is that in our experiment the defective clones occurred only twice. We experienced that clones in industrial and open-source systems have often multiple occurrences. The chance of a complete removal of a cloned bug in a real scenario is most probably lower than in our study because more instances of the bug may exist at various locations. Incomplete fixes of such clones may leave the system in a defective state or even introduce new or other defects based on inconsistent changes. In such cases, it may be more beneficial to be provided with clone management tools to make sure that all occurrences of a cloned bug have been fixed or at least are known and kept track of. This will reduce the risk that a system remains defective after applying changes to clones.

Apart from the keyword search feature that was frequently used, the logs related to the activities of the participants do not show clear strategies or patterns. In contrary, different approaches were used from participant to participant. Some used features like searching or debugging whereas others just browsed the code and heavily switched between files without using tool support. Similarly, testing was done quite extensively or just very selectively.

6.5   Threats to Validity

In this section we discuss the threats to validity related to our study and how we tried to mitigate these.

6.5.1   Construct Validity

Our Eclipse plugin is designed such that only the time needed to complete a whole task is recorded. A more fine-grained measurement capturing the time the subjects spent on each individual activity (e.g., program comprehension, bug reproduction and localization, changing and testing the code) may expose further insights. However, in this study we are interested in the overall time needed to finish a complete maintenance task including all involved activities and in the final results produced for each task.

6.5.2   Internal Validity

Selection. The subjects were randomly assigned to two groups A and B without any blocking. However, we ensured that all subjects participated for the first time in a controlled experiment related to code clones. Due to the small number of participants and the simple randomized sampling used, the groups may not be balanced regarding experience and skills of the subjects. The risk of unequal experience was minimized by the fact that all subjects were required to be familiar with Java and Eclipse. Moreover, the tasks were designed such that no knowledge beyond the standard Java class library was needed.

Maturation. To avoid the risk of learning bias, the subjects were provided with different systems for each task. Both groups were provided with clone information for the systems in switching order to rule out a bias based on a different complexity of the systems. The order in which clone information was available may have affected the expectations for the second task to work on.

Instrumentality. Due to organizational reasons all subjects were required to use the Eclipse IDE prepared for the experiment. Although experience in working with Eclipse was mandatory to participate, different levels of knowledge with it may result in differences related to the performances. However, the recording of data (e.g., time) was done in the background and did not influence the subject's behavior.

Experimenter bias. To avoid bias based on the interaction between the subjects and us, we gave a scripted talk at the beginning of each session that was identical for all participants. Afterwards the subjects were guided through the whole experiment by instructions on the Eclipse plugin. The relevant data to analyze the results were automatically recorded by the plugin as well and, therefore, not exposed to our subjectivity.

6.5.3   External Validity

In this study we used two rather small software systems from the same domain with rather low complexity. The given tasks were quite simple, too. However, the costs of preparing, executing and evaluating such experiments is still quite high. Each participant spent about three hours considering the introduction, execution as well as a feedback session afterwards. A more complex experiment design (more systems, more clones, etc.) would have gone beyond the time constraints of such an experiment. Still, we prepared the defects such that they are quite realistic—wrong indices in loops, for instance, off-by-one errors, and incorrect uses of signs when computing movement patterns are fairly common defects. Nonetheless, most industrial as well as open-source systems are larger in size and normally of higher complexity. Moreover, developers are generally familiar with the systems they are working on while the participants of our study got in touch with the subject systems for the first time.

The clones in these systems occurred only twice in the source code, but from our experience clones often occur more than twice in many systems [26, 29]. Due to the high cost of involving participants for human-based studies, the number of subjects was rather small and all of them were students. A different (especially larger) sample of professional subjects may produce different results.

These threats suggest that our results may not necessarily be generalized to other systems and populations. Further studies are necessary to reduce these threats and allow for a more general understanding.

6.6   Summary

We conducted a controlled experiment to investigate the use of clone information on the performance of developers in common bug-fixing tasks in terms of time and correctness. For this purpose, we extended a previous study on the use of clone information by changing the experiment design to overcome various shortcomings. To the best of our knowledge, we are the first to evaluate the support of contextual clone information integrated in an IDE in a human-based controlled experiment.

The experiment shows that developers are quite capable to compensate missing clone information in certain situations through testing to provide correct solutions (although our experimental design does not allow to generalize this finding to cases in which defects were cloned more than once). Clone information potentially helps to detect cloned defects faster, although developers may exploit semantic code relations such as inheritance to uncover cloned defects only slightly slower if they do not have clone information. If cloned defects lurk in semantically unrelated places however, clone information helps to find them faster at statistical significance. Developers without clone information needed more than 9 minutes longer on average or about 55 % more time in relative terms to complete the task. Although the findings might be regarded quite expected, they still need to be proven by empirical research to rule out possible misjudgments [251].

In future research further human-based studies should be directed to the use of clone information and clone management tools to widen and deepen the insights gained. For instance, maintenance tasks other than bug-fixing need to be looked at to capture a more complete picture of how programmers work with clones. Also, more effort is needed to research the impact of different design patterns and code structures, such as inheritance, on the performance of developers when dealing with cloned code. Our work is preliminary regarding this aspect.

Chapter 7

Approximative Code Search

Various studies analyzed duplicated code fragments and proposed tools facilitating clone management activities such us performing consistent changes to clone fragments of the same clone class (see Chapter 2). They found that these inconsistencies were often unwanted and resulted from missing propagation of the modifications to all clone fragments. For instance, different studies show that defects are often corrected in a single place only, whereas other instances of the defect existed—and consequently remained—in the system [19, 29, 87, 130, 164, 250]. To support developers several clone detection techniques were introduced capable of providing clone information for a single version of a software system as well as for multiple versions by tracking fragments over time and building an evolution model. Considering the evolution of software systems is very important since defects may exist unknowingly in the source cod for a long time, a defect found in the current version of the program may also exist in previous versions and other branches of the source code where it needs to be fixed. In the automotive domain, for instance, a defect detected in the current release may have been present in the software for a long time without being noticed and may be operating in different cars controlled by older releases. If the defect represents a safety risk, it must be corrected in all releases where it occurs. In such cases, the defective code fragment must be searched for in all the previous releases hat may be affected. Moreover, products in the embedded software domain frequently form a product family, and often variant software of such families is managed as different branches in the version control system. Then the defect must be searched for in many releases of multiple branches in the version control system.

Apart from defect correcting activities other changes may be applied to various code fragments and code locations as well, for instance, adding new features. However, detecting all locations a change or a fix needs to be applied to is further complicated by copy-and-paste programming, because one cannot safely assume that the affected code is identical at every places, especially considering different releases and branches. That is, a code fragment a developer is looking for may exist multiple times at different locations, but with various modifications such that the code fragments are not identical but still similar. In addition, most clone detectors are based on syntactical similarity, thus, the number of identified clone fragments is rather high, for large systems with several millions lines of source code in particular. The huge amount of clone data limits the usefulness of clone detection results for developers looking for a specific code fragment since it is impractical or not even feasible to filter the relevant information related to that specific code fragment. For this reason, an approximate code search within the history of a program is needed. The detection of syntactical arbitrary code fragments represents an alternative to traditional clone detection. Developer define syntactical arbitrary code fragments they are interested in and all similar fragments are automatically located. This ensures that no irrelevant data is provided which again reduces the amount of data delivered to an user drastically.

Our human-based experiment described in Section 6.4 confirms the usefulness of a targeted search for relevant source code since many participants decided to use the keyword search provided by ECLIPSE to locate certain code (suspected to be defective). Although every IDE, text editor, and tools like GREP provide search functionality, they are only of limited use in our scenario. First, they are text-based and, thus, unable to tolerate differences in layout or comments. Second, they can identify only exact matches. Every toleration of differences has to be encoded by the user—for example, using regular expressions. This requires the user to be aware of any possible difference that may occur. Furthermore, existing techniques just allow for searching in single versions either defining single keywords or a complete source code line, that is, it is not possible to search for code fragments encompassing multiple lines. Consequently, we need a technique to efficiently locate all approximate matches of an syntactical arbitrary code fragment in the program's history as they may need to be changed as well.

We received the demand for our kind of approximate search for defective code from an industrial partner. The software of the industrial partner is a product line where each variant is developed in a different branch in the version control system. The software is embedded in a controller that is shipped in different releases. A defect affecting safety must be corrected in all releases that have already been shipped.

In summary, the research problem is to develop a technique that efficiently locates all approximate matches of an arbitrary token sequence (the code fragment) in a large token sequence (the source code of a program). We identified the following requirements for such a technique:

(1) The query fragment should be specified as an arbitrary sequence of tokens. This way, the user can simply select the defective part of the source code and use it as query pattern.

(2) The search should ignore differences in layouts and comments. In addition, it should tolerate a certain amount of differences to find approximate matches.

(3) The technique should efficiently search matches in different versions and branches of the source code by exploiting similarities between versions.

In this chapter an approximate whole-program code search in multiple releases and branches and its implementation in the tool APPROX is presented giving the answer to Question 18. Our algorithm to locate approximate matches of an arbitrary defective code fragment can be separated into different phases. The approximate search algorithm is based on an algorithm developed by Chang and Lawler as described in [47, 48, 101]. We will describe the different phases of the algorithm of Chang and Lawler in detail, before we explain how these phases are integrated in our tool APPROX. Chang and Lawler used this algorithm in computational biology, for instance, to search for similar DNA or protein sequences in genomic databases. Here we adapt and modify their technique to find similar token sequences in source code databases. In the following, we use terminology adjusted to our domain. Furthermore, we evaluate our approach for real-world defects of various large and realistic programs having multiple releases and branches to answer Question 19. We report runtime measurements and recall using varying levels of allowable differences of the approximate search.

7.1 Search Algorithm

Chang and Lawler propose to split the search of an arbitrary code fragment in a large text into the following three phases, *Partitioning*, *Searching*, and *Checking*. The initial situation of the algorithm is as follows:

- a text T of length m is to be searched

- all occurrences of a given query pattern P of length n with $n < m$ need to be found in T

- an occurrence of P in T is found if, and only if, the edit distance between P and a substring T' of T is within a given threshold k; the edit distance between two strings is the minimal number of deletions, additions, and modifications to transform one string into the other string [178, 235].

In the following we will describe each of the proposed phases in detail.

7.1.1 Partitioning

The partitioning phase prepares the text T that needs to be searched for the query pattern P so that irrelevant regions of the text can be efficiently eliminated by the upcoming search phase. This is done by partitioning T into consecutive regions of a specific length. The length proposed by Chang and Lawler is $n/2$. A region length of $n/2$ assures that no matter how P is aligned to T at least one region is completely covered by P. Figure 7.1 shows different alignments of P to T that illustrate this property. The next section describes how partitioned regions can be excluded from the search.

7.1.2 Searching

Chang and Lawler take advantage of the partitioning phase to identify regions in T that cannot be part of an occurrence of P. This is done by checking the region that is completely covered by a substring P' of P in a certain alignment. For instance, in the second alignment of P in Figure 7.1, only the second visible region of T would be

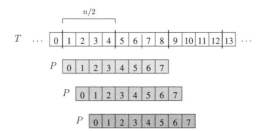

Figure 7.1 – Different alignments of P to regions of length $n/2$ of T.

considered. P' would consist of the elements in the range 4 and 7 of P spanning the whole second visible region. If the edit distance between the spanned region and P' already exceeds the given threshold k, it is obvious that this region cannot be part of an occurrence of P in T with an edit distance less than or equals to k. Locating and eliminating those regions is done in the search phase.

The actual algorithm to identify and eliminate irrelevant regions needs the *matching statistics* of T. The matching statistics for a position i in T, denoted by $T[i]$, is the length of the longest substring T' starting at i in T present somewhere in P. That means that there is no substring T'' in T at position i with $|T''| > |T'|$ that is also present in P. The starting index of T' in P is denoted by $p(i)$. For each i in T the length of T' is denoted by $ms(i)$. T' starting at i in T can only be an occurrence of P in T if $ms(i) = n$. Using a suffix tree for P, all values $ms(i)$ of T can be determined in linear time and space. To implement the matching statistics in linear time it is needed that the suffix tree is constructed by an algorithm that provides the suffix tree with so called suffix links. Suffix links enables a linear time traversal of the suffix tree and, hence, string matching in linear time. There are different algorithms published, for instance, by McCreight [195] or Ukkonen [257]. Our implementation has both variants. For the measurements reported in Chapter 7, the algorithm by McCreight was used. Details of our implementation of the suffix tree and its attributes including suffix links are given in [25, 79, 96, 101].

The linear worst-case complexity is the main reason why matching statistics are very attractive to use in a string matching algorithm. Using the matching statistics of T, Chang and Lawler give an algorithm to eliminate irrelevant regions of T in linear time. A region is relevant and needs to be included in the search of approximate matches of P in T if it is divided by mismatches into at most $k + 1$ intervals of consecutive matches. The reason is that the edit distance k limits the number of mismatches that can interrupt an interval of matches between a specific region and P. The matching statistics of T are used to identify the length of intervals without any mismatches and hence no further string comparisons are needed to decide whether a region is relevant or not. Figure 7.2 shows an example alignment of P to T with a region T' that is divided into five intervals of matches by four mismatches. Figure 7.3 shows an algorithm in pseudo code to eliminate irrelevant regions of T.

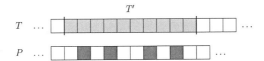

Figure 7.2 – P is aligned to T in a way that it covers a substring T' completely. The dark squares represent mismatches between P and T' which interrupt intervals of matches.

1   $i, j \leftarrow$ Start position of T';
2   *counter* $\leftarrow 0$;
3   **while** *counter* $\neq k \vee i - j < n/2$ **do**
     // Use matching statistics ms
4      $i \leftarrow i + ms(i) + 1$;
5   *counter* $\leftarrow$ *counter* $+ 1$;
6   **if** $i - j < n/2$ **then**
7   Eliminate T';

Figure 7.3 – Pseudocode of the algorithm of Chang and Lawler to eliminate irrelevant regions of T.

7.1.3   Checking

In the last phase those regions that were not eliminated in the search phase are checked for approximate occurrences of P. Considering that a surviving region can form an occurrence of P by combining it with a part of an eliminated region, the check phase does not only search the surviving regions but also an area of length $n/2$ before and after them. This is sufficient because P can completely cover at most two regions at once.

    P is detected in T using a *hybrid dynamic programming* algorithm. The hybrid dynamic programming combines the basic *dynamic programming* approach with the use of suffix trees. The basic dynamic programming consists of three components:

    Recurrence relation: The recurrence relation describes the recursive attribute of an algorithm to solve a problem by using the dynamic programming approach. The recurrence relation denotes the edit distance of two strings by $D(i, j)$, for i being the starting index of the first string and j the starting index of the second string. $D(i, j)$ is calculated using results of previous calculations of $D(i - 1, j)$, $D(i, j - 1)$ and $D(i - 1, j - 1)$.

    Tabular computation: Using the recurrence relation, values of every index pair $D(i, j)$ are calculated by a bottom-up approach and stored in a table. By saving intermediate values that are used by the recurrence relation to determine subsequent values, redundant calculation of values is avoided and the process of determining the edit distance of two strings is accelerated. Notice that storing and reusing intermediate results instead of calculating them by a recursive algorithm is a trade-off between runtime performance and memory consumption.

Traceback: During the tabular computation each value stored in a cell in the resulting table is calculated using the values of its predecessor cells. To be able to trace the path from an arbitrary cell back to the first cell $(0,0)$, a pointer can be set from one cell to those predecessor cells from which the values are used to calculate the value of the current cell.

The concept of dynamic programming is extended by the additional use of suffix trees. Suffix trees are used as part of the tabular computation to solve different subproblems during the process of determining the edit distance of two strings. A study of different use cases of the suffix tree as part of the hybrid dynamic programming is published in [46, 244]. In our case the suffix tree is used to answer *lowest common ancestor* queries in constant time after linear preprocessing. The lowest common ancestor query finds the common parent w with maximum depth for two arbitrary nodes x and y in the suffix tree. To answer lowest common ancestor queries, we reduce the problem of lowest common ancestor queries to the more general *range minimum query* problem. The algorithm presented in [34] introduces the reduction of the lowest common ancestor problem to the range minimum query and is used in our implementation to answer lowest common ancestor queries in constant time after a linear preprocessing phase.

The lowest common ancestor queries, again, are needed to answer *longest common extension* queries in constant time. A longest common extension query for an arbitrary index pair (i, j) related to two strings S_1 and S_2 returns the length l of the longest common substring starting at index i in S_1 and index j in S_2. Answering longest common extension queries is the base precondition of the hybrid dynamic programming to determine the edit distance between two strings in linear time. The linear time complexity of $O(k \cdot m)$ for the hybrid dynamic programming was first proved in [169, 170, 208]. Details concerning the algorithms used to implement the hybrid dynamic programming as well as the lowest common ancestor query and the longest common extension are given in [59, 101, 242].

7.2   Implementation

This section describes how the different concepts and algorithms described in the previous section are combined and implemented in the tool APPROX. APPROX is integrated into the *Bauhaus Project*. Because it is desirable to locate an arbitrary code fragment not only in one but in multiple versions of a given software, APPROX works in an incremental way to reduce the runtime t compared to an algorithm which processes each version of the given software individually. The idea of working incremental is to analyze the software for the first version, which is to be searched for the query pattern, completely and then analyze only those parts of the software that have been modified from one version to the next one. Given that our assumption is correct and our incremental approach reduces the runtime t considering j revisions, it is considered the following relation should hold: $t_{incremental} < j \cdot t_{individual}$.

Consequently, APPROX needs information about the changes that have been applied to the source code from one version to the next. This information is used to avoid redundant processing of files that did not change between two versions and, hence, do not contain any new or modified source code that could result in new matches of the given query pattern. Accordingly, only those files of two consecutive versions that have been added or modified are searched. In the first version, all source files are considered as changed. Besides the information about changes, APPROX expects the tolerated edit distance between the code pattern and any match in the software as input.

To provide approximate search in an incremental way APPROX processes the program's source code in four main phases. The first step is to preprocess the query pattern, before in the following phase the first version of the software is analyzed. After that all upcoming versions are analyzed considering only their changes. Finally the results are filtered and printed. In the following we will describe each phase of APPROX in more detail.

7.2.1   Preprocessing

The first main phase in APPROX is the processing of the query pattern. The code of the query pattern is read from a source file and transformed into a token stream stored in a token table. Having the tokens of the query pattern, the suffix tree can be constructed in time linear to the number of tokens of the pattern. Since the query pattern is usually relatively small, suffix tree construction can be neglected in runtime considerations.

As described in Section 7.1, the tree is needed to calculate the matching statistics for the text T and this can be done by string matching using a suffix tree. In our case it is better to construct a suffix tree for the query pattern P and not for the text T. This is due to two main reasons. On the one hand, the query pattern P will likely be significantly smaller in size compared to the text T. On the other hand, the query pattern is not changed during the analysis and so the suffix tree neither requires any updates, whereas the source code of the software does change between different versions.

Apart from string matching, the suffix tree is needed in this phase to calculate the range minimum query table. After all values of the range minimum query table are calculated, lowest common ancestor queries can be answered for any pair of two nodes in the suffix tree in constant time. Therefore, answering lowest common ancestor queries does not influence the runtime of the following phases of APPROX after a linear preprocessing in this phase.

7.2.2   First Version Analysis

The first version of a software that is analyzed is processed differently compared to all following versions, because there is no previous version from which information about changed files could be extracted and, hence, data and structures needed by APPROX have to be calculated for every source file of this version.

The first step is to tokenize the complete source code of the first version and save all tokens in token tables, just like it is done with the query pattern. Each file is stored in a separate token table. After all files have been tokenized the matching statistics values for the source code are calculated and saved in corresponding tables. The matching statistics are calculated by comparing the token type of the tokens of the source code to those in the suffix tree of the query pattern for each file. By comparing the token types instead of their values we abstract from identifiers and literals.

Using the suffix links in the suffix tree, the traversal and, hence, the comparison can be done in linear time with respect to the number of tokens of the source code. With the help of the matching statistics of the complete source code, the algorithm by Chang and Lawler to eliminate irrelevant regions can be used to reduce the size of source code that needs to be checked for approximate matches of the search pattern. To do so the indexes of all surviving regions are saved into tables. The index consists of a token table identifier and a position within that token table, since we have multiple token tables, one for each file.

Finally, the hybrid dynamic programming algorithm described previously is used to search for approximate occurrences of the query pattern in the surviving regions of the source code. Each match that is located during this phase is added to the result set together with its location in the analyzed software, including the version it was found in, the file and the path to it, starting and ending line as well as starting and ending column within the file. In addition to the location, each match in the result set gives information about the edit distance between itself and the query pattern.

Version i Analysis

Every version i, except the first one, uses information about modifications that have been introduced to the source code while analyzing version $i - 1$. That way it is possible to search for approximate occurrences of the query pattern in an incremental way. The implementation of the incremental approach uses information about changes between two consecutive versions and processes only files that have been changed and thus need to be analyzed again. APPROX considers and deals with three different kinds of changes in version $i + 1$ compared to version i:

A new file has been added: Every file that is added in version $i + 1$ is analyzed by creating all data structures needed to search for approximate matches of the query pattern: the token tables, the matching statistics, and the surviving regions. Afterward, hybrid dynamic programming is used search the matches which are then included in the result set.

An existing file has been deleted: Files that have been deleted from a revision to the next are not needed any more because they cannot influence the result set in any way. Neither will new matches be added nor will existing matches be deleted because the information of these matches will still be provided at the end of the run of APPROX. Hence, in the case of a file deletion, APPROX simply deletes unneeded data structures. These are the token tables as well as the tables of the matching statistics, the surviving regions and the hybrid dynamic programming data.

An existing file has been modified: If the source code of a file in version $i + 1$ is modified, this file needs to be analyzed by APPROX to assure that matches that might have been newly created are found. Because the available data of the previous version i cannot easily be updated in parts and without major changes to the algorithms introduced in Section 7.1, all data structures concerning the modified file are created from scratch. Unfortunately, we are not aware of any incremental algorithm to update

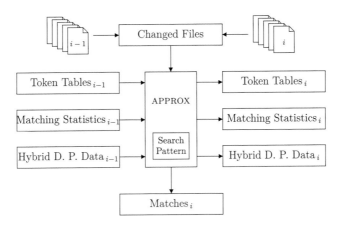

Figure 7.4 – Overview of APPROX' incremental processing when finding approximate matches of the query pattern in the source code of version i

these data structures. In other words, a modification of a file is handled by deleting the data structures of the file from version i and creating them for version $i + 1$ from scratch. Again, the involved data structures are the token tables, the tables of the matching statistics, the surviving regions and the hybrid dynamic programming data.

Figure 7.4 shows the involved components of APPROX to analyze a version of the source using intermediate data of the previously analyzed version.

7.2.3 Postprocessing

The implementation of the approximate search as described so far finds every occurrence of the query pattern in the source code. Therefore, there are matches among the result set that are completely contained in other matches and do not differ in their edit distance related to the query pattern. These submatches, or *non-maximal* matches are of no interest and are removed from the result set in a post-processing step. After this filtering, only maximal matches remain in the result set, which are then sorted by different criteria. First, the matches that belong to the same version are grouped. Matches within the same group are ordered by their edit distance related to the query pattern, starting from smallest to largest. Finally, the result set is presented to the user in a text-based format.

7.3   Complexity

The complexity of APPROX depends on the size of the source code and the query pattern as well as on the edit distance k. The string matching implemented in APPROX uses token sequences as representation of the source code and the query pattern. For this reason, the size of both is measured in tokens. In the following, m denotes the number of tokens of the source code and n the number of tokens of the query pattern.

The first phase of APPROX preprocesses the search pattern, that means that mainly the suffix tree is constructed and the range minimum query table for the suffix tree is calculated. Both steps are done in linear time related to n. The steps of tokenizing the source code and creating the matching statistics tables are linear in time with respect to m. The construction of the tables for the surviving regions and the hybrid dynamic programming depend additionally on k and thus have a worst-case complexity of $O(k \cdot m)$, where k is typically small.

7.4   Study Setup

Due to confidentiality reasons, we could not use the software of our industrial partner who initially asked for the tool to evaluate it. Instead we selected two open-source systems that offered a similar setting. The selection criteria were as follows:

- The systems should be open-source and implemented either in Java, C, or C++.

- Multiple revisions of the systems are publicly available.

- They contain multiple branches and tags[1].

- The average size of a single branch or tag is above 100 KSLOC.

- They have an associated bug tracker and links between repository revisions and fixed bugs.

We selected two subject systems for our study, namely JEDIT[2] and DRJAVA[3]. JEDIT is a text editor, whereas DRJAVA is a lightweight developing environment. Both systems are written in Java.

We selected the revisions for our case study in the following way, where the term *revision* encompasses *trunk*, *branches*, and *tags* according to SUBVERSION. From the perspective of APPROX, there is no difference between *trunk*, *branches*, and *tags*. For each system, we selected one initial revision that contained a change correcting a defect. Then we selected nine predecessor revisions (not consecutive) of the initial revision. All of them needed to contain a defect correction, too. We selected predecessor revisions of revisions containing a defect correction instead of successor revisions to make sure that revisions are included containing a defect which we already know is fixed at some later point in time. The ten revisions containing fixes were selected by analyzing the commit messages of the bug tracker. They were selected only if the commit message was a clear indication of a correction and contained no feature change. In addition to the commit message, we also checked the changed source code.

Because the runtime of APPROX depends on the amount of source code changes between two consecutive revisions when multiple revisions are supposed to be searched,

---

[1]A tag denotes a snapshot of a project in time that is supposed to be kept and marked with a meaningful name, for instance, a release together with its version number such as "releasr-1.1".

[2]http://www.jedit.org/

[3]http://www.drjava.org/

System	Files	KSLOC	Branches	Tags
JEDIT	4140 – 11680	829 – 2365	3 – 13	6 – 14
DRJAVA	1434 – 14387	184 – 1795	5 – 19	5 – 14

Table 7.1 – Size of subject systems evaluating APPROX.

we selected predecessor revisions such that between every pair of selected revisions, there is a gap of approximately 100 revisions. Our initial test with APPROX showed that a gap of approximately 100 revisions ensures two important properties. First, there are enough aggregated changes that make APPROX' runtime measurable. Second, the amount of changes between two consecutive revisions varies sufficiently to evaluate the influence of the number of changes on the runtime.

To sum it up, a predecessor revision of the initial revision n with a corrective change was selected only if it was a revision containing a defect correction, too, and if its revision number m fulfills the constraint $m = n - i \cdot 100$ for $i \in \mathbb{N}$ and $1 \leq i \leq 9$.

After selecting ten revisions, we added three more revisions with the revision numbers $n - i \cdot 100$ for $10 \leq i \leq 12$. These revisions may or may not contain a corrective change. We added these revisions to ensure that APPROX would be able to search for the defects corrected in the older revisions, too.

In summary, we analyzed 13 revisions for each system of which the last ten revisions contain a defect-correcting change that was to be searched by APPROX. Table 7.1 provides the minimum and maximum size for the selected revisions of both subject systems.

7.5   Performance

In this section, we analyze APPROX's performance when searching approximate matches of a given code fragment. Since APPROX is an incremental approach, its runtime depends on the amount of changed source code between consecutive revisions. Figure 7.5 and Figure 7.6 show the number of tokens in changed files for each revision of JEDIT and DRJAVA, respectively. Both figures show that the number of changes varies between revisions.

We first conducted an approximate search to analyze how the runtime depends on the number of changes and which phases contribute most to the runtime. For both systems, we executed APPROX with ten different query patterns. Each query pattern represents a defective code fragment taken from one version of the subject system's history. The query patterns were derived from the defective code fragment by identifying the enclosing syntactic unit, for instance, an if-else statement that includes the defective code. Please note that although we have used this syntactic procedure to derive our search patterns, APPROX accepts arbitrary token sequences as query pattern. Furthermore, we executed APPROX three times for each query pattern to detect approximate matches in all 13 revisions of the corresponding system. That is, to analyze the influence of the tolerated differences, we measured the runtime using three different

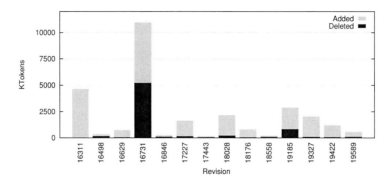

Figure 7.5 – Tokens in changed files for each version of JEDIT

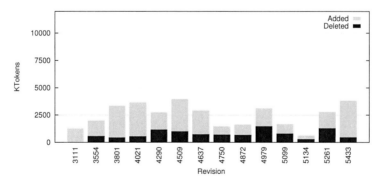

Figure 7.6 – Tokens in changed files for each version of DRJAVA

thresholds for tolerated differences k: 0%, 10%, and 20% of the pattern's length. Each search was conducted on a machine with an Intel 3 GHz 64 bit CPU and 64 GB of main memory. The current implementation of APPROX uses a single CPU only.

Due to the large amount of gathered data points, we present detailed results for one search per system only. For both systems, we selected the search with the query pattern extracted from the last defect-correcting revision and ran APPROX using the three different thresholds as described above. Due to the similarity of the results obtained for the other query patterns in terms of the performance of APPROX during its different phases, we do not present them in this thesis in detail. However, we made the detailed performance evaluation publicly available on our website[4].

For JEDIT, our query pattern was 84 tokens (13 lines of code) long. The corresponding runtime is shown in Figure 7.7. It can be seen, that the runtime for each revision primarily depends on the number of changed tokens—that is, the pattern of the bars in Figure 7.7 is similar to the pattern of the light-gray bars in Figure 7.5. When allowing more differences, the runtime increases notably. In total, it took 60 seconds to find identical matches, 94 seconds to find matches with at most 10% differences, and 213 seconds to find matches with at most 20% differences in all revisions, which add up to approximately 3.7 million SLOC that were actually processed. Our approach processes only files of the first revision and then all files that were changed later on. Summing up the total source code size of all revisions would result in 16 million SLOC.

Looking at the different phases, tokenizing the source code requires most of the time when searching for identical matches. Please note that for all searches, the tokenizing phase of the first revision includes a search for relevant source files. Due to technical reasons, this cannot be easily measured separately. Creating the matching statistics requires significantly less time while the other phases are hardly recognizable. When more differences are tolerated, the time needed for tokenizing and creating the matching statistics remains constant for a given revision as it depends only on the size of the source code that is searched and not on k. However, the time needed for the matching phase itself increases notably. This suggests that the amount of tolerated differences should be chosen carefully.

For DRJAVA the results follow the same pattern. The pattern we used for our search was 116 tokens (17 lines of code) long. The corresponding runtime of the search is shown in Figure 7.8. In total, it took 65 seconds to find identical matches, 120 seconds to find matches with at most 10% differences, and 311 seconds to find matches with at most 20% differences in all revisions, which add up to approximately 3.3 million SLOC that were actually processed.

The results support our previous findings as well as the complexity description of APPROX as given in Section 7.3. That is, constructing the suffix tree for the query pattern is linear in time to its size and tokenizing the source code is linear in time to the size of the code—both measured in tokens. Since the size of the query pattern is most probably very small compared to the size of the source code that is searched, we can basically consider the runtime of both phases linear in time with respect to the size of the source code. The runtime of the approximative search heavily depends on the

---

[4]http://softwareclones.org/approx-results.php

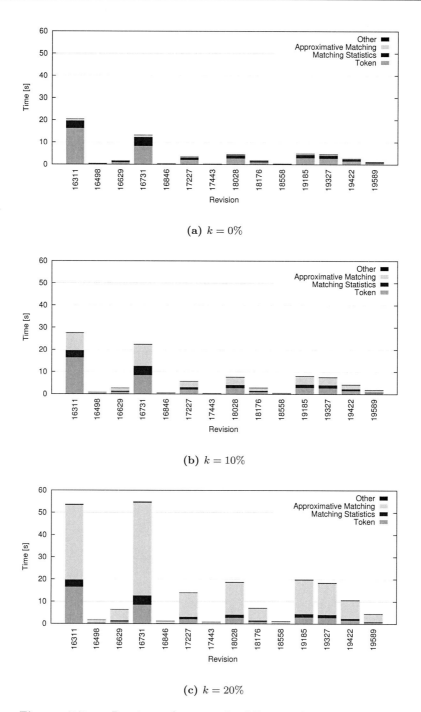

(a) $k = 0\%$

(b) $k = 10\%$

(c) $k = 20\%$

Figure 7.7 – Runtime of APPROX's different phases when finding approximate matches in JEDIT.

number of tolerated differences between the defined query and any of its occurrences in the source code. The results illustrate very well that the less differences are tolerated the less time is needed. However, the size of the query pattern is a natural upper bound for the number of possibly tolerated differences. Realistically the number of tolerated differences is much smaller than the actual size of the query pattern—we consider 20% to be a rather high value already.

Although the detailed analysis of the runtime is interesting from a technical perspective, the total time needed for a search is more relevant from a practical point of view. In addition, it is important to know how the total runtime is influenced by the pattern (mainly its size but also of frequentl code fragments in the subject source code are similar or identical to it) and the number of tolerated differences—basically, the parameters the user is in control of. Therefore, we measured the total search time for each of the patterns—each representing a defective fragment derived from a version of the subject system's history—using different similarity thresholds. Figure 7.9 shows the results for JEDIT, where the x-axis indicates the pattern size and the y-axis shows the corresponding runtime. The three graphs correspond to 0%, 10%, and 20% tolerated differences. The ten data points from our searches are indicated by the points in the graphs.

Looking at 0% tolerated differences—identical matches—we observe that the runtime remains almost constant. That is, the runtime is hardly influenced by the size of the pattern when identical matches are searched. When we allow 20% differences, we see that the runtime is higher compared to searching only identical matches and notably increases with increasing pattern sizes. The runtime when allowing 10% differences falls in-between those two. It also increases with increasing pattern size but not as steep and steady compared to tolerating 20% differences.

When looking at the results for DRJAVA shown in Figure 7.10, we can observe a similar pattern. When only identical matches are searched, the size of the query pattern does not influence the runtime. Allowing more differences increases the runtime as well as the influence of the pattern size on the runtime. We conclude that the amount of tolerated differences has to be chosen carefully and with regard to the size of the query pattern. In summary, we conclude that APPROX has a reasonable performance that allows searching approximate matches of a code fragment in a large body of source code in reasonable time.

7.6   Incomplete Defect Correction

Regarding our envisioned usage scenario, APPROX is useful only if it can find matches that are truly missing propagations of defect corrections. To show that APPROX can really detect these situations, we have analyzed the approximate matches that APPROX found in our subject systems in more detail. In this section, we present examples of defects that were corrected in one place, but should have been corrected in at least one other location as well. We used the very same setup as in our performance evaluation. The examples are taken from the matches that were found by APPROX.

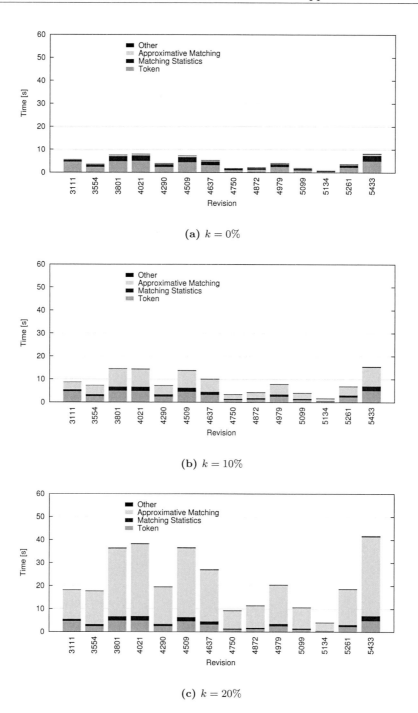

(a) $k = 0\%$

(b) $k = 10\%$

(c) $k = 20\%$

Figure 7.8 – Runtime of APPROX's different phases when finding approximate matches in DRJAVA.

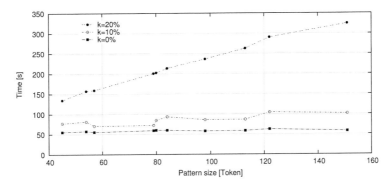

Figure 7.9 – Runtime of APPROX for finding approximate matches in JEDIT considering different pattern sizes and different thresholds.

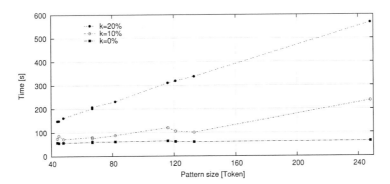

Figure 7.10 – Runtime of APPROX for finding approximate matches in DRJAVA considering different pattern sizes and different thresholds.

Our first example is taken from JEDIT where a defect was corrected in revision 18176. In particular, the highlighted part has been added to the code fragment that is shown in Figure 7.11. The correction prevents the unintentional overwriting of properties. However, the correction was not propagated to another branch, where a copy of the same files resides. The defect still existed in that branch at that time we conducted our study.

```
1   public void unsetProperty(String key)
2   {
3     if (initialized)
4     {
5       String prefix = "mode." + name + '.';
6       jEdit.unsetProperty(prefix + key);
7     }
8     props.remove(key);
9   }
```

Figure 7.11 – Defect correction in revision 18176 of JEDIT

The second example is also taken from JEDIT and shown in Figure 7.12. The defect was corrected in revision 18558 by changing the highlighted comparison operator from > to >=. The defective code fragment was found by APPROX in multiple other branches, one of which was still active at the time of our evaluation.

```
1   while(--start >= 0)
2   {
3     char c = text.charAt(start);
4     int index = openBrackets.indexOf(c);
```

Figure 7.12 – Defect correction in revision 18558 of JEDIT

Our third example is taken from DRJAVA where a defect was corrected in revision 4979. The corresponding code fragment is shown in Figure 7.13. The defect was corrected by adding a missing *null* check—the highlighted part. Although the correction was propagated to most other branches, the defect was not corrected in one branch where it existed until our study at least.

7.7   Discussion

In this section we discuss the results of our case study with respect to our research questions 18 and 19. We have shown that APPROX is able to find approximate matches of arbitrary code fragments from real systems in millions of lines of code in reasonable time—usually between one and five minutes using our study setup. Therefore, we consider the application of APPROX feasible for the envisioned use case of finding approximate matches of a given code fragment that need to be changed as well. Apart

```
1   boolean open = false;
2   for (OpenDefinitionsDocument doc :
3          model.getOpenDefinitionsDocuments()) {
4     if ((doc.getFile()!=null) &&
5          (doc.getFile().equals(error.file())) )) {
6       open = true;
7       break;
8     }
```

Figure 7.13 – Defect correction in revision 4979 of DRJAVA

from the length of the search pattern, its structure may also influence APPROX' runtime. Certain characteristics—for example repetitiveness—may affect the runtime.

We have found many situations where defect corrections were not propagated to the branches of our program. We have shown that these situations exist and that APPROX is very helpful in finding them. Nevertheless, we were not able to classify any of these situations as unambiguously harmful, which has to do with the way branching is used in our subject–and most likely in many similar—systems. The main purpose of the branches we have analyzed was trying things out without affecting the main line of development. Although these branches sometimes contain a notable number of changes, they become inactive very quickly compared to the project's lifetime. Many of the matches that APPROX has found were located in "dead" branches that still exist in the repository but are not maintained any longer. In a realistic setting, APPROX would be applied only to branches that are alive.

In other projects—industrial projects—in particular, branching is used much more extensively, for example, to maintain variants of a product line for different customers. Often, there is a significantly larger number of branches in industrial projects and the branches are much longer active compared to the branches of our subject systems. In fact, the use case for APPROX and the motivation for our work originates from one of our industrial partners. Unfortunately, we are not able to publish any data due to non-disclosure reasons. Using our two subject systems, however, we have shown that it is technically possible to detect missing propagations of defect-correcting changes using APPROX.

7.8   Threats to Validity

In this section we discuss the threats to validity related to our study and how we tried to mitigate these.

7.8.1   Internal Validity

The query pattern has—together with the choice of k—a notable influence on the recall and precision of APPROX. Using a smaller query pattern increases recall and decreases precision. Increasing the size of the search pattern has the opposite effect. Thus, recall and precision values are meaningful only if we use a reasonable query pattern. This requires an in-depth analysis of which query patterns are reasonable. We believe this question can be answered only for individual systems and defects with the help of system experts.

Our approximate search allows differences between the search fragment and any match of up to k different tokens. The syntactic similarity, however, does not necessarily correspond to the semantic similarity. Consequently, APPROX may not detect some matches although they are semantically similar, because the syntactic difference is too high. These situations might, for example, arise when a semantic-preserving reordering of statements is performed. The syntactic differences prevent APPROX from detecting these kinds of matches.

7.8.2 External Validity

We evaluated our approach using two software systems both written in the Java programming language. Therefore, we cannot assert that our findings can be generalized to other software systems—especially those written in another programming language than Java. However, with our study we pioneered the approximative code fragment search in the evolution of a system's source code. Certainly, more research is necessary to extend but also replicate results.

7.9 Summary

In this case study, we evaluated our tool APPROX for finding approximate matches of a given source fragment in a large body of source code. The use case for APPROX is finding sections of source code similar to a defective source code fragment. We have shown that APPROX can detect approximate matches of a given code fragment in millions of lines of code in reasonable time—usually between one and five minutes.

We have also shown that APPROX is able to detect many situations where a defect-correcting change was not propagated to other parts of the system. Consequently, we think that APPROX is a valuable addition to software maintenance as it helps to ensure that defects are removed completely. The approximative code search is a good alternative to traditional clone detection techniques also. It enables the user to focus on a specific code segment which might be of interest in certain situations, thus, reducing the amount of the output drastically in contrast to using a traditional clone detector. The challenge, however, is to define an appropriate query pattern which may not be straight forward in some cases. Applying traditional clone detection avoids specifying a query pattern in terms of determining its bounds. Accordingly, it really depends on the use case which approach is to be preferred.

Part III

Finale

Chapter 8

Conclusion

This chapter summarizes the findings and conclusions of this thesis with respect to the research problems stated in Section 1.1. Taken together we showed that software clones are an existing issue since commonly be present in the source code of software systems. To investigate their effect we presented a new technique to map identical as well as non-identical clones avoiding the previous shortcomings. The approach has been evaluated and used in several case studies on real-world software systems. Findings help to improve the understanding of the cloning phenomenon and its effects on software systems and on software maintainability in particular.

8.1 Clone Rates

In a large-scale study on clone rates in open-source software we were able to show that cloning is an existing and even common phenomenon. In contrast to previous studies presenting rather high numbers on clone rates, we conclude that cloning is common but at a lower scale than reported so far. However, in some cases outliers with exceptionally high rates were find caused by cloning whole software entities, for instance, subdirectories. In addition, applied statistical significance tests to find differences of clone rates among programming languages and found C# having the highest and C the lowest clone rates. Finally, we were able to validate that clones tend to be in close proximity with cloned token sequences being mostly in the same source file.

8.2 Clone Evolution

Although previous studies introduced approaches to map software clones across multiple versions and also analyzed the evolution of several systems, non-identical clones have been neglected widely. These studies presented evolution patterns and empirical data mainly for identical clones, some also considered clones of type 2. Clone mapping has previously been done by finding best matches between clones of two versions using their positions while considering the deltas between consecutive versions. Furthermore, studies were based on data gathered by using one set of parameter settings only, prohibiting any conclusion on their influence on results. To be able to draw a more complete picture of the effects of cloning on software maintainability, it is necessary to detect and map all relevant clone types in a system accurately and investigate the effect of parameters used on the results.

We introduced an approach to build an evolution model appropriate for mapping clones of type 1 to 3. The mapping avoids the problem of possible ambiguity mappings for non-identical clones by extending it to consider clone class memberships in addition to the use of position information. Based on our new mapping we adapted the *Late Propagation* evolution pattern such that it can automatically be uncovered for non-identical clones as well which was not possible before. To make use of the advantages of incremental detection techniques, we integrated our mapping approach and the detection of the *Late Propagation* pattern into our existing incremental clone detector.

To analyze how type-3 clones evolve and whether their evolution differs from the evolution of type-1 and type-2 clones, we tracked individual clone fragments of seven open-source systems over a period of four years. Moreover, we repeated the analysis for each subject system using different parameters determining the clone detection thresholds. Comparing identical clones to non-identical clones it was found hat the majority of detected clones were non-identical clone fragments and that the number of non-identical clones also tended to grow faster over time. Similar results were obtained investigating the lifetime and change frequency of clones. That is, non-identical clone fragments were generally more persistent and underwent more changes, most of them being inconsistent, than identical clones.

Our observations suggest that non-identical clones tend to be the dominating clone type regarding the analyzed aspects and therefore clone management tools might pay higher attention to them. Finally, we observed that different parameter settings regarding the minimum clone length and the minimum identical block length (for non-identical clones) have influenced the results but conserved the relations.

8.3   Relevant Clones

We further extended our research on clone evolution by focusing on refactorings that removed existing software clones. Analyzing 16 software systems over a period of two years, it was found that the main share of code clones were either replaced by calls to newly introduced methods or by methods in the corresponding superclass. Interestingly, there was no difference in the frequency and type of the applied refactorings when comparing deliberate and accidental clone removals. Trying to determine metrics that are useful to detect relevant clones in terms of being good candidates for a removal, results were mainly different between systems and no clear conclusions could be made. However, we found non-identical clones were more often removed than identical clones. This observation is a bit surprising as non-identical clones usually require more sophisticated refactorings compared to identical ones.

In addition, we tracked and analyzed code fragments that have been introduced by clone removing refactorings in the same time period. On the one hand, we found that only half of the tracked fragments changed after they were introduced which indicates that maintenance costs are not decreased by removing duplication in many cases. On the other hand, those fragments that did change later most probably decreased maintenance costs by reducing the system's size and control flow complexity while the complexity of removing the duplications was rather small.

Investigating clone removals, we also identified refactorings that missed some clone fragments that could have been removed as well. Based on this observation, we conducted a controlled experiment to the use of clone information on the performance— in terms of time and correctness—of developers in common defect-correcting tasks. The results show that developers are able to compensate missing clone information, for instance, through testing and exploiting semantic code relations such as inheritance. Thus, clone information were helpful when cloned defects lurked in semantically unrelated locations. Moreover, using clone information led to less time spent on detecting cloned defects. Recording the developers actions while searching for the defective code, it was also observed that they often used keyword-search mechanisms to locate relevant code fragments. According to this observation, we presented a technique to detect arbitrary code fragments in the history of software systems. The approach is capable of detecting all identical as well as similar occurrences of defined code fragments within a few minutes. Evaluating the approach we were also able to show that it can be used to identify situations where defect-correcting changes were not propagated to other parts of the system.

8.4   Future Work

This section summarizes opportunities for extending our work on software clones in the future.

8.4.1   Closed-source Projects

In this thesis our studies are commonly based on open-source systems. To verify and extend findings closed-source systems need to be analyzed as well. The development of open-source and closed-source systems often differs in some characteristics. For instance, the policies for contributing to the corresponding system vary. While for closed-source projects there is often a well-defined team with certain access rights and tasks, for instance, adding features, testing, or writing documentation, there is basically no such rigid team defined for open-source projects. These usually have a few core members that take care of the development process, granting access rights to others willing to contribute. However, in most cases open-source projects follow a *pull request* policy. That is, changes performed by someone not part of the core members are merged to the source code after granted by a core member responsible for doing a review ahead. The different policies used in closed-source and open-source projects may lead to fairly different numbers of contributors in turn. Plenty of developers may contribute to an open-source project depending on its size and lifetime. For closed-source projects the development team usually do not change that often and often smaller than the total number of contributors of an open-source project. Since the development policy and the number of different contributors may affect software maintenance findings of the studies presented in this thesis may turn out to be totally different for closed-source software system—or they turn out to be rather similar which would be very interesting as well.

8.4.2   Human-based Studies

Still most studies are based on statistical data, e.g., metrics, using retrospective approaches. A developer's view is yet often disregarded. There are some challenges preventing researchers from doing more human-based based such as controlled experiments, for instance, finding appropriate participants in acceptable numbers. Nonetheless, gathering developer centric data most probably add further and different insights into the cloning phenomenon. Various methods could be used to extract a developer's knowledge and opinion on specific use cases, among others controlled experiments, questionnaires, and observations.

In this thesis we contributed to that issue by investigating how developers perform with respect to fixing cloned defects (Chapter 6). In future research further human-based studies should be directed to the use of clone information and clone management tools to widen and deepen the insights gained. Knowledge obtained by such studies can be used to improve clone detection and management tools and these in turn to improve the quality of statistical data gathered. That is, a combination of traditional studies based on statistical data and human-based studies may capture more insights than both research disciplines on their own.

8.4.3   IDE Integration

Clone detection and visualization tools may unfold their usefulness for programmers at daily work even more when they are smoothly integrated into their standard development environment. Existing and well-known development environments could be extended by clone detection or code search features by plugins that can be developed independently from the actual development environment. Though, basic characteristics, e.g., the user interface, of the development environment should be considered such that a homogeneous workflow and expectation conformity are preserved. Besides improving the usability, the integration of detection tools in a development environment is a good way to facilitate the inspection of results as current clone detection tools provide a large amount of findings.

The integration of our detection tools is already in progress but still preliminary. We developed an ECLIPSE plugin encompassing some of our clone detection features focusing on context related information (described in Section 6.1.5). First insights collected during our controlled experiment (Chapter 6) showed that little introduction is needed to apply the cone detection features and interpreting its results when the users are familiar with ECLIPSE in general. Further features may be integrated as well as visualization support. However, extending features should be done in small steps to spot just the right amount before the entry thresholds becomes an obstacle for users.

Appendix A

Experiment

A.1 Handout

Figure A.1 shows the first page and Figure A.2 the second page of the handout given to the participants of the experiment. The handout was used to gather the basic steps that were needed to be taken care of by each subject. It represents a summary of the slide presentation given at the beginning of the experiment and, thus, makes sure that every subject knows what to do even if information were missed during the presentation.

A.2 Pre-study Questionnaire

Figure A.3 shows the general questions the subjects have been asked before starting the actual experiment. Using this questionnaire the subjects assessed their Java skills and whether they have experience working with the Eclipse IDE. A unique number (put in the corresponding text field *Number*) was generated by us and assigned to every subject. The e-mail address was not mandatory since we performed an anonymized experiment and was only meant to send the subjects their results after evaluating the data.

A.3 Post-study Questionnaire

Figure A.4 shows the questions the subjects have been asked after finishing each of the two tasks. That is, for each task the same questionnaire was presented since the answers relate to each task. The first four questions concern a self-assessment of the subjects towards their own performance and the overall level of difficulty of the tasks. They were also asked to state whether they believe to accomplished the tasks or not. In addition, we asked each subject to summarize how they approached the tasks.

Arbeitsgruppe Softwaretechnik
Software Engineering Group

EXPERIMENT

Preparation

- Insert the DVD delivered to you in the envelop. If you do not have a DVD drive, please ask for a USB stick. Both include the same materials.
- Either copy **workspace.zip** or **workspace.tar** to your local drive. Both are identical except for their archive type used for compression.
- Copy the right Eclipse (based on your OS) to your local drive. You have to use the provided Eclipse.
- Extract both files (Eclipse and the workspace) on your local drive
- Start Eclipse:
  - Double-click on eclipse/eclipse.exe in the extracted Eclipse directory.
  - Alternative: In the Linux Shell type **./eclipse** in the extracted directory.
  - Eclipse asks for the Workspace to be used. Insert the path to the extracted Workspace.

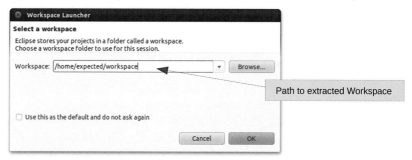

- Eclipse is ready..

Main Part

You will see the standard Eclipse UI. Located on the bottom-right you will find the "Experiment View". The "Experiment View" will guide you through the entire experiment. Follow the instructions presented in this view carefully. When you finished the instructions currently presented, click "next" to proceed.

Figure A.1 – First page of the experiment handout.

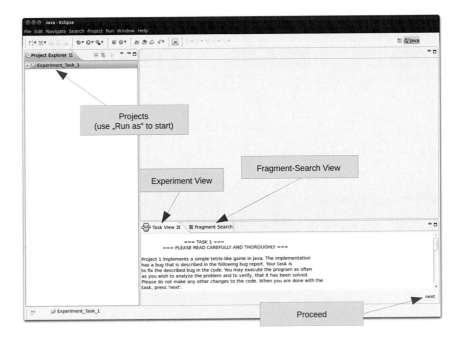

Finishing

As soon as you completed both tasks and followed the instructions given, perform the following two steps:

- Close Eclipse
- Let us know that you finished and we will collect your Workspace.

After collecting the Workspace, the Experiment is done.
Thank you for participating!

Figure A.2 – Second page of the experiment handout.

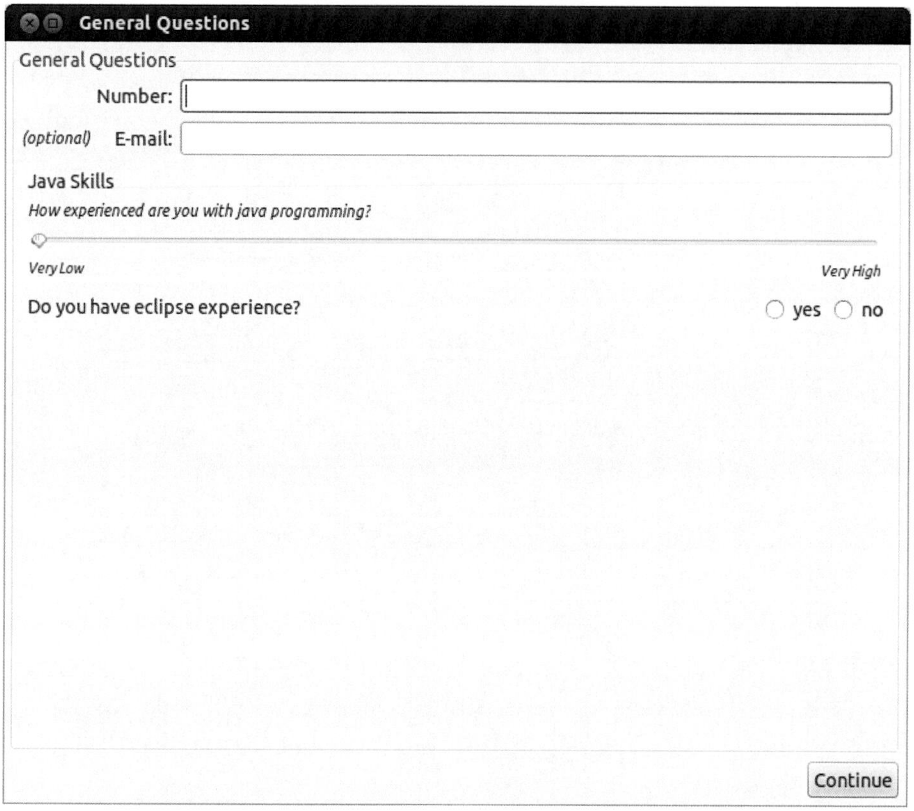

Figure A.3 – Screenshot of the pre-study questionnaire integrated into our Eclipse plugin used in the experiment to record user data and interactions.

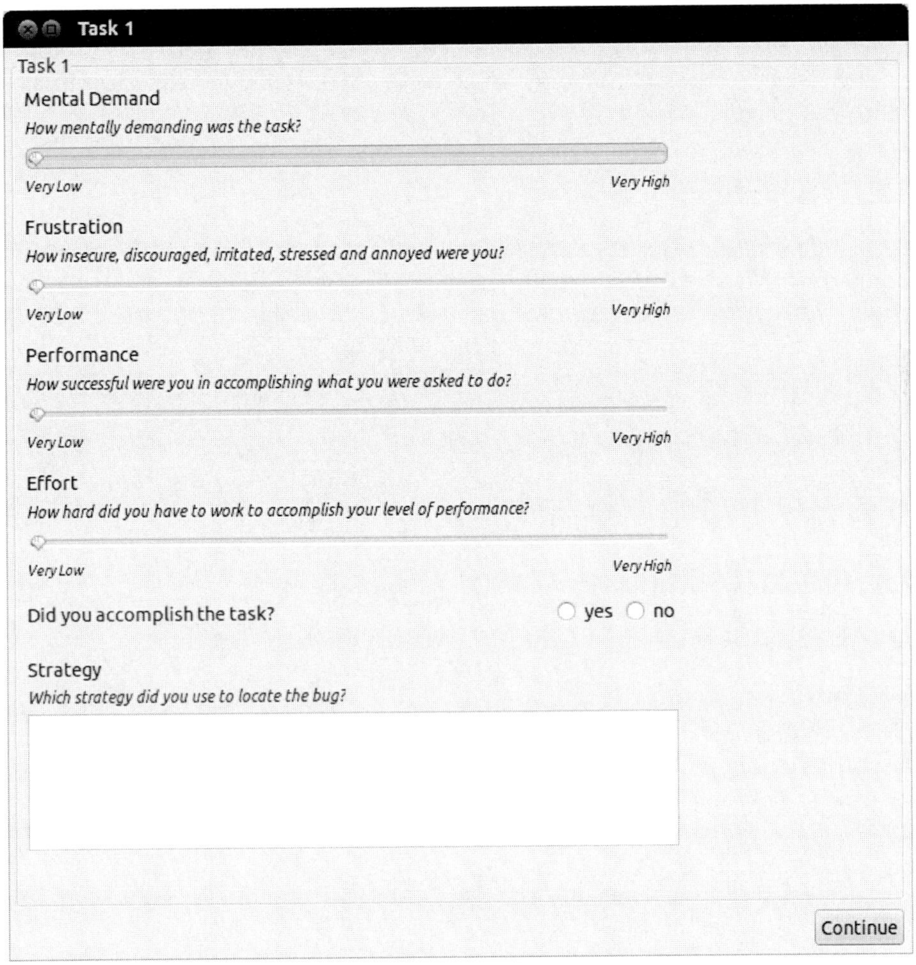

Figure A.4 – Screenshot of the post-study questionnaire integrated into our Eclipse plugin used in the experiment to record user data and interactions.

A.4   Introduction

A.4.1   Frozen Bubble

The program of the upcoming task is Frozen Bubble. Before the task starts you get the opportunity to familiarize with a fully functional version of the game. To start the game click the 'Run' button below. Note, that you need to select the game window with a click. To play the game use the arrow keys: "Up" to start a new game and to fire. The "Left" and "Right" arrows to navigate the launcher. Make some moves to learn how the game works. Please do not play longer than 3 minutes.

A.4.2   Pacman

The program of the next task is Pacman. Before the task starts you get the opportunity to familiarize with a fully functional version of the game. Please start Pacman using the "Run" button below and make some moves using the arrow keys to learn how the game works. Please do not play longer than 3 minutes.

A.5   Bug Report

The bug reports given for the two tasks.

A.5.1   Frozen Bubble

=== PLEASE READ CAREFULLY AND THOROUGHLY ===

Project 1 implements a simple tetris-like game in java. The implementation has a bug that is described in the following bug report. Your task is to fix the described bug in the code. You may execute the program as often as you wish to analyze the problem and to verify, that it has been solved. Please do not make any other changes to the code. When you are done with the task, press 'next'.

Bug Report #421:

There are eight differently colored bubbles in the game. When a level starts, only gray bubbles appear on top. The launcher at the bottom will also fire only gray bubbles. Obviously not all available bubbles are loaded.

FrozenBubble is the main class. On startup all managers (from the manager package) are initialized: LifeManager, LevelManager etc. and the initial screen (SplashScreen from the screens package) is loaded. To start the game the user has to press a key. This event creates a new instance of the FrozenGame class.

Hints:

- The bug is located in the default package. You do not have to modify the packages lib, manager, or screens.

- The class BubbleSprite handles the top bubble area but does not load the bubbles itself. The constructor of the BubbleSprite class takes a BubbleManager as an argument and the BubbleManager takes the already loaded bubbles as an argument. So it may help to find out where the BubbleManager is initialized.

Click 'next' to start the task.

A.5.2   Pacman

=== PLEASE READ CAREFULLY AND THOROUGHLY ===

Project 2 implements a simple Pacman game in java. The implementation has a bug that is described in the following bug report. Your task is to fix the described bug in the code. You may execute the program as often as you wish to analyze the problem and to verify, that it has been solved. Please do not make any other changes to the code. When you are done with the task, press 'next'.

Bug Report #237:

For all game characters the movement up and left does not work correctly. Instead of moving up or left the characters move in the opposite direction in a flickering motion. Moving down and right works fine for all characters.

Hints:

- To solve the problem, it is important to know how the movement works. The game has an underlying map grid, which is used to decide in which direction a character can currently move and to check if two characters are at the same position. The cells are the same size as the characters and each character is assigned to one cell in the grid at a time. On every move, the characters move some pixels in one direction on the screen. When they have moved enough pixels to reach the next map cell, they will be assigned to that new cell.

- The bug is located in the package 'pacman.actors', you should only search for it there.

Click 'next' to start the task.

List of Figures

List of Tables

List of Examples

Glossary

AST

An AST (Abstract Syntax Tree) represents the syntactic structure of a program [96].

Bad Smell

Code and design anomalies that may have a negative effect on the comprehensibility and changeability of software systems.

CEG

→ *Clone Evolution Graph*

Clone Class

Similarity relation between two or more *fragments* [96].

Clone Evolution Graph

Comprehensive model for clone evolution. Nodes are the occurrences of cloned *fragments*. Different types of edges tell which fragments occur in the same version, are similar to each other, and are ancestors of each other [96].

Clone Pair

Similarity relation between exactly two *fragments* [96].

Consistent Change

A change applied to every fragment of a *clone class* or a *clone pair* in exactly the same way.

cyclone

Tool for multi-perspective analysis of clone evolution data [96].

Extensible

> A *clone class* or *clone pair* is extensible, if it is *left-extensible*, *right-extensible*, or both [96].

Fragment

> Contiguous section of source code (*token* sequence) with a well-defined location characterized by the file that contains the fragment, as well as a start and end position within that file [96].

Gapped Clone

> → *Type-3 Clone*

Generalized Suffix Tree

> Data structure for efficient extraction of identical subsequences within a set of sequences of elements [96].

Ghost Fragment

> Source code fragment that has previously been part of a clone class but is now without similar counterpart due to an inconsistent change [96].

iClones

> Implementation of *IDA* [96].

IDA

> Our Incremental Detection Algorithm which detects clones in multiple versions of a system and extracts information about their ancestry and change characteristics [96].

Inconsistent Change

> A change that is either applied to a subset of fragments of a *clone class* or a *clone pair* or to all but in a different way.

Late Propagation

> Resolves an earlier *inconsistent change* by propagating the change to all fragments of a *clone class* or *clone pair* [96].

Left-Extensible

> A set of *fragments* is left-extensible, if the tokens directly before the starting position of each fragment are equal [96].

LOC

LOC (Lines of Code) denotes a size metric for source code which counts all lines in a corresponding source file.

Maximal

A *clone class* or *clone pair* is maximal, if it is not *extensible* [96].

Near-Miss Clone

→ *Non-Identical Clone*

Non-Identical Clone

Collective term for clones with certain differences, namely *type-2 clones* and *type-3 clones* [96].

PDG

A PDG (Program Dependency Graph) represents control or data dependencies between different entities of a program [96].

Refactoring

Code restructuring to improve non-functional characteristics of a system—for example, maintainability [96].

Right-Extensible

A set of *fragments* is right-extensible, if the tokens directly after the end position of each fragment are equal [96].

ROD (Removal of Duplication)

A situation where one or more cloned source code fragments have been deliberately removed [96].

SLOC

SLOC (Source Lines of Code) denotes a size metric for source code which counts all source lines in a corresponding source file that contain at least a non-comment token.

Suffix Tree

Data structure for efficient extraction of identical subsequences within a sequence of elements [96].

System

Arbitrary collection of source code files within which clones should be detected [96].

Token

> Atomic syntactic element of a programming language—for example, a keyword, an operator, or an identifier [96].

Token Table

> Stores a sequence of tokens along with their properties [96].

Type-1 Clone

> *Clone class* or *clone pair* whose *fragments* have identical *token* sequences disregarding comments and whitespace [96].

Type-2 Clone

> *Clone class* or *clone pair* whose *fragments* have identical *token* sequences disregarding comments, whitespace, and the textual representation of identifiers and literals [96].

Type-3 Clone

> *Clone class* or *clone pair* whose *fragments* have similar token sequences but some tokens do not occur in all fragments (gaps) [96].

Version

> State of a *system*'s source code at a specific point in time [96].

Bibliography

[1] Eytan Adar and Miryung Kim. Softguess: Visualization and exploration of code clones in context. In *ICSE*, pages 762–766. IEEE Computer Society, 2007.

[2] Alfred V. Aho, Ravi Sethi, and Jeffrey D. Ullman. *Compilers: Principles, Techniques, and Tools*. Addison-Wesley Longman Publishing Co., Inc., Boston, MA, USA, 1986.

[3] Farouq Al-Omari, Iman Keivanloo, Chanchal K. Roy, and Juergen Rilling. Detecting clones across microsoft .net programming languages. In *WCRE*, pages 405–414. IEEE Computer Society, 2012.

[4] G. Antoniol, G. Casazza, M. Di Penta, and E. Merlo. Modeling clones evolution through time series. In *Proceedings of the International Conference on Software Maintenance*, pages 273–280. IEEE Computer Society, 2001.

[5] G. Antoniol, U. Villano, E. Merlo, and M. Di Penta. Analyzing cloning evolution in the linux kernel. *Information and Software Technology*, 44(13):755–765, 2002.

[6] Muhammad Asaduzzaman, Chanchal K. Roy, and Kevin A. Schneider. Viscad: Flexible code clone analysis support for nicad. In *Proceedings of the 5th International Workshop on Software Clones*, pages 77–78. ACM, 2011.

[7] L. Aversano, L. Cerulo, and M. Di Penta. How clones are maintained: An empirical study. In *Proceedings of the 11th European Conference on Software Maintenance and Reengineering*, pages 81–90. IEEE Computer Society, 2007.

[8] R. A. Baeza-Yates, A., and C. H. Perleberg. Fast and practical approximate string matching. *Information Processing Letters*, 59(1):21–27, 1996.

[9] Muhammad Yasin Bahtiyar. Clone: Syntax tree based clone detection for java. Master's thesis, Linnæus University, 2010.

[10] B. S. Baker. A program for identifying duplicated code. In *Computing Science and Statistics: Proceedings of the 24th Symposium on the Interface*, volume 24, pages 49–57, 1992.

[11] B. S. Baker. On finding duplication and near-duplication in large software systems. In *Proceedings of the 2nd Working Conference on Reverse Engineering*, pages 86–95. IEEE Computer Society, 1995.

[12] B. S. Baker. Parameterized pattern matching: Algorithms and applications. *Journal of Computer and System Sciences*, 52(1):28–42, 1996.

[13] B. S. Baker. Parameterized duplication in strings: Algorithms and an application to software maintenance. *SIAM Journal on Computing*, 26(5):1343–1362, 1997.

[14] T. Bakota, R. Ferenc, and T. Gyimóthy. Clone smells in software evolution. In *Proceedings of the 23rd International Conference on Software Maintenance*, pages 24–33. IEEE Computer Society, 2007.

[15] M. Balazinska, E. Merlo, M. Dagenais, B. Lagüe, and K. Kontogiannis. Measuring clone based reengineering opportunities. In *Proceedings of the 6th International Symposium on Software Metrics*, pages 292–304. IEEE Computer Society, 1999.

[16] M. Balazinska, E. Merlo, M. Dagenais, B. Lagüe, and K. Kontogiannis. Partial redesign of java software systems based on clone analysis. In *Proceedings of the 6th Working Conference on Reverse Engineering*, pages 326–336. IEEE Computer Society, 1999.

[17] M. Balazinska, E. Merlo, M. Dagenais, B. Lagüe, and K. Kontogiannis. Advanced clone-analysis to support object-oriented system refactoring. In *Proceedings of the 7th Working Conference on Reverse Engineering*, pages 98–107. IEEE Computer Society, 2000.

[18] M. Balint, R. Marinescu, and T. Gîrba. How developers copy. In *Proceedings of the 14th IEEE International Conference on Program Comprehension*, pages 56–68. IEEE Computer Society, 2006.

[19] Liliane Barbour, Foutse Khomh, and Ying Zou. Late propagation in software clones. In *ICSM*, pages 273–282. IEEE, 2011.

[20] H. A. Basit, S. J. Puglisi, W. F. Smyth, A. Turpin, and S. Jarzabek. Efficient token based clone detection with flexible tokenization. In *Proceedings of the 6th Joint Meeting on European Software Engineering Conference and the ACM SIGSOFT Symposium on the Foundations of Software Engineering*, pages 513–516. ACM, 2007.

[21] H. A. Basit, D. C. Rajapakse, and S. Jarzabek. Beyond templates: A study of clones in the stl and some general implications. In *Proceedings of the 27th International Conference on Software Engineering*, pages 451–459. ACM, 2005.

[22] Hamid Abdul Basit, Muhammad Hammad, and Rainer Koschke. A survey on goal-oriented visualization of clone data. In *Proceedings of the 3rd Working Conference on Software Visualization*, pages 46–55, 2015.

[23] Hamid Abdul Basit, Damith C. Rajapakse, and Stan Jarzabek. An empirical study on limits of clone unification using generics. In *SEKE*, pages 109–114, 2005.

[24] I. D. Baxter, A. Yahin, L. Moura, M. Sant'Anna, and L. Bier. Clone detection using abstract syntax trees. In *Proceedings of the International Conference on Software Maintenance*, pages 368–377. IEEE Computer Society, 1998.

[25] Saman Bazrafshan. Codefragment-suche in der programmhistorie. Diploma thesis, University of Bremen, 2010.

[26] Saman Bazrafshan. Evolution of near-miss clones. In *Proceedings of the 12th IEEE International Conference on Source Code Analysis and Manipulation*, pages 74–83. IEEE Computer Society Press, 2012.

[27] Saman Bazrafshan. Late propagation of type-3 clones. *Softwaretechnik-Trends*, 32(2):2 Seiten, 2012.

[28] Saman Bazrafshan. No clones, no trouble? In *Proceedings of the 7th International Workshop on Software Clones*, pages 37–38. IEEE Computer Society, 2013. Position Paper.

[29] Saman Bazrafshan and Rainer Koschke. An empirical study of clone removals. In *Proceedings of the 29th International Conference on Software Maintenance*, pages 50–59. IEEE Computer Society Press, 2013.

[30] Saman Bazrafshan and Rainer Koschke. Effect of clone information on the performance of developers fixing cloned bugs. In *Proceedings of the 14th Conference on Source Code Analysis and Manipulation*, pages 1–10. IEEE Computer Society Press, 2014.

[31] Saman Bazrafshan and Rainer Koschke. Clone removals and their return on investment. *Journal of Software Evolution and Process*, 2016.

[32] Saman Bazrafshan, Rainer Koschke, and Nils Göde. Approximate code search in program histories. In *Proceedings of the 18th Working Conference on Reverse Engineering*, pages 109–118. IEEE Computer Society Press, 2011.

[33] S. Bellon, R. Koschke, G. Antoniol, J. Krinke, and E. Merlo. Comparison and evaluation of clone detection tools. *IEEE Transactions on Software Engineering*, 33(9):577–591, 2007.

[34] M. A. Bender and M. Farach-Colton. The LCA problem revisited. In *Proceedings of the 4th Latin American Symposium on Theoretical Informatics*, pages 88–94, 2000.

[35] N. Berger. Klonmanagement: Klonerkennung für eingebettete systeme. Diploma thesis, University of Bremen, 2007.

[36] N. Bettenburg, W. Shang, W. Ibrahim, B. Adams, Y. Zou, and A. E. Hassan. An empirical study on inconsistent changes to code clones at release level. In *Proceedings of the 25th Working Conference on Reverse Engineering*, pages 85–94. IEEE Computer Society, 2009.

[37] Barry W. Boehm. *Software Engineering Economics*. Prentice Hall, Englewood Cliffs, NJ, 1981.

[38] Salah Bouktif, Giuliano Antoniol, Ettore Merlo, and Markus Neteler. A novel approach to optimize clone refactoring activity. In *GECCO*, pages 1885–1892. ACM, 2006.

[39] R. Brixtel, M. Fontaine, B. Lesner, C. Bazin, and R. Robbes. Language-independent clone detection applied to plagiarism detection. In *Proceedings of the 10th International Working Conference on Source Code Analysis and Manipulation*, pages 77–86. IEEE Computer Society, 2010.

[40] M. Bruntink. Aspect mining using clone class metrics. In *Proceedings of the 1st Workshop on Aspect Reverse Engineering*, 2004.

[41] M. Bruntink, A. van Deursen, T. Tourwé, and R. van Engelen. An evaluation of clone detection techniques for identifying crosscutting concerns. In *Proceedings of the 20th IEEE International Conference on Software Maintenance*, pages 200–209. IEEE Computer Society, 2004.

[42] M. Bruntink, A. van Deursen, R. van Engelen, and T. Tourwé. On the use of clone detection for identifying crosscutting concern code. *IEEE Transactions on Software Engineering*, 31(10):804–818, 2005.

[43] E. Burd and M. Munro. Investigating the maintenance implications of the replication of code. In *Proceedings of the International Conference on Software Maintenance*, pages 322–329. IEEE Computer Society, 1997.

[44] E. Buss, R. De Mori, W. M. Gentleman, J. Henshaw, H. Johnson, K. Kontogiannis, E. Merlo, H. A. Müller, J. Mylopoulos, S. Paul, A. Prakash, M. Stanley, S. R. Tilley, J. Troster, and K. Wong. Investigating reverse engineering technologies for the cas program understanding project. *IBM Syst. J.*, 33(3):477–500, 1994.

[45] Jeffrey Carver, Debarshi Chatterji, and Nicholas A. Kraft. On the need for human-based empirical validation of techniques and tools for code clone analysis. In James R. Cordy, Katsuro Inoue, Stanislaw Jarzabek, and Rainer Koschke, editors, *IWSC*, pages 61–62. ACM, 2011.

[46] W. I. Chang and J. Lampe. Theoretical and empirical comparisons of approximate string matching algorithms. In *Proceedings of the Third Symposium on Combinatorial Pattern Matching*, pages 175–184. Springer LNCS 644, 1992.

[47] W. I. Chang and E. L. Lawler. Approximate string matching in sublinear expected time. In *Proceedings of the 31st Annual Symposium on Foundations of Computer Science*, pages 116–124. IEEE Computer Society, 1990.

[48] W. I. Chang and E. L. Lawler. Sublinear approximate string matching and biological applications. *Algorithmica*, 12(4):327–344, 1994.

[49] Debarshi Chatterji, Jeffrey C. Carver, Nicholas A. Kraft, and Jan Harder. Effects of cloned code on software maintainability: A replicated developer study. In *Proceedings of the 20th Working Conference on Reverse Engineering*, pages 112–121, 2013.

[50] Debarshi Chatterji, Beverly Massengill, Jason Oslin, Jeffrey C. Carver, and Nicholas A. Kraft. Measuring the efficacy of code clone information: an empirical study. In *ESEM*, pages 20–29, 2011.

[51] W. Chen, B. Li, and R. Gupta. Code compaction of matching single-entry multiple-exit regions. In *Proceedings of the 10th International Conference on Static Analysis*, pages 401–417. Springer-Verlag, 2003.

[52] Yaowen Chen, Iman Keivanloo, and Chanchal Kumar Roy. Near-miss software clones in open source games: An empirical study. In *27th Canadian Conference on Electrical and Computer Engineering*, pages 1–7, 2014.

[53] DV. Cicchetti. Guidelines, criteria, and rules of thumb for evaluating normed and standardized assessment instruments in psychology. *Psychological Assessment*, 6(4):284–290, 1994.

[54] A. Ciu and D. Hirtle. Beyond clone detection. Technical report, University at Waterloo, Ontario, Canada, 2007.

[55] J. R. Cordy. Comprehending reality – practical barriers to industrial adoption of software maintenance automation. In *Proceedings of the 11th IEEE International Workshop on Program Comprehension*, pages 196–205. IEEE Computer Society, 2003.

[56] J. R. Cordy. The TXL source transformation language. *Science of Computer Programming*, 61(3):190–210, 2006.

[57] J. R. Cordy, T. R. Dean, and N. Synytskyy. Practical language-independent detection of near-miss clones. In *Proceedings of the Conference of the Centre for Advanced Studies on Collaborative Research*, pages 1–12. IBM Press, 2004.

[58] James R. Cordy. Live scatterplots. In *IWSC*, pages 79–80. ACM, 2011.

[59] T. Cormen, C. Leiserson, and R. Rivest. *Introduction to Algorithms*. MIT Press and McGraw Hill, Cambridge, MA, USA, 1992.

[60] M. Dagenais, E. Merlo, B. Laguë, and D. Proulx. Clones occurrence in large object oriented software packages. In *Proceedings of the Conference of the Centre for Advanced Studies on Collaborative Research*. IBM Press, 1998.

[61] Mayur Datar, Nicole Immorlica, Piotr Indyk, and Vahab S. Mirrokni. Locality-sensitive hashing scheme based on p-stable distributions. In *Proceedings of the Twentieth Annual Symposium on Computational Geometry*, pages 253–262. ACM, 2004.

[62] N. Davey, P. Barson, S. Field, R. Frank, and S. Tansley. The development of a software clone detector. *International Journal of Applied Software Technology*, 1995.

[63] I. J. Davis and M. W. Godfrey. Clone detection by exploiting assembler. In *Proceedings of the 4th International Workshop on Software Clones*, pages 77–78. ACM, 2010.

[64] I. J. Davis and M. W. Godfrey. From whence it came: Detecting source code clones by analyzing assembler. In *Proceedings of the 17th Working Conference on Reverse Engineering*, pages 242–246. IEEE Computer Society, 2010.

[65] M. de Wit, A. Zaidman, and A. van Deursen. Managing code clones using dynamic change tracking and resolution. In *Proceedings of the International Conference on Software Maintenance*, pages 169–178. IEEE Computer Society, 2009.

[66] Saumya K. Debray, W. Evans, R. Muth, and B. de Sutter. Compiler techniques for code compaction. *ACM Transactions on Programming Languages and Systems*, 22(2):378–415, 2000.

[67] F. Deissenboeck, B. Hummel, E. Juergens, M. Pfaehler, and B. Schaetz. Model clone detection in practice. In *Proceedings of the 4th International Workshop on Software Clones*, pages 57–64. ACM, 2010.

[68] F. Deissenboeck, B. Hummel, E. Juergens, B. Schätz, S. Wagner, Jean-François Girard, and Stefan Teuchert. Clone detection in automotive model-based development. In *Proceedings of the 30th International Conference on Software Engineering*, pages 603–612. ACM, 2008.

[69] G. A. Di Lucca, M. Di Penta, and A. R. Fasolino. An approach to identify duplicated web pages. In *Proceedings of the 26th International Computer Software and Applications Conference on Prolonging Software Life: Development and Redevelopment*, pages 481–486. IEEE Computer Society, 2002.

[70] C. Domann, E. Juergens, and J. Streit. The curse of copy&paste—cloning in requirements specifications. In *Proceedings of the 3rd International Symposium on Empirical Software Engineering and Measurement*, pages 443–446. IEEE Computer Society, 2009.

[71] E. Duala-Ekoko and M. P. Robillard. Tracking code clones in evolving software. In *Proceedings of the 29th International Conference on Software Engineering*, pages 158–167. IEEE Computer Society, 2007.

[72] E. Duala-Ekoko and M. P. Robillard. Clonetracker: Tool support for code clone management. In *Proceedings of the 30th International Conference on Software Engineering*, pages 843–846. ACM, 2008.

[73] E. Duala-Ekoko and M. P. Robillard. Clone region descriptors: Representing and tracking duplication in source code. *ACM Transactions on Software Engineering and Methodology*, 20(1):1–31, 2010.

[74] Yael Dubinsky, Julia Rubin, Thorsten Berger, Slawomir Duszynski, Martin Becker, and Krzysztof Czarnecki. An exploratory study of cloning in industrial software product lines. In *Proceedings of the 2013 17th European Conference on Software Maintenance and Reengineering*, pages 25–34. IEEE Computer Society, 2013.

[75] S. Ducasse, M. Rieger, and S. Demeyer. A language independent approach for detecting duplicated code. In *Proceedings of the International Conference on Software Maintenance*, pages 109–118. IEEE Computer Society, 1999.

[76] H. Ebbinghaus, H.A. Ruger, and C.E. Bussenius. *Memory: A Contribution to Experimental Psychology*. Columbia University. Teachers College. Educational reprints. Teachers College, Columbia University, 1913.

[77] R. Falke, P. Frenzel, and R. Koschke. Empirical evaluation of clone detection using syntax suffix trees. *Empirical Software Engineering*, 13(6):601–643, 2008.

[78] R. Fanta and V. Rajlich. Removing clones from the code. *Journal of Software Maintenance*, 11(4):223–243, 1999.

[79] P. Ferragina, R. Grossi, and M. Montagero. A note on updating suffix tree labels. In *Proceedings of the 3rd Italian Conference on Algorithms and Complexity*, pages 181–192. Springer-Verlag, 1997.

[80] Jeanne Ferrante, Karl J. Ottenstein, and Joe D. Warren. The program dependence graph and its use in optimization. *ACM Trans. Program. Lang. Syst.*, 9(3):319–349, 1987.

[81] M. Fowler. *Refactoring: Improving the Design of Existing Code*. Addison-Wesley, Boston, MA, USA, 1999.

[82] Y. Fukushima, R. Kula, S. Kawaguchi, K. Fushida, M. Nagura, and H. Iida. Code Clone Graph Metrics for Detecting Diffused Code Clones. In *Software Engineering Conference, 2009. APSEC '09. Asia-Pacific*, pages 373–380, 2009.

[83] R. Geiger, B. Fluri, H. Gall, and M. Pinzger. Relation of code clones and change couplings. *Lecture Notes in Computer Science*, 3922:411–425, 2006.

[84] Simon Giesecke. Generic modelling of code clones. In *Duplication, Redundancy, and Similarity in Software*, number 06301 in Dagstuhl Seminar Proceedings. Internationales Begegnungs- und Forschungszentrum für Informatik (IBFI), Schloss Dagstuhl, Germany, 2007.

[85] David Gitchell and Nicholas Tran. Sim: A utility for detecting similarity in computer programs. *SIGCSE Bull.*, 31(1):266–270, 1999.

[86] N. Göde. Incremental clone detection. Diploma thesis, University of Bremen, 2008.

[87] N. Göde. Evolution of type-1 clones. In *Proceedings of the 9th International Working Conference on Source Code Analysis and Manipulation*, pages 77–86. IEEE Computer Society, 2009.

[88] N. Göde. Mapping code clones using incremental clone detection. *Softwaretechnik-Trends*, 29(2):28–29, 2009.

[89] N. Göde. Clone removal: Fact or fiction? In *Proceedings of the 4th International Workshop on Software Clones*, pages 33–40. ACM, 2010.

[90] N. Göde and J. Harder. Clone stability. In *Proceedings of the 15th European Conference on Software Maintenance and Reengineering*, pages 65–74. IEEE Computer Society, 2011.

[91] N. Göde and J. Harder. Oops!... I changed it again. In *Proceedings of the 5th International Workshop on Software Clones*, 2011. Accepted for publication.

[92] N. Göde and R. Koschke. Incremental clone detection. In *Proceedings of the 13th European Conference on Software Maintenance and Reengineering*, pages 219–228. IEEE Computer Society, 2009.

[93] N. Göde and R. Koschke. Studying clone evolution using incremental clone detection. *Journal of Software Maintenance and Evolution: Research and Practice*, 2010. Published online.

[94] N. Göde and R. Koschke. Frequency and risks of changes to clones. In *Proceedings of the 33rd International Conference on Software Engineering*, 2011. Accepted for puplication.

[95] N. Göde and M. Rausch. Clone evolution revisited. *Softwaretechnik-Trends*, 30(2):60–61, 2010.

[96] Nils Göde. *Clone Evolution*. Dissertation (University of Bremen). Logos-Verlag, 2011.

[97] Nils Göde, Benjamin Hummel, and Elmar Jürgens. What clone coverage can tell. In *International Workshop of Software Clones*, pages 90–91. IEEE, 2012.

[98] M. W. Godfrey and Q. Tu. Growth, evolution, and structural change in open source software. In *Proceedings of the 4th International Workshop on Principles of Software Evolution*, pages 103–106. ACM, 2001.

[99] Todd L. Graves, Alan F. Karr, J. S. Marron, and Harvey Siy. Predicting fault incidence using software change history. *IEEE Trans. Softw. Eng.*, 26(7):653–661, 2000.

[100] Kevin Greenan. Method-level code clone detection on transformed abstract syntax trees using sequence matching algorithms. Technical report, University of California, 2005.

[101] Dan Gusfield. *Algorithms on Strings, Trees and Sequences: Computer Science and Computational Biology.* Cambridge University Press, New York, NY, USA, 2008.

[102] J. Harder and N. Göde. Quo vadis, clone management? In *Proceedings of the 4th International Workshop on Software Clones*, pages 85–86. ACM, 2010.

[103] J. Harder and N. Göde. Efficiently handling clone data: RCF and cyclone. In *Proceedings of the 5th International Workshop on Software Clones*, 2011. Accepted for publication.

[104] J. Harder and N. Göde. Cloned code: stable code. *Journal of Software: Evolution and Process*, 2012. Published online. DOI: 10.1002/smr.1551.

[105] Jan Harder and Rebecca Tiarks. A controlled experiment on software clones. In *ICPC*, pages 219–228. IEEE Press, 2012.

[106] R. Heller, Y. Heller, and M. Gorfine. A consistent multivariate test of association based on ranks of distances. *Biometrika*, 100(2):503–510, 2013.

[107] Felienne Hermans, Ben Sedee, Martin Pinzger, and Arie van Deursen. Data clone detection and visualization in spreadsheets. In *Proceedings of the 2013 International Conference on Software Engineering*, pages 292–301. IEEE Press, 2013.

[108] Y. Higo, T. Kamiya, S. Kusumoto, and K. Inoue. Aries: Refactoring support environment based on code clone analysis. In *Proceedings of the 8th International Conference on Software Engineering and Applications*, pages 222–229, 2004.

[109] Y. Higo, T. Kamiya, S. Kusumoto, and K. Inoue. Refactoring support based on code clone analysis. *Lecture Notes in Computer Science*, 3009:220–233, 2004.

[110] Yoshiki Higo and Shinji Kusumoto. Enhancing quality of code clone detection with program dependency graph. In *Proceedings of the 16th Working Conference on Reverse Engineering*, pages 315–316, 2009.

[111] Yoshiki Higo, Hiroaki Murakami, and Shinji Kusumoto. Revisiting capabilities of pdg-based clone detection. Technical report, Graduate School of Information Science and Techology, Osaka University, 11 2013.

[112] Yoshiki Higo, Yasushi Ueda, Toshihro Kamiya, Shinji Kusumoto, and Katsuro Inoue. On software maintenance process improvement based on code clone analysis. In *Proc. Int'l Conf. Product Focused Software Process Improvement*, volume 2559 of *Lecture Notes in Computer Science*, pages 185–197. Springer-Verlag, 2002.

[113] D. Hofmann. Entwurf und implementierung der klonerkennung mittels suffix-arrays. Diploma thesis, University of Stuttgart and University of Bremen, 2010.

[114] W. Hordijk, M. L. Ponisio, and R. Wieringa. Harmfulness of code duplication – a structured review of the evidence. In *Proceedings of the 13th International Conference on Evaluation and Assessment in Software Engineering*. IEEE Computer Society, 2009.

[115] K. Hotta, Y. Sano, Y. Higo, and S. Kusumoto. Is duplicate code more frequently modified than non-duplicate code in software evolution?: An empirical study on open source software. In *Proceedings of the Joint Workshop on Software Evolution and International Workshop on Principles of Software Evolution*, pages 73–82. ACM, 2010.

[116] D. Hou, P. Jablonski, and F. Jacob. CnP: Towards an environment for the proactive management of copy-and-paste programming. In *Proceedings of the 17th International Conference on Program Comprehension*, pages 238–242. IEEE Computer Society, 2009.

[117] B. Hummel, E. Juergens, L. Heinemann, and M. Conradt. Index-based code clone detection: Incremental, distributed, scalable. In *Proceedings of the 26th International Conference on Software Maintenance*. IEEE Computer Society, 2010.

[118] P. Jablonski and D. Hou. CReN: A tool for tracking copy-and-paste code clones and renaming identifiers consistently in the ide. In *Proceedings of the OOPSLA Workshop on Eclipse Technology Exchange*, pages 16–20. ACM, 2007.

[119] F. Jacob, D. Hou, and P. Jablonski. Actively comparing clones inside the code editor. In *Proceedings of the 4th International Workshop on Software Clones*, pages 9–16. ACM, 2010.

[120] S. Jarzabek and S. Li. Unifying clones with a generative programming technique: a case study. *Journal of Software Maintenance and Evolution: Research and Practice*, 18(4):267–292, 2006.

[121] L. Jiang, G. Misherghi, Z. Su, and S. Glondu. DECKARD: Scalable and accurate tree-based detection of code clones. In *Proceedings of the 29th International Conference on Software Engineering*, pages 96–105. IEEE Computer Society, 2007.

[122] Zhen Ming Jiang and Ahmed E. Hassan. A framework for studying clones in large software systems. In *Proceedings of the Seventh IEEE International Working Conference on Source Code Analysis and Manipulation*, pages 203–212. IEEE Computer Society, 2007.

[123] J. H. Johnson. Identifying redundancy in source code using fingerprints. In *Proceedings of the Conference of the Centre for Advanced Studies on Collaborative Research*, pages 171–183. IBM Press, 1993.

[124] J. H. Johnson. Visualizing textual redundancy in legacy source. In *Proceedings of the Conference of the Centre for Advanced Studies on Collaborative Research*, pages 32–41. IBM, 1994.

[125] J. Howard Johnson. Navigating the textual redundancy web in legacy source. In *CASCON*, page 16. IBM, 1996.

[126] Landis JR. and Koch GG. The measurement of observer agreement for categorical data. *Biometrics*, 33(1):159–174, 1977.

[127] E. Juergens and F. Deissenboeck. How much is a clone? In *Proceedings of the 4th International Workshop on Software Quality and Maintainability*, 2010.

[128] E. Juergens, F. Deissenboeck, M. Feilkas, B. Hummel, B. Schaetz, S. Wagner, Christoph Domann, and Jonathan Streit. Can clone detection support quality assessments of requirements specifications? In *Proceedings of the 32nd International Conference on Software Engineering*, pages 79–88. ACM, 2010.

[129] E. Juergens, F. Deissenboeck, and B. Hummel. Clonedetective – a workbench for clone detection research. In *Proceedings of the 31st International Conference on Software Engineering*, pages 603–606. IEEE Computer Society, 2009.

[130] E. Juergens, F. Deissenboeck, B. Hummel, and S. Wagner. Do code clones matter? In *Proceedings of the 31st International Conference on Software Engineering*, pages 485–495. IEEE Computer Society, 2009.

[131] Elmar Juergens. Research in cloning beyond code: A first roadmap. In *Proceedings of the 5th International Workshop on Software Clones*, pages 67–68. ACM, 2011.

[132] N. Juillerat and B. Hirsbrunner. An algorithm for detecting and removing clones in java code. In *Proceedings of the 3rd International Workshop on Software Evolution through Transformations*, pages 63–74, 2006.

[133] Krippendorff K. *Content analysis: An introduction to its methodology.* Sage Publications, Beverly Hills, CA, 1980.

[134] T. Kamiya, S. Kusumoto, and K. Inoue. CCFinder: A multilinguistic token-based code clone detection system for large scale source code. *IEEE Transactions on Software Engineering*, 28(7):654–670, 2002.

[135] C. J. Kapser, P. Anderson, M. Godfrey, R. Koschke, M. Rieger, F. van Rysselberghe, and P. Weißgerber. Subjectivity in clone judgment: Can we ever agree? In R. Koschke, E. Merlo, and A. Walenstein, editors, *Duplication, Redundancy, and Similarity in Software*, number 06301 in Dagstuhl Seminar Proceedings, Dagstuhl, Germany, 2007. Internationales Begegnungs- und Forschungszentrum für Informatik (IBFI), Schloss Dagstuhl, Germany.

[136] C. J. Kapser and M. W. Godfrey. Toward a taxonomy of clones in source code: A case study. In *Proceedings of the Workshop on Evolution of Large-scale Industrial Software Applications*, pages 67–78, 2003.

[137] C. J. Kapser and M. W. Godfrey. Aiding comprehension of cloning through categorization. In *Proceedings of the 7th International Workshop on Principles of Software Evolution*, pages 85–94. IEEE Computer Society, 2004.

[138] C. J. Kapser and M. W. Godfrey. Improved tool support for the investigation of duplication in software. In *Proceedings of the 21st International Conference on Software Maintenance*, pages 305–314. IEEE Computer Society, 2005.

[139] C. J. Kapser and M. W. Godfrey. "Cloning considered harmful" considered harmful. In *Proceedings of the 13th Working Conference on Reverse Engineering*, pages 19–28. IEEE Computer Society, 2006.

[140] C. J. Kapser and M. W. Godfrey. Supporting the analysis of clones in software systems: a case study. *Journal of Software Maintenance and Evolution: Research and Practice*, 18(2):61–82, 2006.

[141] Richard M. Karp. Combinatorics, complexity, and randomness. *Commun. ACM*, 29(2):98–109, 1986.

[142] Richard M. Karp and Michael O. Rabin. Efficient randomized pattern-matching algorithms. *IBM J. Res. Dev.*, 31(2):249–260, 1987.

[143] S. Kawaguchi, T. Yamashina, H. Uwano, K. Fushida, Y. Kamei, M. Nagura, and Hajimu Iida. SHINOBI: A tool for automatic code clone detection in the ide. In *Proceedings of the 16th Working Conference on Reverse Engineering*, pages 313–314. IEEE Computer Society, 2009.

[144] Iman Keivanloo, Juergen Rilling, and Philippe Charland. Internet-scale real-time code clone search via multi-level indexing. In *WCRE*, pages 23–27. IEEE Computer Society, 2011.

[145] Iman Keivanloo, Chanchal Kumar Roy, and Juergen Rilling. Sebyte: Scalable clone and similarity search for bytecode. *Sci. Comput. Program.*, 95:426–444, 2014.

[146] M. G. Kendall and J. D. Gibbons. *Rank Correlation Methods*. Griffin, London, 5th ed edition, 1990.

[147] Joshua Kerievsky. *Refactoring to Patterns*. Pearson Higher Education, 2004.

[148] M. Kim, L. Bergman, T. Lau, and D. Notkin. An ethnographic study of copy and paste programming practices in OOPL. In *Proceedings of the International Symposium on Empirical Software Engineering*, pages 83–92. IEEE Computer Society, 2004.

[149] M. Kim and D. Notkin. Using a clone genealogy extractor for understanding and supporting evolution of code clones. *SIGSOFT Software Engineering Notes*, 30(4):1–5, 2005.

[150] M. Kim, V. Sazawal, D. Notkin, and G. C. Murphy. An empirical study of code
      clone genealogies. In *Proceedings of the Joint 10th European Software Engineering
      Conference and the 13th ACM SIGSOFT Symposium on the Foundations of
      Software Engineering*, pages 187–196. ACM, 2005.

[151] R. Komondoor and S. Horwitz. Semantics-preserving procedure extraction. In
      *Proceedings of the 27th ACM SIGPLAN-SIGACT Symposium on Principles of
      Programming Languages*, pages 155–169. ACM, 2000.

[152] R. Komondoor and S. Horwitz. Effective, automatic procedure extraction.
      In *Proceedings of the 11th IEEE International Workshop on Program
      Comprehension*, pages 33–42. IEEE Computer Society, 2003.

[153] R. V. Komondoor. *Automated duplicated code detection and procedure extraction*.
      PhD thesis, The University of Wisconsin, Madison, 2003.

[154] R. V. Komondoor and S. Horwitz. Using slicing to identify duplication in source
      code. In *Proceedings of the 8th International Symposium on Static Analysis*, pages
      40–56. Springer-Verlag, 2001.

[155] K. Kontogiannis. Evaluation experiments on the detection of programming
      patterns using software metrics. In *Proceedings of the 4th Working Conference on
      Reverse Engineering*, pages 44–54. IEEE Computer Society, 1997.

[156] K. Kontogiannis, R. Demori, E. Merlo, M. Galler, and M. Bernstein. Pattern
      matching for clone and concept detection. *Automated Software Engineering*, 3(1–
      2):77–108, 1996.

[157] R. Koschke. Survey of research on software clones. In R. Koschke, E. Merlo,
      and A. Walenstein, editors, *Duplication, Redundancy, and Similarity in Software*,
      number 06301 in Dagstuhl Seminar Proceedings, Dagstuhl, Germany, 2007.
      Internationales Begegnungs- und Forschungszentrum für Informatik (IBFI),
      Schloss Dagstuhl, Germany.

[158] R. Koschke. Frontiers of software clone management. In *Proceedings of Frontiers
      of Software Maintenance*, pages 119–128. IEEE Computer Society, 2008.

[159] R. Koschke. Software-clone rates in open-source programs written in c or c++.
      In *Proceedings of the 10th International Workshop on Software Clones*. IEEE
      Computer Society, 2016. accepted for publication.

[160] R. Koschke, R. Falke, and P. Frenzel. Clone detection using abstract syntax suffix
      trees. In *Proceedings of the 13th Working Conference on Reverse Engineering*,
      pages 253–262. IEEE Computer Society, 2006.

[161] Rainer Koschke. Large-scale inter-system clone detection using suffix trees and
      hashing. *Journal of Software: Evolution and Process*, 26(8):747–769, 2014.

[162] Rainer Koschke and Saman Bazrafshan. A large-scale statistical analysis of software clone rates and localization in open-source programs written in c, c++, c#, or java. *Transactions on Software Engineering*, 2016.

[163] J. Krinke. Identifying similar code with program dependence graphs. In *Proceedings of the 8th Working Conference on Reverse Engineering*, pages 301–309. IEEE Computer Society, 2001.

[164] J. Krinke. A study of consistent and inconsistent changes to code clones. In *Proceedings of the 14th Working Conference on Reverse Engineering*, pages 170–178. IEEE Computer Society, 2007.

[165] J. Krinke. Is cloned code more stable than non-cloned code? In *Proceedings of the 8th International Working Conference on Source Code Analysis and Manipulation*, pages 57–66. IEEE Computer Society, 2008.

[166] Giri Panamoottil Krishnan and Nikolaos Tsantalis. Refactoring clones: An optimization problem. In *Proceedings of the 29th International Conference on Software Maintenance*, pages 360–363, 2013.

[167] Giri Panamoottil Krishnan and Nikolaos Tsantalis. Unification and refactoring of clones. In *Proceedings of the 22nd Conference on Software Maintenance, Reengineering, and Reverse Engineering*, pages 104–113, 2014.

[168] B. Laguë, D. Proulx, J. Mayrand, E. Merlo, and J. Hudepohl. Assessing the benefits of incorporating function clone detection in a development process. In *Proceedings of the International Conference on Software Maintenance*, pages 314–321. IEEE Computer Society, 1997.

[169] G. Landau and U. Vishkin. Introducing efficient parallelism into approximate string matching and a new serial algorithm. In *Proceedings of ACM Symposium on the Theory of Computing*, pages 220–230, Berkeley, CA, USA, 1986.

[170] G. M. Landau, U. Vishkin, and R. Nussinov. An efficient string matching algorithm with k differences for nucleotide and amino acid sequences. *Nucleic Acids Research*, 14(1):31–46, 1986.

[171] F. Lanubile and T. Mallardo. Finding function clones in web applications. In *Proceedings of the 7th European Conference on Software Maintenance and Reengineering*, pages 379–386. IEEE Computer Society, 2003.

[172] T. D. LaToza, G. Venolia, and R. DeLine. Maintaining mental models: a study of developer work habits. In *Proceedings of the 28th International Conference on Software Engineering*, pages 492–501. ACM, 2006.

[173] M. Lee, J. Roh, S. Hwang, and S. Kim. Instant code clone search. In *Proceedings of the 18th International Symposium on Foundations of Software Engineering*, pages 167–176. ACM, 2010.

[174] Sukhee Lee, Gigon Bae, Heung Seok Chae, Doo-Hwan Bae, and Yong Rae Kwon. Automated scheduling for clone-based refactoring using a competent GA. *Softw., Pract. Exper.*, 41(5):521–550, 2011.

[175] M. M. Lehman and L. A. Belady, editors. *Program Evolution: Processes of Software Change*. Academic Press Professional, Inc., San Diego, CA, USA, 1985.

[176] Meir M. Lehman, Dewayne E. Perry, and Juan F. Ramil. On evidence supporting the feast hypothesis and the laws of software evolution. In *Proc. IEEE Symp. Software Metrics*. IEEE Computer Society Press, 1998.

[177] Antonio Menezes Leitao. Detection of redundant code using R2D2. In *Detection of redundant code using r2d2*, pages 183–192. IEEE Press, 2003.

[178] V. I. Levenstein. Binary codes capable of correcting deletions insertions and reversals. *Sov. Phys. Dokl.*, 10:707–710, 1966.

[179] Z. Li, S. Lu, S. Myagmar, and Y. Zhou. CP-Miner: A tool for finding copy-paste and related bugs in operating system code. In *Proceedings of the 6th Conference on Opearting Systems Design & Implementation*, pages 20–33. USENIX Association, 2004.

[180] Z. Li, S. Lu, S. Myagmar, and Y. Zhou. CP-Miner: Finding copy-paste and related bugs in large-scale software code. *IEEE Transactions on Software Engineering*, 32(3):176–192, 2006.

[181] Zhenmin Li, Shan Lu, Suvda Myagmar, and Yuanyuan Zhou. CP-Miner: Finding copy-paste and related bugs in large-scale software code. *IEEE Transactions on Software Engineering*, 32(3):176–192, 2006.

[182] C. Liu, C. Chen, J. Han, and P. S. Yu. GPLAG: Detection of software plagiarism by program dependence graph analysis. In *Proceedings of the 12th ACM SIGKDD International Conference on Knowledge Discovery and Data Mining*, pages 872–881. ACM, 2006.

[183] H. Liu, Z. Ma, L. Zhang, and W. Shao. Detecting duplications in sequence diagrams based on suffix trees. In *Proceedings of the 13th Asia Pacific Software Engineering Conference*, pages 269–276. IEEE Computer Society, 2006.

[184] S. Livieri, Y. Higo, M. Matsushita, and K. Inoue. Analysis of the linux kernel evolution using code clone coverage. In *Proceedings of the 4th International Workshop on Mining Software Repositories*, pages 22–25. IEEE Computer Society, 2007.

[185] S. Livieri, Y. Higo, M. Matushita, and K. Inoue. Very-large scale code clone analysis and visualization of open source programs using distributed CCFinder: D-CCFinder. In *Proceedings of the 29th International Conference on Software Engineering*, pages 106–115. IEEE Computer Society, 2007.

[186] A. Lozano and M. Wermelinger. Assessing the effect of clones on changeability. In *Proceedings of the 24th International Conference on Software Maintenance*, pages 227–236. IEEE Computer Society, 2008.

[187] A. Lozano, M. Wermelinger, and B. Nuseibeh. Evaluating the harmfulness of cloning: A change based experiment. In *Proceedings of the 4th International Workshop on Mining Software Repositories*, pages 18–21. IEEE Computer Society, 2007.

[188] Angela Lozano, Fehmi Jaafar, Kim Mens, and Yann-Gaël Guéhéneuc. Clones and macro co-changes. *Electronic Communications of the EASST*, 63, 2014.

[189] U. Manber. Finding similar files in a large file system. In *Proceedings of the USENIX Winter 1994 Technical Conference*, pages 1–10, 1994.

[190] A. Marcus and J. I. Maletic. Identification of high-level concept clones in source code. In *Proceedings of the 16th IEEE International Conference on Automated Software Engineering*, pages 107–114. IEEE Computer Society, 2001.

[191] Lionel Marks, Ying Zou, and Iman Keivanloo. An empirical study of the factors affecting co-change frequency of cloned code. In *Proceedings of the 2013 Conference of the Center for Advanced Studies on Collaborative Research*, pages 161–175. IBM Corp., 2013.

[192] R. C. Martin. *Clean Code: A Handbook for Agile Software Craftmanship*. Prentice Hall, 2008.

[193] J. Mayrand, C. Leblanc, and E. Merlo. Experiment on the automatic detection of function clones in a software system using metrics. In *Proceedings of the International Conference on Software Maintenance*, pages 244–253. IEEE Computer Society, 1996.

[194] T.J. McCabe. A complexity measure. *Software Engineering, IEEE Transactions on*, SE-2(4):308–320, 1976.

[195] E. McCreight. A space-economical suffix tree construction algorithm. *Journal of the ACM*, 32(2):262–272, 1976.

[196] Thilo Mende, Felix Beckwermert, Rainer Koschke, and Gerald Meier. Supporting the grow-and-prune model in software product lines evolution using clone detection. In *European Conference on Software Maintenance and Reengineering*, pages 163–172. IEEE Computer Society Press, 2008.

[197] Thilo Mende, Rainer Koschke, and Felix Beckwermert. An evaluation of code similarity identification for the grow-and-prune model. *Journal on Software Maintenance and Evolution*, 21(2):143 – 169, March–April 2009.

[198] E. Merlo, G. Antoniol, M. Di Penta, and V. F. Rollo. Linear complexity object-oriented similarity for clone detection and software evolution analyses. In *Proceedings of the 20th International Conference on Software Maintenance*, pages 412–416. IEEE Computer Society, 2004.

[199] E. Merlo, M. Dagenais, P. Bachand, J. S. Sormani, S. Gradara, and G. Antoniol. Investigating large software system evolution: The linux kernel. In *Proceedings of the 26th International Computer Software and Applications Conference on Prolonging Software Life: Development and Redevelopment*, pages 421–426. IEEE Computer Society, 2002.

[200] E. Merlo and T. Lavoie. Computing structural types of clone syntactic blocks. In *Proceedings of the 16th Working Conference on Reverse Engineering*, pages 274–278. IEEE Computer Society, 2009.

[201] M. Mondal, C. K. Roy, and K. A. Schneider. Dispersion of changes in cloned and non-cloned code. In *Proceedings of the 6th International Workshop on Software Clones*, pages 29–35. IEEE, 2012.

[202] Manishankar Mondal, Chanchal K. Roy, and Kevin A. Schneider. Insight into a method co-change pattern to identify highly coupled methods: An empirical study. In *Proceedings of the 21st International Conference on Program Comprehension*, pages 103–112, 2013.

[203] Manishankar Mondal, Chanchal K. Roy, and Kevin A. Schneider. Automatic ranking of clones for refactoring through mining association rules. In *2014 Software Evolution Week - Conference on Software Maintenance, Reengineering, and Reverse Engineering*, pages 114–123, 2014.

[204] Manishankar Mondal, Chanchal K. Roy, and Kevin A. Schneider. Prediction and ranking of co-change candidates for clones. In *Proceedings of the 11th Working Conference on Mining Software Repositories*, pages 32–41. ACM, 2014.

[205] A. Monden, D. Nakae, T. Kamiya, S. Sato, and K. Matsumoto. Software quality analysis by code clones in industrial legacy software. In *Proceedings of the 8th International Symposium on Software Metrics*, page 87. IEEE Computer Society, 2002.

[206] Leon Moonen. Generating robust parsers using island grammars. In *Proceedings of the Eighth Working Conference on Reverse Engineering (WCRE'01)*, WCRE '01, pages 13–22. IEEE Computer Society, 2001.

[207] Hsiao Hui Mui, Andy Zaidman, and Martin Pinzger. Studying late propagations in code clone evolution using software repository mining. In *Proceedings of the 8th International Workshop on Software Clones*, 2014.

[208] E. W. Myers. An O(ND) difference algorithm and its variations. *Algorithmica*, 1(2):251–266, 1986.

[209] E. W. Myers. A sublinear algorithm for approximate keyword searching. *Algorithmica*, 12(4):345–374, 1994.

[210] S. M. Nasehi, G. R. Sotudeh, and M. Gomrokchi. Source code enhancement using reduction of duplicated code. In *Proceedings of the 25th Conference on IASTED International Multi-Conference: Software Engineering*, pages 192–197. ACTA Press, 2007.

[211] H. A. Nguyen, T. T. Nguyen, N. H. Pham, J. M. Al-Kofahi, and T. N. Nguyen. Accurate and efficient structural characteristic feature extraction for clone detection. In *Proceedings of the 12th International Conference on Fundamental Approaches to Software Engineering*, pages 440–455. Springer-Verlag, 2009.

[212] Hoan Anh Nguyen, Tung Thanh Nguyen, Nam H. Pham, Jafar Al-Kofahi, and Tien N. Nguyen. Clone management for evolving software. *IEEE Trans. Softw. Eng.*, 38(5):1008–1026, 2012.

[213] T. T. Nguyen, H. A. Nguyen, J.M. Al-Kofahi, N. H. Pham, and T. N. Nguyen. Scalable and incremental clone detection for evolving software. In *Proceedings of the International Conference on Software Maintenance*, pages 491–494. IEEE Computer Society, 2009.

[214] T. T. Nguyen, H. A. Nguyen, N. H. Pham, J. M. Al-Kofahi, and T. N. Nguyen. Cleman: Comprehensive clone group evolution management. In *Proceedings of the 23rd International Conference on Automated Software Engineering*, pages 451–454. IEEE Computer Society, 2008.

[215] T. T. Nguyen, H. A. Nguyen, N. H. Pham, J. M. Al-Kofahi, and T. N. Nguyen. Clone-aware configuration management. In *Proceedings of the 24th International Conference on Automated Software Engineering*, pages 123–134. IEEE Computer Society, 2009.

[216] Ge Nong, Sen Zhang, and Wai Hong Chan. Two efficient algorithms for linear suffix array construction. *IEEE Transactions on Computers*, 60(10):1471–1484, 2011.

[217] J.-F. Patenaude, E. Merlo, M. Dagenais, and B. Laguë. Extending software quality assessment techniques to java systems. In *Proceedings of the 7th International Workshop on Program Comprehension*, pages 49–56. IEEE Computer Society, 1999.

[218] P. Pevzner and M. Waterman. Multiple filtration and approximate pattern matching. *Algorithmica*, 13(1):135–154, 1995.

[219] N. H. Pham, H. A. Nguyen, T. T. Nguyen, J. M. Al-Kofahi, and T. N. Nguyen. Complete and accurate clone detection in graph-based models. In *Proceedings of the 31st International Conference on Software Engineering*, pages 276–286. IEEE Computer Society, 2009.

[220] L. Prechelt, G. Mahlpohl, and M. Philippsen. Finding plagiarisms among a set of programs with JPlag. *Journal of Universal Computer Science*, 8(11):1016–1038, 2002.

[221] Simon J. Puglisi, William F. Smyth, and Munina Yusufu. Fast optimal algorithms for computing all the repeats in a string. In *Prague Stringology Conference*, pages 161–169, 2008.

[222] Jochen Quante. Do dynamic object process graphs support program understanding? - a controlled experiment. In *ICPC*, 2008.

[223] F. Rahman, C. Bird, and P. Devanbu. Clones: What is that smell? In *Proceedings of the 7th International Working Conference on Mining Software Repositories*, pages 72–81. IEEE Computer Society, 2010.

[224] Md. Saidur Rahman, Amir Aryani, Chanchal K. Roy, and Fabrizio Perin. On the relationships between domain-based coupling and code clones: an exploratory study. In *ICSE*, pages 1265–1268. IEEE / ACM, 2013.

[225] M. Rieger. *Effective Clone Detection Without Language Barriers*. PhD thesis, University of Bern, 2005.

[226] C. K. Roy and J. R. Cordy. A survey on software clone detection research. Technical report, Queens University at Kingston, Ontario, Canada, 2007.

[227] C. K. Roy and J. R. Cordy. NICAD: Accurate detection of near-miss intentional clones using flexible pretty-printing and code normalization. In *Proceedings of the 16th International Conference on Program Comprehension*, pages 172–181. IEEE Computer Society, 2008.

[228] C. K. Roy and J. R. Cordy. Are scripting languages really different? In *Proceedings of the 4th International Workshop on Software Clones*, pages 17–24. ACM, 2010.

[229] C. K. Roy, J. R. Cordy, and R. Koschke. Comparison and evaluation of code clone detection techniques and tools: A qualitative approach. *Science of Computer Programming*, 74(7):470–495, 2009.

[230] Chanchal K. Roy and James R. Cordy. Near-miss function clones in open source software: an empirical study. *Journal on Software Maintenance*, 22(3):165–189, 2010.

[231] Chanchal K. Roy, Minhaz F. Zibran, and Rainer Koschke. The vision of software clone management: Past, present, and future (keynote paper). In *2014 Software Evolution Week - Conference on Software Maintenance, Reengineering, and Reverse Engineering, CSMR-WCRE 2014*, pages 18–33. IEEE, 2014.

[232] A. Sæbjørnsen, J. Willcock, T. Panas, D. Quinlan, and Z. Su. Detecting code clones in binary executables. In *Proceedings of the 18th International Symposium on Software Testing and Analysis*, pages 117–128. ACM, 2009.

[233] R. K. Saha, M. Asaduzzaman, M. F. Zibran, C. K. Roy, and K. A. Schneider. Evaluating code clone genealogies at release level: An empirical study. In *Proceedings of the 10th International Working Conference on Source Code Analysis and Manipulation*, pages 87–96. IEEE Computer Society, 2010.

[234] R. K. Saha, C. K. Roy, and K. A. Schneider. An automatic framework for extracting and classifying near-miss clone genealogies. In *Proc. of the 27th ICSM*, pages 293–302. ACM, 2011.

[235] D. Sankoff and J. Cedergren. *Time Warps, String Edits, and Macromolecules: The Theory and Practice of Sequence Comparison*. Addison-Wesley, Reading, MA, USA, 1975.

[236] S. Schleimer, D. S. Wilkerson, and A. Aiken. Winnowing: Local algorithms for document fingerprinting. In *Proceedings of the 2003 ACM SIGMOD International Conference on Management of Data*, pages 76–85. ACM, 2003.

[237] S. Schulze and M. Kuhlemann. Advanced analysis for code clone removal. *Softwaretechnik-Trends*, 29(2):26–27, 2009.

[238] Sandro Schulze, Martin Kuhlemann, and Marko Rosenmüller. Towards a refactoring guideline using code clone classification. In *Proceedings of the 2Nd Workshop on Refactoring Tools*, pages 6:1–6:4. ACM, 2008.

[239] Niko Schwarz, Mircea Lungu, and Romain Robbes. On how often code is cloned across repositories. In *Proceedings of the 34th International Conference on Software Engineering*, pages 1289–1292. IEEE Press, 2012.

[240] D. M. Shawky and A. F. Ali. An approach for assessing similarity metrics used in metric-based clone detection techniques. In *Proceedings of the 3rd International Conference on Computer Science and Information Technology*, pages 580–584. IEEE Computer Society, 2010.

[241] PE Shrout and JL Fleiss. Intraclass correlations: Uses in assessing rater reliability. *Psychological Bulletin*, 86(2):420–428, 1979.

[242] S. S. Skiena. *The Algorithm Design Manual*. Springer, New York, NY, USA, 2008.

[243] Matthew Stephan and James R. Cordy. Identification of simulink model antipattern instances using model clone detection. In *Proceedings of the 18th International Conference on Model Driven Engineering Languages and Systems*, pages 276–285, 2015.

[244] G. A. Stephen. *String searching algorithms*. World Scientific, River Edge, NJ, USA, 1994.

[245] H. Störrle. Towards clone detection in UML domain models. In *Proceedings of the Fourth European Conference on Software Architecture: Companion Volume*, pages 285–293. ACM, 2010.

[246] N. Synytskyy, J. R. Cordy, and T. Dean. Resolution of static clones in dynamic web pages. In *Proceedings of the International Workshop on Web Site Evolution*, pages 49–56. IEEE Computer Society, 2003.

[247] R. Tairas and J. Gray. Phoenix-based clone detection using suffix trees. In *Proceedings of the 44th ACM Annual Southeast Regional Conference*, pages 679–684. ACM, 2006.

[248] Robert Tairas and Jeff Gray. Get to know your clones with cedar. In *OOPSLA Companion*, pages 817–818. ACM, 2009.

[249] Robert Tairas, Jeff Gray, and Ira D. Baxter. Visualizing clone detection results. In *Proceedings of the Twenty-second IEEE/ACM International Conference on Automated Software Engineering*, pages 549–550. ACM, 2007.

[250] S. Thummalapenta, L. Cerulo, L. Aversano, and M. Di Penta. An empirical study on the maintenance of source code clones. *Empirical Software Engineering*, 15(1):1–34, 2010.

[251] Walter F. Tichy. Should computer scientists experiment more? - 16 excuses to avoid experimentation. *IEEE Computer*, 31:32–40, 1997.

[252] M. Toomim, A. Begel, and S. L. Graham. Managing duplicated code with linked editing. In *Symposium on Visual Languages and Human Centric Computing*, pages 173–180. IEEE Computer Society, 2004.

[253] John Tukey. Comparing individual means in the analysis of variance. *Biometrics*, 5(2):99–114, 1949.

[254] Md. Sharif Uddin, Chanchal K. Roy, Kevin A. Schneider, and Abram Hindle. On the effectiveness of simhash for detecting near-miss clones in large scale software systems. In *WCRE*, pages 13–22. IEEE Computer Society, 2011.

[255] Y. Ueda, T. Kamiya, S. Kusumoto, and K. Inoue. Gemini: Maintenance support environment based on code clone analysis. In *Proceedings of the 8th Symposium on Software Metrics*, pages 67–76, 2002.

[256] Y. Ueda, T. Kamiya, S. Kusumoto, and K. Inoue. On detection of gapped code clones using gap locations. In *Proceedings of the 9th Asia-Pacific Software Engineering Conference*, pages 327–336. IEEE Computer Society, 2002.

[257] E. Ukkonen. On-line construction of suffix trees. *Algorithmica*, 14(3):249–260, 1995.

[258] V. Wahler, D. Seipel, J. W. v. Gudenberg, and G. Fischer. Clone detection in source code by frequent itemset techniques. In *Proceedings of the 4th International Workshop on Source Code Analysis and Manipulation*, pages 128–135. IEEE Computer Society, 2004.

[259] A. Walenstein and A. Lakhotia. The software similarity problem in malware analysis. In R. Koschke, E. Merlo, and A. Walenstein, editors, *Duplication, Redundancy, and Similarity in Software*, number 06301 in Dagstuhl Seminar Proceedings, Dagstuhl, Germany, 2007. Internationales Begegnungs- und Forschungszentrum für Informatik (IBFI), Schloss Dagstuhl, Germany.

[260] Chao Wang and Han Pan. Visualization of text duplicates in documents. Master's thesis, Växjö University, School of Mathematics and Systems Engineering, 2009.

[261] Tiantian Wang, Mark Harman, Yue Jia, and Jens Krinke. Searching for better configurations: A rigorous approach to clone evaluation. In *Foundations on Software Engineering*, pages 455–465. ACM Press, 2013.

[262] W. Wang and M. W. Godfrey. A study of cloning in the linux scsi drivers. In *Proceedings of the 11th International Working Conference on Source Code Analysis and Manipulation*, pages 95–104. IEEE, 2011.

[263] V. Weckerle. CPC an eclipse framework for automated clone life cycle tracking and update anomaly detection. Diploma thesis, Freie Universität Berlin, 2008.

[264] C. Wohlin, P. Runeson, M. Host, C. Ohlsson, B. Regnell, and A. Wesslén. *Experimentation in Software Engineering: an Introduction.* Kluver Academic Publishers, 2000.

[265] S. Wu and U. Manber. Fast text searching: allowing errors. *Communications of the ACM*, 35(10):83–91, 1992.

[266] S. Xie, F. Khomh, and Y. Zou. An empirical study of the fault-proneness of clone mutation and clone migration. In *Proceedings of the 10th Working Conference on Mining Software Repositories*, pages 149–158. IEEE, 2013.

[267] Zhenchang Xing, Yinxing Xue, and Stan Jarzabek. Distilling useful clones by contextual differencing. In *WCRE*, pages 102–111. IEEE Computer Society, 2013.

[268] W. Yang. Identifying syntactic differences between two programs. *Software – Practice & Experience*, 21(7):739–755, 1991.

[269] Norihiro Yoshida, Yoshiki Higo, Toshihiro Kamiya, Shinji Kusumoto, and Katsuro Inoue. On refactoring support based on code clone dependency relation. In *Proceedings of the 11th IEEE International Software Metrics Symposium*, pages 16–. IEEE Computer Society, 2005.

[270] Feng Zhang, Audris Mockus, Iman Keivanloo, and Ying Zou. Towards building a universal defect prediction model. In *Proceedings of the 11th Working Conference on Mining Software Repositories*, pages 182–191. ACM, 2014.

[271] G. Zhang, X. Peng, Z. Xing, and W. Zhao. Cloning practices: Why developers clone and what can be changed. In *Proceedings of the 28th International Conference on Software Maintenance*, pages 285–294. IEEE Computer Society, 2012.

[272] Yali Zhang, Hamid Abdul Basit, Stan Jarzabek, Dang Anh, and Melvin Low. Query-based filtering and graphical view generation for clone analysis. In *ICSM*, pages 376–385. IEEE Computer Society, 2008.

[273] Minhaz F. Zibran and Chanchal K. Roy. A constraint programming approach to conflict-aware optimal scheduling of prioritized code clone refactoring. In *Proceedings of the 2011 IEEE 11th International Working Conference on Source Code Analysis and Manipulation*, pages 105–114. IEEE Computer Society, 2011.

[274] Minhaz F. Zibran and Chanchal K. Roy. Conflict-aware optimal scheduling of prioritised code clone refactoring. *IET Software*, 7(3), 2013.

Chapter 10
AI Literacy from Educators' Perspectives

After understanding AI literacy from the perspective of human-design factor, this chapter presents a conceptual framework introducing an expanded view of AI literacy from educators' perspectives. It moves beyond technological competencies and tries to identify a more holistic and broader understanding about AI literacy education. When using these novel AI tools to teach, educators need to be equipped with adequate technological literacy skills and knowledge. In this way, they can teach AI literacy and promote other digital competencies such as collaboration and communication among their students in AI-driven environments. Since teachers may not have rich technical knowledge to apply AI educational applications to facilitate their teaching. As one of the most important twenty-first-century competencies, AI literacy can be conceptualized as the knowledge, skills, and attitudes necessary to be competitive in the twenty-first-century workforce. Teacher education and professional development should be reworked to incorporate training in teaching key digital competencies.

10.1 Understanding Teachers' AI Digital Competencies

Artificial intelligence technology has gained its popularity in education in recent years. It reshapes education which helps educators to automate nonteaching tasks to reduce their workload and enhance learning analysis and teaching optimization (Kexin et al., 2020). Further, it helps promote students' personalized learning (Ahmad et al., 2022) and advance students' knowledge acquisition using AI-empowered systems (e.g., Chen et al., 2020; Hwang et al., 2020). However, these technologies are novel to educators who may not have enough knowledge and skills to manipulate these AI-driven educational applications for learning and teaching purposes (Ally, 2019; Seo et al., 2021). They may not have rich technological experience to design AI-driven learning environments, construct learning analysis.

© The Author(s), under exclusive license to Springer Nature Switzerland AG 2022
D. T. K. Ng et al., *AI Literacy in K-16 Classrooms*,
https://doi.org/10.1007/978-3-031-18880-0_10

and set the rules in various AI-enhanced systems to automate responses, assignments, and feedback (Seo et al., 2021), not to mention developing students' AI literacy (Yau et al., 2022). Moreover, challenges were identified such as AI-based
misunderstandings and misleadingness, limitations, and hidden ethical issues
behind different platforms (Akgun & Greenhow, 2021; Sijing & Lan, 2018).

To develop student' AI literacy, educators need to upskill and reskill their knowledge to design relevant instruction (e.g., pedagogy, content, activities) for their students (Williamson & Eynon, 2020). Research examples were used to identify what
types of AI digital competencies should be emphasized for teachers. A set of teachers' AI digital competencies is proposed based on the P21's Framework for the 21st
Century Learning. This chapter aims to extend the proposal of viewing AI literacy
as an important twenty-first-century skill set (Ng et al., 2021a, b). As mentioned in
Chap. 4, AI literacy moves toward a broader understanding that identifies other
nontechnical, critical, and complex literacy that K–16 learners need to learn to
manipulate AI technologies ethically and effectively. Toward a holistic picture,
teachers should not view AI literacy as an independent domain but an avenue to
develop other important skill sets such as life and career skills, multidisciplinary
skills, learning, and innovation skills. With the P21 framework, teachers can use it
as a guideline to equip themselves with necessary digital competencies to facilitate
better instruction (Lindfors et al., 2021).

Several digital competency frameworks have been used in teacher education,
such as DigCompEdu (Caena & Redecker, 2019) and the International Society for
Technology in Education (ISTE) standards (Crompton, 2017) to update the necessary digital competencies for today's digital world. These frameworks inform educators how AI should be incorporated in their subject areas and levels of study.
According to the DigCompEdu standards, teachers' digital competencies can be
categorized in six areas that facilitate their professional activities (Mishou &
Paliouras, 2022): (1) professional engagement, using AI for communication, collaboration, and professional development; (2) resource management, sourcing, creating, and sharing AI-empowered resources; (3) teaching and learning, managing
the use of AI for teaching/learning; (4) assessment, using AI to enhance automatic
assessment and analysis; (5) empowering learners, Using AI to enhance inclusion,
personalization, and learning engagement; and (6) facilitating learners' AI competence, enabling learners to create their own intelligent agents responsibly and use AI
for information sharing, communication, content creation, and problem-solving.
The ISTE standards consider AI as a new digital competence requirement to develop
citizens' necessary knowledge, skills, and attitudes (Riina et al., 2022). These
frameworks offer a common understanding across the European Union and beyond
of what digital competence needs to frame digital skills policy, curricula development, and assessment of digital skills (Riina et al., 2022).

Among these models, this Chapter proposes the P21's Framework for the 21st
Century Learning illustrates the knowledge and skills that educators need to suc-
ceed in working, learning, and living (National Research Council, 2012). The
framework is famous for educators and business leaders to identify learning standards for implementing curriculum, instruction, assessments, and learning

environments. This chapter does not focus on the technical perspectives for fostering students' AI literacy. Instead, it aims to focus on broader digital competencies (e.g., communication, collaboration, critical thinking, life, and career skills) that support teachers to conduct teaching using AI technologies and implement AI literacy education. In this way, teachers should not only know and use AI applications to empower their students and prepare related teaching resources. They should also master other AI digital competencies such as applying AI knowledge in their disciplines and life and career skills to prepare students to enter the future workforce and communicating and collaborating with their peers.

10.2 Essential AI Digital Competencies for Educators (P21)

Recent scholars proposed the need to reconsider teachers' professional development programs to meet the educational standards and expectations in the new digital era. For example, Trujillo-Cabezas (2020) suggested some teacher's AI digital competencies such as using basic applications, managing information, creating learning content, and connecting their students via technology. Ng et al. (2021b) incorporated AI literacy development into the TPACK model which guides teachers to consider related teaching content, pedagogy, and technology. Using the P21's Framework, this section investigates what teacher competencies are desired for effective online teaching with AI technology. Four key competencies are identified. The key competencies of teachers should focus not only on the acquisition of basic AI knowledge and skills but also on the cultivation of the capabilities necessary for the teacher's adaptation to, survival in, and control over the future society and their lifelong professional development.

Core Subjects, 3Rs, and Twenty-First-Century Themes To be a successful student and adult in the future, educators have a role to help students to master the core subjects and twenty-first-century themes. AI has commonly become a topic in computer science education, but it has already become part of these core subjects of education. In schools, teachers are from diverse educational backgrounds and subjects, and they need to collaborate and work together to adopt, adapt, and implement interdisciplinary materials and approaches. Artificial intelligence technologies could be new to most teachers, and it takes effort for educators to incorporate AI into their knowledge domains and other twenty-first-century themes such as global awareness and financial, environmental, civic, and health literacy. For example, Ng et al. (2022) designed a digital story writing program to develop students' AI concepts, and students can use these concepts to write their stories. When writing their books, translation tools and recommendation systems can help students reduce grammatical errors and generate ideas and artworks in their digital stories which involve the efforts of language and computer teachers.

Moreover, teachers who are more capable of using AI can empower students' learning using AI-driven technologies (e.g., recommendation systems, intelligent agents)

in their classrooms. They can enable students to apply their multidisciplinary knowledge and help them reach higher cognition levels such as critical thinking, creativity, collaboration, and communication. In higher education, AI literacy education is addressed across different subject areas such as healthcare (Rampton et al., 2020), financial and business (Guerrero-Roldán et al., 2021), and legal education (Demchenko et al., 2021). Higher education educators need to empower their students to use AI applications throughout their life cycle, harness opportunities of using AI technologies in their fields, and be aware of ethical implications and risks (Zawacki-Richter et al., 2019). Concurrently, teachers, regardless of their subject domains, need to develop certain AI digital competencies in order to instruct and assess their students using AI technologies. Ultimately, teachers should be able to guide students on how to manipulate different AI-driven systems and machines that would play a part in their future workplaces.

Nowadays, AI can empower students' reading, writing, and arithmetic abilities (3Rs). For example, e-book systems consist of AI-empowered recommendations that suggest reading materials, practices, and assignments based on students' reading habits (Wu & Peng, 2017). Moreover, AI writing software helps people generate ideas and content for writing articles, novels, blogs, and emails to optimize their work. It can produce compelling articles with the right tone and style, ensure them to be grammatically correct, paraphrase texts, reduce grammatical errors, generate citations automatically, and enhance formatting that improve readability (Nazari et al., 2021; Lin & Chang, 2020). In arithmetic calculation, other applications (e.g., Wolfram Alpha, Symbolab) enable students to take photos of mathematical formulas and questions to generate steps and solve them automatically. However, these applications are too convenient for students to plagiarize in their assignments and examinations (Wu et al., 2021). Teachers should be more sensitive to these AI-enhanced submissions and differentiate whether it is the students' original ideas. It is important for teachers to remind students with correct mindsets and ethical concerns when using these applications to facilitate their learning and living.

Learning and Innovation Skills (4Cs) Scholars have strived the importance of critical, creative thinking, collaboration, and communication in particular to prepare students for today's ever-changing workforce (Van Laar et al., 2017). The skill sets can enable students to create and adapt to changes and encourage students to apply their existing knowledge with peers to solve problems creatively and critically. Studies have shown the effectiveness of using AI technologies to enhance students' learning and innovation skills. For example, when AI is used in music education, it empowers student learning experience through interactive composition, performances, mixing, and appreciation (Zulić, 2019).

Demchenko et al. (2021) identified a digital transformation in legal education that teachers need to equip their students with AI digital competencies. There is a need for law schools to innovate and form stronger interdisciplinary collaboration with AI expertise to enhance their effective professional and everyday activities such as using AI-based tools for criminal justice and identifying algorithmic bias (Deeks, 2019). In business education, AI has a wide range of uses in business to complete

authentic tasks such as aggregating business data, managing customer relationships, and predicting future trends. Business educators need to update their knowledge and enable students to integrate AI into their workplace and create a new user experience for their clients (Williamson & Eynon, 2020; Uzialko, 2022). In medical education, there is a greater demand for digital health applications to promote social distancing during the pandemic. Medical educators need to timely update their knowledge and skills to help their e-patients via AI-driven medical applications such as infection rate prediction, computed tomography image recognition, robotics for patient assessment and drug delivery, and X-ray interpretation (Ahuja & Nair, 2021). These knowledge and skills are useful for teachers and students to become professionals/leaders in their knowledge fields to implement complex cognitive and decision-making tasks and adapt to present scenarios.

Information, Media, and Technology Skills Educators need to prepare themselves to become digital ready so that they are able to teach students related skills such as information, media, and ICT literacy (Gleason & Von Gillern, 2018). Especially in recent years, teachers and students need to adapt to digital transformation and develop related technological skills. In AI-driven classrooms, teachers need to manipulate different AI-enhanced systems to design assessments and examine students' performance using their historical and current data using the adaptive learning system (Guerrero-Roldán et al., 2021). In another study, teachers adopt an automatic mode in an AI-driven service called IBM RXN to enable students to draw target molecules and generate chemical reactions and structure representations (Healy & Blade, 2020). Kostopoulos et al. (2021) mentioned the use of an AI-driven system called DevOps to equip smart city professionals and educators with adequate technological skills to visualize urban innovation in an 11-week online course. Further, teachers need to acquire better technology skills and enable them to intervene early to enhance students' performance and retention (Jokhan et al., 2022). They need to learn how to use different AIED technologies to design their instruction, examine students' learning outcomes, and premise intelligent support for collaborative working. These examples showed that university educators from different disciplines need to equip themselves with technological skills to enable their students to express knowledge, solve problems, and manipulate AI-driven applications so that they are ready to work in AI-driven environments.

Life and Career Skills Life and career skills are important to prepare students to engage as citizens in a dynamic global community and meet different challenges and opportunities in the workforce. Students need to develop positive mindsets, attitudes, and other competencies (e.g., flexibility, adaptability, self-direction, social skills, productivity, responsibility) to navigate complex life and work environments (Van Laar et al., 2017). First, studies suggested that AI has the potential to transform youth employment and students need to develop relevant skills to adapt to this change. For example, Singh et al. (2020) suggested that AI profiling will move away from merely information collection about formal qualifications to a more holistic approach of capturing skills and life experiences. Educators need to upgrade their

students to fit the future job market. Second, improving students' self-efficacy and self-regulation is important when using AI-driven systems to support students' online learning since these systems usually do not consist of a physical teacher to monitor their learning (Guerrero-Roldán et al., 2021). Third, Cetinkamar et al. (2022) highlighted four sets of workplace capabilities associated with AI: techno-logical skills (e.g., data collection, analytics, ethics, security), work-related skills (e.g., decision-making, critical thinking, teamwork), human-machine interaction (e.g., situation assessments, affordance analysis, adaptive expertise), and learning-related capabilities (e.g., lifelong learning, self-learning ability). Other studies also mentioned the importance of life and career skills in the fourth industrial revolution such as problem-solving (Mohammed et al., 2021), emotional intelligence, judg-ment, service orientation, negotiating and cognitive flexibilities (Webber-Youngman, 2017), as well as communication and teamwork skills (Seo et al., 2021). Teachers can enable their students to become adaptive thinkers who equip themselves with technological literacies to solve problems, think critically, lead their teammates, and implement reflective practice (Li & Du, 2017). With these life and workplace skills, students become more digitally ready to contribute to their fields and companies after graduation.

These four essential digital competencies suggest how higher education policymak-ers consider the necessary educational standards and goals in their universities and schools and provide relevant professional training to develop teachers' readiness in today's AI world. At the classroom level, the framework serves as a guideline to help instructional designers to design suitable curriculum and materials for their students and create positive learning environments. Moreover, such educational standards are important to serve as a basis of educational reform and digital transi-tion to help practitioners to identify the necessary learning outcomes to meet the goals set by the governments, regions, and markets. For example, it helps fulfill job demands in the market, enhance learners' competitiveness, equipping students with futuristic skills, and educate the next generation to become responsible citizens. To achieve these goals, educators need to cultivate their TPACK knowledge to incorpo-rate meaningful learning elements (e.g., assessments, curriculum, instruction) for their students. Since teachers may not be familiarized with these novel technologies, practices for teacher education (e.g., teacher program, professional community, guideline) are important to support educators to equip with necessary knowledge and skills for students' learning and achieve teaching and learning outcomes. Moreover, collaboration from different professionals from higher education institu-tions, schools, government, industries, and companies could co-design these profes-sional development programs and guidelines to develop meaningful materials, tools, and platforms to support teachers AI literacy education.

10.3 Conclusion

The existing frameworks focused more on students' learning; few of them investigate how to enhance teachers' AI digital competence in professional development programs. However, it is important to promote frontline educators and decision-makers' professional growth so as to improve their pedagogical, content, and technological knowledge to incorporate AI into their classrooms. Research shows that professional development could lead to better instruction, thus improving student learning outcomes (e.g., Kutaka et al., 2017; Gore et al., 2021). Teachers become more capable of connecting their teaching materials to AI and understand the educational standards that guide their teaching, assess, and design students' learning experiences with novel technologies. Further, they can use it wisely to solve teaching problems (e.g., lack of social isolation and motivation in online learning). With AI, teachers can analyze students' behaviors and performance to adapt their teaching and give students immediate assistance to meet learning needs for individual learners.

This Chapter proposed the P21's Framework for 21st Century Learning. Research examples are suggested for each competence to show what teachers should learn before teaching their students. Teachers need to learn technological skills to access AI devices and software (e.g., learning analytic) to improve their teaching and working efficiency (Kexin et al., 2020). On top of technical skills, there is a need to include broader digital competencies such as communication, life and career skills, ethical concerns, teacher identity, attitudes, and mindsets as components of teacher education in AI literacy education (e.g., Akgun & Greenhow, 2021; Seo et al., 2021).

References

Ahmad, S. F., Alam, M. M., Rahmat, M. K., Mubarik, M. S., & Hyder, S. I. (2022). Academic and administrative role of artificial intelligence in education. *Sustainability, 14*(3), 1101.

Ahuja, V., & Nair, L. V. (2021). Artificial intelligence and technology in COVID Era: A narrative review. *Journal of Anaesthesiology, Clinical Pharmacology, 37*(1), 28.

Akgun, S., & Greenhow, C. (2021). Artificial intelligence in education: Addressing ethical challenges in K-12 settings. *AI and Ethics*, 1–10.

Ally, M. (2019). Competency profile of the digital and online teacher in future education. *The International Review of Research in Open and Distance Learning, 20*(2).

Caena, F., & Redecker, C. (2019). Aligning teacher competence frameworks to 21st century challenges: The case for the European digital competence framework for educators (Digcompedu). *European Journal of Education, 54*(3), 356–369.

Cetindamar, D., Kitto, K., Wu, M., Zhang, Y., Abedin, B., & Knight, S. (2022). Explicating AI literacy of employees at digital workplaces. *IEEE Transactions on Engineering Management.*

Chen, X., Xie, H., Zou, D., & Hwang, G. J. (2020). Application and theory gaps during the rise of artificial intelligence in education. *Computers and Education: Artificial Intelligence, 1*, 100002.

Crompton, H. (2017). *ISTE standards for educators: A guide for teachers and other professionals.* International Society for Technology in Education.

Demchenko, M. V., Gulieva, M. E., Larina, T. V., & Simaeva, E. P. (2021). Digital transformation of legal education: Problems, risks and prospects. *European Journal of Contemporary Education*, 10(2), 297-307.

Deeks, A. (2019). The judicial demand for explainable artificial intelligence. *Columbia Law Review*, 119(7), 1829-1850.

Gleason, B., & Von Gillern, S. (2018). Digital citizenship with social media: Participatory practices of teaching and learning in secondary education. *Journal of Educational Technology & Society*, 21(1), 200-212.

Gore, J. M., Miller, A., Fray, L., Harris, J., & Prieto, E. (2021). Improving student achievement through professional development: Results from a randomised controlled trial of quality teaching rounds. *Teaching and Teacher Education*, 101, 103297.

Guerrero-Roldán, A. E., Rodríguez-González, M. E., Bañeres, D., Elasri-Ejjaberi, A., & Cortadas, P. (2021). Experiences in the use of an adaptive intelligent system to enhance online learners' performance: A case study in economics and business courses. *International Journal of Educational Technology in Higher Education*, 18(1), 1-27.

Healy, E. F., & Blade, G. (2020). Tips and tools for teaching organic synthesis online. *Journal of Chemical Education*, 97(9), 3163-3167.

Hwang, G. J., Xie, H., Wah, B. W., & Gašević, D. (2020). Vision, challenges, roles and research issues of artificial intelligence in education. *Computers and Education: Artificial Intelligence*, 1, 100001.

Jokhan, A., Chand, A. A., Singh, V., & Mamun, K. A. (2022). Increased digital resource consumption in higher educational institutions and the artificial intelligence role in informing decisions related to student performance. *Sustainability*, 14(4), 2377.

Kexin, L., Yi, Q., Xiaoou, S., & Yan, L. (2020). Future education trend learned from the Covid-19 pandemic: Take artificial intelligence online course as an example. In *2020 International Conference on Artificial Intelligence and Education (ICAIE)* (pp. 108-111). IEEE.

Kostopoulos, G., Panagiotakopoulos, T., Kotsiantis, S., Pierrakeas, C., & Kameas, A. (2021). Interpretable models for early prediction of certification in MOOCs: A case study on a MOOC for Smart City professionals. *IEEE Access*, 9, 165881-165891.

Kutaka, T. S., Smith, W. M., Albano, A. D., Edwards, C. P., Ren, L., Beattie, H. L., Lewis, W. J., Heaton, R. M., & Stroup, W. W. (2017). Connecting teacher professional development and student mathematics achievement: A 4-year study of an elementary mathematics specialist program. *Journal of Teacher Education*, 68(2), 140-154.

Li, D., & Du, Y. (2017). *Artificial intelligence with uncertainty*. CRC Press.

Lin, M. P. C., & Chang, D. (2020). Enhancing post-secondary writers' writing skills with a chatbot. *Journal of Educational Technology & Society*, 23(1), 78-92.

Lindfors, M., Pettersson, F., & Olofsson, A. D. (2021). Conditions for professional digital competence: The teacher educators' view. *Education Inquiry, 12*(4), 390-409.

Mishtou, S., & Paliouras, A. (2022). Teaching Artificial Intelligence in K-12 Education: Competences and Interventions. In *Interactive Mobile Communication, Technologies and Learning*, Springer, Cham, pp. 887-896.

Mohammed, Z., Arafa, A., Atlam, E. S., El-Qerafi, N., El-Shazly, M., Al-Hazazi, O., & Ewis, A. (2021). Psychological problems among the university students in Saudi Arabia during the COVID-19 pandemic. *International Journal of Clinical Practice, 75*(11), e14853.

National Research Council. (2012). *Education for life and work: Developing transferable knowledge and skills in the 21st century*. National Academies Press.

Nazari, N., Shabbir, M. S., & Setiawan, R. (2021). Application of artificial intelligence powered digital writing assistant in higher education: Randomized controlled trial. *Heliyon, 7*(5), e07014.

Ng, D. T. K., Leung, J. K. L., Chu, S. K. W., & Qiao, M. S. (2021a). AI literacy: definition, teaching, evaluation and ethical issues. *Proceedings of the Association for Information Science and Technology, 58*(1), 504-509.

Ng, D. T. K., Leung, J. K. L., Chu, S. K. W., & Qiao, M. S. (2021b). Conceptualizing AI literacy: An exploratory review. *Computers and Education: Artificial Intelligence, 2*, 100041.

Ng, D. T. K., Luo, W., Chan, H. M. Y., & Chu, S. K. W. (2022). Using digital story writing as a pedagogy to develop AI literacy among primary students. *Computers and Education: Artificial Intelligence, 3*, 100054.

Rampton, V., Mittelman, M., & Goldhahn, J. (2020). Implications of artificial intelligence for medical education. *The Lancet Digital Health, 2*(3), e111–e112.

Riina, V., Stefano, K., & Yves, P. (2022). DigComp 2.2: the digital competence framework for citizens – With new examples of knowledge, skills and attitudes. Retrieved from https://publications.jrc.ec.europa.eu/repository/handle/JRC128415

Seo, K., Tang, J., Roll, I., Fels, S., & Yoon, D. (2021). The impact of artificial intelligence on learner–instructor interaction in online learning. *International Journal of Educational Technology in Higher Education, 18*(1), 1–23.

Sijing, L., & Lan, W. (2018). Artificial intelligence education ethical problems and solutions. In *2018 13th International Conference on Computer Science & Education (ICCSE)* (pp. 1–5). IEEE.

Singh, S., Sharma, P. K., Yoon, B., Shojafar, M., Cho, G. H., & Ra, I. H. (2020). Convergence of blockchain and artificial intelligence in IoT network for the sustainable smart city. *Sustainable Cities and Society, 63*, 102364.

Trujillo-Cabezas, R. (2020, June). Towards the development of future trend scenarios through dynamic analysis: A proposal of integration of Artificial Intelligence, Data Sciences and the field of Futures Studies to adapt to new environments. In *2020 15th Iberian Conference on Information Systems and Technologies (CISTI)* (pp. 1–6). IEEE.

Uzialko, A. (2022). *How artificial intelligence will transform businesses*. Retrieved from https://www.businessnewsdaily.com/9402-artificial-intelligence-business-trends.html

Van Laar, E., Van Deursen, A. J., Van Dijk, J. A., & De Haan, J. (2017). The relation between 21st-century skills and digital skills: A systematic literature review. *Computers in Human Behavior, 72*, 577–588.

Webber-Youngman, R. C. W. (2017). Life skills needed for the 4th industrial revolution. *Journal of the Southern African Institute of Mining and Metallurgy, 117*(4), iv–v.

Williamson, B., & Eynon, R. (2020). Historical threads, missing links, and future directions in AI in education. *Learning, Media and Technology, 45*(3), 223–235.

Wu, J. Y., & Peng, Y. C. (2017). The modality effect on reading literacy: Perspectives from students' online reading habits, cognitive and metacognitive strategies, and web navigation skills across regions. *Interactive Learning Environments, 25*(7), 859–876.

Wu, J. S., Chien, T. H., Chien, L. R., & Yang, C. Y. (2021). Using artificial intelligence to predict class loyalty and plagiarism in students in an online blended programming course during the COVID-19 pandemic. *Electronics, 10*(18), 2203.

Yau, K. W., Chai, C. S., Chiu, T. K., Meng, H., King, I., & Yam, Y. (2022). A phenomenographic approach on teacher conceptions of teaching artificial intelligence (AI) in K-12 schools. *Education and Information Technologies*, 1–24.

Zawacki-Richter, O., Marín, V. I., Bond, M., & Gouverneur, F. (2019). Systematic review of research on artificial intelligence applications in higher education–where are the educators? *International Journal of Educational Technology in Higher Education, 16*(1), 1–27.

Zulić, H. (2019). How AI can change/improve/influence music composition, performance and education: three case studies. *INSAM Journal of Contemporary Music, Art and Technology, 1*(2), 100–114.

Chapter 11
Summary and Conclusions

In the end, we hope to have taken our readers through a journey of discovering the origins and development of AI literacy and, more importantly, positioning the unique role that AI literacy education plays in our rapidly changing, digitized, twenty-first-century education. Part I has posited that AI literacy is different from AI education; while they share overlapping domains, they are differentiated by the scope, aim, and outcomes of the two. Hence, we borrowed concepts from other literacies to introduce a holistic view of AI learning for a wide range of learners and also the stakeholders involved in supporting them. That brings us to Part II, where AI literacy is being discussed in depth according to four distinct educational levels (kindergarten, primary, secondary, and nonengineering undergraduate). We applied similar research methodology throughout the four levels to search for existing publications, which led us to a considerable number of results for thematic analyses. The information obtained from Part II acted as a bridge. Not only does it confirm the arguments and proposals on the growing importance of AI literacy stated in Part I but also provides an ample amount of evidence to generate insights for us to navigate the avenue towards an AI-literate future. At last in Part III is where we synthesized. We gathered evidence, our insights, and international educational standards and frameworks such as Bloom's taxonomy, TPACK model, and P21's Framework, altogether and ultimately to suggest methods, approaches, guidelines, etc. for stakeholders of interest to make efficient use of our data.

Our foremost intention to write this book is to propose a set of guidelines of AI literacy instructional design that can be applied in today's K–16 educational settings. For researchers, the book provides research-driven recommendations to consider theoretical and pedagogical bases for future studies. The methodology used was by no means the only effective approach in consolidating data nor the single way to interpret it. Plus, such a fast-growing industry requires more scholars to collectively contribute to analyzing the landscape of AI literacy from different angles methodologically, timely, geographically, etc.

Another notion we advocate is that AI literacy or even AI education should not be viewed as an independent subject. We used the linkage between characteristics of AI literacy and twenty-first-century skills as a gateway to enter students' core and foundation curriculum. Technological knowledge, skill acquisition (in a digital perspective), and broader competencies such as life and career, multidisciplinary, the four Cs learning, and innovation skills (in a critical perspective) are all important aspects to the development of appropriate teaching tools and platforms, meaningful learning activities, and assessments. We have also discussed the instructional designs in terms of teaching practices and human-centered (or even student-centered) considerations to meet students' needs and scaffold on the foundations of their learning. On this note, this book has put forward a range of pedagogical recommendations that facilitate twenty-first-century skills education from early childhood education to higher education to meet the needs of the industries and society.

To confirm the significance of this AI literacy arena, prior to the publication of this book, the DigCompEdu and the International Society for Technology in Education (ISTE) standards updated their guidelines and plans to include AI literacy as the latest educational standards with regard to the digital upskilling of the population. Furthermore, national education strategies across the United States, China, and European Union and beyond have updated their plans to frame policy and curriculum development to devise and affirm the role of artificial intelligence in promoting AI literacy to citizens and fostering the next generation's AI digital competence. Inspired by the National Education Technology Plan, there are some general recommendations for different stakeholders in terms of learning, teaching, leadership, assessment, and infrastructure (Smith, 2015) (see Table 11.1).

Further, human-centered design consideration has a large role in the newly updated plans, which suggests instructional designers (including developers and teachers) to design their instruction and learning environments that meet learners'

Table 11.1 Recommendations based on national education technology plan

Domains	Recommendations
Learning	Developing high-quality government-endorsed curricula to meet the needs of their students
	Using AI technology to transform learning experiences with the goal of providing greater equity and accessibility
	Universally offering equitable access to AI technology inside and outside of school, regardless of students' backgrounds
	Implementing universal design principles for student-centered learning
Teaching	Designing teacher professional developments to develop minimum standards for educators to take full advantage of AI-empowered learning environments
Leadership	Leaders need to create a shared vision for AI technology to best meet the needs of all students and to devise a plan to execute it
Assessment	Designing useful assessments and tools to examine students' AI learning outcomes to improve their learning effectiveness and reduce challenges to students' learning
Infrastructure	Establishing a robust AI-driven technology infrastructure for today's schools, meeting current connectivity goals, and augmenting it for future demands

needs (Yang et al., 2021). It is also our goal of this book to provide educators across the globe with pedagogies, learning content, technologies, and assessment strategies supported by state-of-the-art research evidence. We believe that this book will facilitate stakeholders to design and implement AI literacy education more effectively that grows our students up to become educated digital citizens with positive knowledge, attitude, and skills learning gain in core AI-empowered curriculum domains as well as twenty-century technological skills. Here, we summarize and make recommendations for stakeholders who have responsibility in changing the AI-driven landscape of today's digital world. These stakeholders include, but not limited to, educators, policymakers, researchers, and parents.

11.1 For Teachers

Teachers play an important role in making decisions about what learning elements such as assessments, curriculum, pedagogy, and technology used in their classrooms for the needs to foster students' AI literacy skills as their learning outcomes. However, teachers may not have computer science educational backgrounds to develop suitable technology driven curricula and learning materials for their students. To enable a smooth digital transition to make our teaching professionals ready and confident and help them adapt to changes in this era, teacher education in AI literacy is important. A particular reason is that supporting students requires teachers to become more digitally advanced so as to serve more aptly in their competence. As such, professional development programs, guidelines, and schools' support are required to upskill and reskill teachers' technological knowledge, skills, and attitudes. Moreover, there is a need to establish and maintain a community of scholars, developers, and educators for sharing and disseminating best practices to develop and refine AI teaching tools, materials, and assessments that meet students' learning outcomes and needs. Through collaboration, frontline teachers do not need to struggle on designing technology-based content and tools for their students. Instead, they can focus on designing engaging learning activities and materials in their classrooms via meaningful pedagogical approaches (e.g., collaborative learning, inquiry-based learning, gamification) to motivate their students in the learning process.

Students may meet challenges throughout their AI literacy learning journeys. Research suggests that experiential learning can help students have a taste of AI-driven technologies (e.g., chatbot, social robots, music, and artwork generator). In this way, students can scaffold their knowledge and skills whereby students can learn by doing and reflecting on their experiences. As a form of experiential learning, hands-on experiences can help students to move away from teacher-centered approaches and absorb new knowledge with their peers. However, it may not suffice to define a task for students such as simulating machine learning using web-based tools, training a model using datasets, designing an AI-enhanced game, and generating a song using AI. Students need authentic and structured instruction on AI

literacy in order to learn how to successfully know, understand, use, apply, evaluate, and create relevant resources to meet their learning outcomes and create their artifacts. Therefore, after experiencing AI, as suggested by our reviews, interventions involving student inquiry and collaboration to solve authentic problems can stimulate students' positive learning gains (e.g. curiosity, creativity, knowledge acquisition) to apply their knowledge in real-world contexts. In other words, collaborative project-based learning is the most sound and commonly used pedagogical approach that helps students to reach a higher cognitive level.

At the same time, teachers are advised to hold back their worries that AI will replace their job and overemphasize the limitations of AI. Although it may not be possible to transform over one night, educators need to see a possibility to use AI applications to facilitate their everyday routine work, understand learners' needs through data analysis, design an interactive learning environment, and provide automatic and timely feedback for their students. They must learn to welcome the challenge of new technologies that may arise in their teaching process. Teachers who embrace lifelong learning approaches are successful in creating innovative and inclusive classrooms to grow students' digital competence through hard work and be willing to learn and open to changes. With such drive and faith in teachers' adaptation, our next generation will become enthusiastic about AI and technologies to help the society grow better and meet today's educational needs.

11.2   For Higher Education Faculty

Higher education aims to develop talents and professionals who can fill the market demands in their field. As AI is influencing nearly every discipline, it enhances the efficiency of employees in the workplace and automates repetitive tasks and frees us to conduct more complex problems and operations. Through turning complex data into insights, AI can identify important changes in patterns and perform deeper content analysis to uncover changes in today's world and people's behavior that affect their industries so as to optimize their performance and profitability. In law schools, faculty need to innovate and form stronger interdisciplinary collaboration with AI expertise to enhance their effectiveness and use AI-based tools to help with criminal justice and identify algorithmic bias (Deeks, 2019). In medical schools, many health applications are now AI-empowered to help medical practitioners to help their clients with infection rate prediction, computed tomography image recognition, robotics for patient assessment and drug delivery, and X-ray interpretation (Ahuja & Nair, 2021). In art schools, AI is drastically changing the nature of creative processes that facilitate illustrators, designers, and photographers to design digital art packages (Boden & Edmonds, 2019). Many universities have designed AI literacy programs to develop students' skills and mindsets for students from educational diverse backgrounds to develop fundamental AI knowledge and skills. Some courses aim to support students with basic programming skills for science and engineering students to learn the underlying computer science concepts behind the AI

technologies (Long & Magerko, 2020). The AI literacy programs further welcome students without computer science prerequisite knowledge to empower them to become AI literates to serve in their future workplaces after graduation.

Teacher training programs should help higher education faculty, postdocs, and teaching support staff to realize the demands, opportunities, and challenges that their industries face in the twenty-first century. It is necessary to situate education in the times of the students to reflect on their teaching philosophies and practices to better cater for learners' needs. It helps groom faculty's ability to critically rethink education to cultivate and strengthen students with related knowledge and skills that are needed in today's world. The updated twenty-first-century skills frameworks have included AI which are relatively novel to educators who do not receive relevant training before in their teacher training, especially for senior professors who are more likely to struggle in the acquisition of IT skills that can support more on how to make sense of AI technologies into their expertise.

11.3 For Policymakers

Across the country, AI is rapidly changing how businesses operate and help people solve complex problems and work more efficiently. By 2030, 70% of companies expect to use AI according to a PwC's global AI report (2022). Countries are working their best to gain global competitiveness through economic improvement and creating innovation to accelerate industrial growth. With more novel technologies, some of the existing practices and policies will not match past experience. Tomorrow's leaders started to discuss the global competition for AI leadership and the need for educational policy frameworks that support learning and innovation. Governments need to collaborate with universities to update its educational standards, policy, frameworks and guidelines, curricula, and evaluation methods indicating the AI literacy interventions.

Policymakers play their roles to present the notable shift in digital skills to close digital divide gaps in the population and nurture learners' twenty-first-century skills to make them ready for tomorrow's workplace and enhance their competitiveness compared with their counterparts. From the literature, we note that standardized frameworks and guidelines are important for educational institutions to start their AI literacy education. Policymakers should set strategies to develop AI and digital literacy among teachers and students that require more than just making use of AI in education. Without sufficient government support, different stakeholders including developers, schools, investors, communities, and professional associations cannot put their concerted efforts to input their resources and human capital to reach the desired level of digital competence and facilitate the inclusion of AI literacy into K-16 education. Government's policies can align with the global needs and consider its resources and budgets to support educational institutions financially to enhance their infrastructure for AI-empowered classrooms and adjust curriculum and assessment strategies in collaboration with AI professionals.

On top of accelerating talent development, realizing AI ethics and human-centered AI is also crucial to make our society safe, fair, and transparent. Many studies have warned that misuse of AI could cause drastic consequences that make the economy downturn and human lives (Baum, 2017; Dwivedi et al., 2020; Jobin et al., 2019). Standardized AI ethical guidelines are important to make people become responsible and trust their lives to AI-empowered machines. Trust and transparency are crucial elements for citizens and governments to guard against potential AI biases, and AI should help support human's life, rather than replacing human intelligence. From this perspective, there is a need to promote digital citizenship education that helps people to gain understanding of what AI can do and how to use it effectively and responsibly.

11.4 Parents

Researchers have identified the usage of AI for children's health development. However, whether they feel comfortable with AI use in education is still unknown. With AI becoming more a part of our everyday lives, this novel technology may affect the way they parent. In recent years, AI-empowered solutions purport to help parents to free up their time to rest. For example, it assists parents in understanding whether their children might be fussy, hungry, or in pain through analyzing the expressions of babies and acoustic features of the baby's cry. Another AI nanny can analyze a baby's sleep patterns and find reasons for its restlessness at night. Further, AI robotics and toys can engage, educate, and entertain children to learn programming, computational thinking, and AI literacy. However, when students meet learning challenges, parents may not know how to deal with them. Ng et al. (2022) found that students may turn to search online after they know their parents do not know about the topic, and sometimes it is challenging for young learners to critically think about the correctness of the knowledge or information found online. If parents are more technologically educated, they can spend more time with their children to study the content together, handle the misunderstandings, and discuss with them, thus having a good parent-child relationship. Further, parents support their children financially, and parents who are AI literates can think critically about what counts as AI, question the intelligence, and understand the limitations and ethical concerns behind so that they could more wisely purchase these so-called AI-empowered products. Providing support for parents can aid them in supporting their children's learning (Long & Magerko, 2020).

When students grow up in primary and secondary schools, educational applications such as intelligent agents, chatbots, and learning analysis evolve to help parents and teachers to understand their children's learning outcomes and experience. However, there have been discussions about parenting and AI about privacy and transparency issues that children's behaviors may be monitored by developers and technology companies. Moreover, the ways how the so-called AI generates such academic results for students are unexplainable. Sometimes the mechanism of

learning analysis could be a "black-box" or too technical that parents may not have technology knowledge and background to understand.

11.5 Researchers and Developers

Artificial intelligence literacy education is a discipline that needs experts from different fields including educational researchers, technology developers, education policymakers, and educators to collaborate and coordinate so as to ensure the quality of education. On one hand, researchers aim at generating new learning theories and principles to address the global needs of AI literacy education. Through research, we can understand the genuine needs of learners to refine the inputs of education (i.e. pedagogies, learning content, technologies used, assessment strategies, student-centered considerations). In the educational technology field, many studies draw upcoming design-based reach as a methodological paradigm to refine learning effectiveness to advance the existing practices to ensure high-quality learning outcomes for students.

On the other hand, developers should not merely focus on profit making with the trend of AI. Instead, they need to align with research evidence to learn users' backgrounds, interests, and needs and produce and refine the products for students that facilitate their learning, thus making a meaningful and responsible contribution to AI literacy education. In this way, human-centered considerations are important to raise attention to educate citizens to become socially responsible and ethical users such as inclusiveness, fairness, accountability, transparency, and ethics, instead of merely enhancing students' AI abilities and interests.

The evidence referenced in this book employs a systematic scoping method that summarizes the current state-of-the-art literature. As suggested by many scholars, "digital literacy" varies, and so does "AI literacy," and our book has synthesized some of the theoretical frameworks for twenty-first-century skills (Reynolds, 2016). Education researchers have to work actively and collaboratively to identify research questions to provide theory and evidence basis for future research. First, there is a need to update the theoretical, conceptual, and methodological underpinnings of AI literacy education. Second, we need to evaluate the design and implementation of AI literacy education for educators to meet the needs of learners; improve quality of instruction, curricula, technology, and pedagogy utilized in classrooms; and redefine rubrics and assessments (e.g., knowledge tests, questionnaire protocols, project, and content analysis).

Several research gaps were found based on the literature review in this book. First, there is a lack of AI literacy curricula and assessment methods. Although recent studies have started to propose curricula and educational theories to identify what types of content knowledge that should be included in K–16 levels, more empirical studies can be conducted to examine the effectiveness of the learning implementation. Second, AI literacy education is an emerging field and it is understandable that studies could be preliminary and exploratory without rigorous

research methods to investigate the theoretical and empirical perspectives in emerging fields. This suggests why design-based research is useful to explore effective practices, design, reflect, and refine different approaches to teach and learn AI (Ng & Chu, 2021). With rigorous evidence-based research using quantitative and qualitative methods, the effectiveness of AI curricula is carefully and critically examined. In the near future, diverse learning conditions in intervention design (e.g., intervention duration, frequency, curriculum structure, learning resources, teacher involvement) were examined to achieve learners' success for intended learning outcomes. Further, it is foreseen that research designs will shift to be more empirical and interventional (e.g., quasi-experiments, design-based research) with clearly documented treatment and control groups and varied data analysis procedures (e.g., regression, structural equation modeling, t-test, ANOVA). Lastly, to advance the field of AI literacy education, priority should be placed on developing an overarching framework to guide educators in creating lesson designs that offer the most appropriate pedagogies and learning artifacts to foster students' AI literacy. The frameworks proposed in this book may need further evidence to support its theoretical basis. Researchers are encouraged to consider both short- and long-term learning outcomes to examine how students develop their AI literacy under varying twenty-first skills frameworks.

We are working to establish a community of researchers to disseminate good practices and research findings in the countries/regions that promote AI literacy education rigorously (e.g., the United States, China, Hong Kong). Through international collaboration, we strive to share experience and locate comparable studies in different implementation models, curricula, and practices so as to help policymakers and frontline teachers to adopt effective approaches to maximize students' learning outcomes. Comparative studies and analyses across countries/regions and/or different education settings can deepen our understanding of how cultures and education systems take part in AI literacy education that harnesses twenty-first skills development.

11.6   What Is Next?

Educational professionals have to bear in mind that there is no perfect formula that will work in all education systems. Every student is different. They grow differently and possess capabilities and strengths which require varying learning support from policies to classroom practices in light of their developmental and cultural diversities. Although it is not possible to transform our society digitally over one night, a step-by-step approach can help make our world a better place to live in, and continuous and tremendous efforts for leaders in different fields are necessary to implement educational policies and practices that develop talents who suit their places. Digital affordances and constraints of the existing education contexts and AI readiness are diverse across the world.

This book serves as a launching point for AI literacy research in the field of twenty-first skills education. It is possible that in the future more research will be generated that targets new instructional design and theories and principles that address effective design of learning technologies. Educational researchers, technology developers, education policymakers, and educators should work together and help ensure that student learning experiences are of a high quality. We hope to propose useful guidelines to conceptualize AI literacy education, identify reasons why K–16 learners need such digital competence, its current landscape and situation across academia and countries, and its theoretical basis to set for future research and education. Further, the guidelines of pedagogy, content, technology, and assessments used in AI literacy education are put forward to update AI literacy as an important twenty-first-century skill.

As the authors of this book are preparing the book, we are living in a challenging time during the pandemic. As educators, we are dedicated to addressing the rapid changes in today's digital world and preparing the next generation for tomorrow. A good education should always think ahead of time and make people more intelligent to cope with upcoming challenges. When we think about whether, why, and how to incorporate AI into education, we can rethink Alan Turing (the father of AI)'s words in 1950 that defines his famous Turing test: "A computer would deserve to be called intelligent if it could deceive a human into believing that it was human." Artificial intelligence empowers machines and computers to imitate humans and perform like us. It has great potential to become conscious and overcome humans. However, humans make their world a better place to live in to address good values abstract ideas like beauty and life and create new insights that are all irreplaceable by machines. Therefore, on one hand, AI embraces a new vision toward education for the future and a mindset open to positive change to empower our learners with the knowledge, skills, and attitudes to thrive in an increasingly complex and fast paced world. On the other hand, as educators, we need to rethink the purpose of education critically. Should we merely prepare students for the job market and money? Or should education prepare students to be good people, critical thinkers, lifelong learners, responsible citizens, and moral and upstanding human beings?

References

Ahuja, V., & Nair, L. V. (2021). Artificial intelligence and technology in COVID Era: A narrative review. *Journal of Anaesthesiology Clinical Pharmacology, 37*(1), 28.

Boden, M. A., & Edmonds, E. A. (2019). *From fingers to digits: An artificial aesthetic.* MIT Press.

Baum, S. D. (2017). On the promotion of safe and socially beneficial artificial intelligence. *AI & SOCIETY, 32*(4), 543–551.

Deeks, A. (2019). The judicial demand for explainable artificial intelligence. *Columbia Law Review, 119*(7), 1829–1850.

Dwivedi, Y. K., Hughes, D. L., Coombs, C., Constantiou, I., Duan, Y., Edwards, J. S., et al. (2020). Impact of COVID-19 pandemic on information management research and practice:

Transforming education, work and life. *International Journal of Information Management, 55*, 102211.

Jobin, A., Ienca, M., & Vayena, E. (2019). The global landscape of AI ethics guidelines. *Nature Machine Intelligence, 1*(9), 389–399.

Long, D., & Magerko, B. (2020). What is AI literacy? Competencies and design considerations. In *Proceedings of the 2020 CHI conference on human factors in computing systems* (pp. 1–16).

Ng, D. T. K., & Chu, S. K. W. (2021). Motivating students to learn AI through social networking sites: A case study in Hong Kong. *Online Learning, 25*(1), 195–208.

Ng, D. T. K., Luo, W., Chan, H. M. Y., & Chu, S. K. W. (2022). Using digital story writing as a pedagogy to develop AI literacy among primary students. *Computers and Education: Artificial Intelligence, 3*, 100054.

PWC'S Global AI Report. (2022). *Sizing the prize What's the real value of AI for your business and how can you capitalize?* Retried from https://www.pwc.com/gx/en/issues/analytics/assets/pwc-ai-analysis-sizing-the-prize-report.pdf

Reynolds, R. (2016). Defining, designing for, and measuring "social constructivist digital literacy" development in learners: A proposed framework. *Educational Technology Research and Development, 64*(4), 735–762.

Smith, D. F. (2015). 6 ways the new National Education Technology plan could help close achievement gap. *Ed Tech Magazine*. Retrieved from http://www.edtechmagazine.com/k12/article/2015/12/6-ways-new-nationaleducationtechnologyplan-could-help-close-achievement-gap

Yang, S. J., Ogata, H., Matsui, T., & Chen, N. S. (2021). Human-centered artificial intelligence in education: Seeing the invisible through the visible. *Computers and Education: Artificial Intelligence, 2*, 100008.

Printed in the United States
by Baker & Taylor Publisher Services

9.4   Scaffolding Support

While we have investigated the properties of a humanistic, ethical, and responsible design for AI literacy education, K–16 education has consistently viewed scaffolding as essential to support students to master AI knowledge and skills like other subject disciplines. To effectively design instructions and products that help students learn, knowing your end users is important. This section suggests four major considerations that help developers and educators to design their activities, pedagogies, assessments, and teaching materials and customize them to meet student needs: students' backgrounds, interests, and abilities, as well as parental involvement.

9.4.1   Knowing Learners' Backgrounds

Students come to the classroom with a diversity of background knowledge and experiences which influence how they see the world around them and how they believe it works. Barriers and inequities exist when learners lack the critical background knowledge to assimilate or apply new knowledge (Ives & Castillo-Montoya, 2020). To create a better learning experience, instructional designers should consider students' developmental backgrounds such as age, prior knowledge, gender, and cultural background as well as their preconceptions when designing tools and platforms for end users.

First, instructional designers need to consider students' developmental backgrounds. Therefore, most of the K–12 AI educational kits for children use Blockly codes and simple tools that may hide and encapsulate advanced computer science concepts and technical mechanisms of how exactly AI works. These inevitable "black-boxes" are necessary to prevent cognitive overload and develop students' AI knowledge and skills, especially when students do not have the enough technical background knowledge to understand how exactly AI works. For example, ML2Scratch extensions use "train label" block to represent the complex ML models, and chatbots (e.g., Parami, Kore) use conversation flowcharts to represent natural language processing. These simplified algorithms and components are black-box for learners. Some teachers may worry about the transparency of these products and design and challenge that students are merely using technologies without understanding the advanced concepts behind. Although this practice may lead to issues of transparency and misunderstanding, a lower barrier to entry in learning AI is also important. A trade-off balance can be achieved by giving learners the option to inspect and learn about the challenging parts later in higher educational levels or explaining only a few concepts that connect to their learning experience.

Further, designers and educators need to consider design bias when it comes to race, ethnicity and socioeconomic class, and gender orientation. According to Harvard Business Review, there have been many incidents of AI adopting gender and cultural bias from humans since most machines are not women and black researchers contributing. For example, Amazon's Alexa and Apple's Siri associate "men" with "doctors" and "women" with "nurses." Google's Photos app wrongly labeled pictures of black people as "gorillas." Developers need to make sure training samples are diverse and from different backgrounds. Moreover, gender disparity and culture diversity in computing have long been a global concern. To reduce the learning gaps for girls and black children, additional efforts are necessary to address the issues and early outreach to them. For example, after-school computer club and activities, career sharing and mentoring from computer scientists, and culturally responsive design (e.g., using arts, culture, and music as themes to learn AI) can support students to create more interest at a younger age.

Finally, knowing students' preconceptions is important. These days, technology companies are exploiting the current AI craze by exaggerating the scope and capabilities of AI in their products to stimulate their sales, according to a report from Gartner (Patrizio, 2017). Attention should be paid to what students may have sensationalized preconceptions of AI from popular media and advertisements. Educators need to remind students to think critically about what counts as AI and question the intelligence, trustworthiness, and ethical aspects of so-called AI-powered solutions, so that they could be less affected by the media and marketing influences.

9.4.2 Knowing Learners' Interests and Motivation

Enhancing students' interests and motivation to sustain their learning is important. Instructional designers should anchor instruction by linking to students' interests and their prior knowledge when designing AI literacy tools and interventions (e.g., playing or making games, listening to music, drawing). For example, in the past, learners needed to train and program their intelligent agents using syntax-based programming. With technological advances, educational tools provide multiple interesting ways to visualize the complex concepts and develop students' AI understandings. Nowadays, many AI educational kits use playful experience and simulations to explain how AI works. For example, AI for Ocean in Code.org, image stylizer and Quick, Draw, and CodeCombat use interactive and engaging games for students to have fun and explore AI in computer lessons (Ng et al., 2022). Moreover, programming skills can be kept to a minimum so that students can use Blockly codes and web-based tools that help students visualize AI concepts and make their machine learning models.

Researchers have tried to consider motivational factors when designing AI curricula and piloting them in school settings. For example, in primary schools, Lin et al. (2021) proposed six motivational factors and strategies: intrinsic motivation, career motivation, attention, relevance, confidence, and satisfaction among 420 primary students from the piloting schools as references for future development of AI curricula and instruction. In secondary level, Chiu et al. (2022) investigated students' perceived AI knowledge gain, readiness, confidence, relevance, and motivation toward AI among 335 students. Ng et al. (2021a, b) used an AI-adapted

Motivated Strategies for Learning Questionnaire to measure students' intrinsic motivation, learning strategy, self-regulation, satisfaction, and knowledge acquisition. In higher education, Kong et al. (2021) recruited 120 university students with diverse backgrounds to evaluate students' AI concepts, literacy, and empowerment in an AI literacy program.

9.4.3   Knowing Students' Learning Progress

Scaffolding is an instructional method that progressively moves students toward deeper understanding during their learning process. Similar to other disciplines, educators require scaffolding throughout students' knowledge construction which helps students accomplish tasks and assessments. This idea is influenced by Vygotsky's (1978) concept of the zone of proximal development. It is important to acknowledge the areas that learners cannot do, what they can accomplish unaided, and what they can do with assistance in AI literacy education. Knowing about students' backgrounds, interests, and abilities, designers can enable developers and educators to refine their learning materials, activities, tools and platforms, and pedagogies.

Designers should offer ways to customize the display of knowledge through hands-on and minds-on learning activities. For example, educators can explain how intelligent agents make decisions via graphical visualizations, simulations, and multimedia demonstrations. These media-rich materials can aid students in decoding challenging concepts and maximizing their understanding and knowledge transfer. On the other hand, minds-on experiences require the use of higher order skills, reflection, and thinking (e.g., collaboration, communication, creativity) on the tasks through embodied and physical interactions. Guided by the constructionist principle of "learning by doing/making," students can construct tangible and shareable work in the authentic world via engaging in artifact creations with craft materials, web-based AI tools, LEGO bricks, and sensors. Students can put themselves in the intelligent agents' "shoes" so that they can make sense of agents' reasoning, it enables students to mix their technological and creativity while exploring new ways to construct and actively make their artifacts through student-centered, discovery, and project-based learning, while in minds-on learning, the learners can further "think about what they are learning" through students' collaboration and social interaction with their peers.

9.4.4   Parental Involvement

At last, parental involvement in students' learning progress remains the key factor contributing to their success. However, parents have different academic backgrounds, and parental acceptance of technology, robots, and AI is diverse. Research evidence has shown that screen-based technologies and robots can outperform children's story time (Lin et al., 2021; Zhang et al., 2022). Zhang et al. (2022) designed an AI-driven interactive storytelling platform called StoryBuddy to act as a companion or a peer to children as it communicates through natural language dialogues. The system assists parents in asking their children questions, recommending questions to use, and proposing follow-up questions. These supports can help parents come up with better questions to fulfill their skill development and assessment goals and reduce their cognitive load. In this way, parents can allocate more attention to interact with their children to build a good parent-child relationship and keep their child engaged and entertained. Therefore, designers need to work with parents to design meaningful features to support their children's AI learning, benefit family well-being, and enhance equity in children's access to technology.

Overall, we need to engage teachers, learners, parents, and other education stakeholders to work with developers, scientists, and policymakers to develop a framework to facilitate students to develop AI literacy skills.

References

Chen, H., Gomez, C., Huang, C. M., & Unberath, M. (2022). Explainable medical imaging AI needs human-centered design: Guidelines and evidence from a systematic review. *npj Digital Medicine, 5*(1), 1–15.

Chiu, M. C., Hwang, G. J., Hsia, L. H., & Shyu, F. M. (2022). Artificial intelligence-supported art education: A deep learning-based system for promoting university students' artwork appreciation and painting outcomes. *Interactive Learning Environments*, 1–19.

Dam, R., & Siang, T. (2018). *Five stages in the design thinking process*. Retrieved from https://www.interaction-design.org/literature/article/5-stages-in-the-designthinking-process.

Dhungel, A. K., Wessel, D., Zoubir, M., & Heine, M. (2021). Too bureaucratic to flexibly learn about AI? The human-centered development of a MOOC on artificial intelligence in and for public administration. In *Mensch und computer 2021* (pp. 563–567).

Dignum, V. (2019). *Responsible artificial intelligence: How to develop and use AI in a responsible way*. Springer Nature.

Hannafin, M. J., & Land, S. M. (2000). Technology and student-centered learning in higher education: Issues and practices. *Journal of Computing in Higher Education, 12*(1), 3–30.

Ipsita, A., Erickson, L., Dong, Y., Huang, J., Bushinski, A. K., Saradhi, S., Villanueva, A., Peppler, K., Redick, T., & Ramani, K. (2022, April). Towards modeling of virtual reality welding simulators to promote accessible and scalable training. In *CHI conference on Human Factors in Computing Systems* (pp. 1–21).

Ives, J., & Castillo-Montoya, M. (2020). First-generation college students as academic learners: A systematic review. *Review of Educational Research, 90*(2), 139–178.

Jain, A., Way, D., Gupta, V., Gao, Y., de Oliveira Marinho, G., Hartford, J., et al. (2021). Development and assessment of an artificial intelligence–based tool for skin condition diagnosis by primary care physicians and nurse practitioners in teledermatology practices. *JAMA Network Open, 4*(4), e217249–e217249.

Jonassen, D. H. (2000). *Computers as Mindtools for schools: Engaging critical thinking*. Merrill/Prentice-Hall.

Kong, H., Yuan, Y., Baruch, Y., Bu, N., Jiang, X., & Wang, K. (2021). Influences of artificial intelligence (AI) awareness on career competency and job burnout. *International Journal of Contemporary Hospitality Management*.

Lin, P. Y., Chai, C. S., Jong, M. S. Y., Dai, Y., Guo, Y., & Qin, J. (2021). Modeling the structural relationship among primary students' motivation to learn artificial intelligence. *Computers and Education: Artificial Intelligence, 2*, 100006.

Long, D., & Magerko, B. (2020, April). What is AI literacy? Competencies and design considerations. In *Proceedings of the 2020 CHI conference on human factors in computing systems* (pp. 1–16).

Luckin, R. (2017). Towards artificial intelligence-based assessment systems. *Nature Human Behaviour, 1*(3), 1–3.

Miller, T. (2019). Explanation in artificial intelligence: Insights from the social sciences. *Artificial Intelligence, 267*, 1–38.

MIT. (2019). *Computing and artificial intelligence: Humanistic perspectives from MIT*. Retreived from https://news.mit.edu/2019/computing-and-ai-humanistic-perspectives-0924

Morrison, K. (2021). Artificial intelligence and the NHS: A qualitative exploration of the factors influencing adoption. *Future Healthcare Journal, 8*(3), e648.

Ng, D. T. K., Leung, J. K. L., Chu, K. W. S., & Qiao, M. S. (2021a). AI literacy: Definition, teaching, evaluation and ethical issues. *Proceedings of the Association for Information Science and Technology, 58*(1), 504–509.

Ng, D. T. K., Leung, J. K. L., Chu, S. K. W., & Qiao, M. S. (2021b). Conceptualizing AI literacy: An exploratory review. *Computers and Education: Artificial Intelligence, 2*, 100041.

Ng, D. T. K., Luo, W., Chan, H. M. Y., & Chu, S. K. W. (2022). Using digital story writing as a pedagogy to develop AI literacy among primary students. *Computers and Education: Artificial Intelligence, 3*, 100054.

Patrizio, A. (2017). *Beware of companies claiming products have AI capabilities*. Retrieved from https://www.networkworld.com/article/3209713/beware-of-companies-claiming-products-have-ai-capabilities.html

Pérez-Ortiz, M., Rivasplata, O., Shawe-Taylor, J., & Szepesvári, C. (2021). Tighter risk certificates for neural networks. *Journal of Machine Learning Research, 22*.

Renz, A., & Vladova, G. (2021). Reinvigorating the discourse on human-centered artificial intelligence in educational technologies. *Technology Innovation Management Review, 11*(5).

Reinhardt, K. (2022). Trust and trustworthiness in AI ethics. *AI and Ethics*, 1–10. https://doi.org/10.1007/s43681-022-00200-5

Rudin, C. (2019). Stop explaining black box machine learning models for high stakes decisions and use interpretable models instead. *Nature Machine Intelligence, 1*(5), 206–215.

Shneiderman, B. (2020a). Human-centered artificial intelligence: Reliable, safe & trustworthy. *International Journal of Human–Computer Interaction, 36*(6), 495–504.

Shneiderman, B. (2020b). Human-centered artificial intelligence: Three fresh ideas. *AIS Transactions on Human-Computer Interaction, 12*(3), 109–124.

Toreini, E., Aitken, M., Coopamootoo, K., Elliott, K., Zelaya, C. G., & Van Moorsel, A. (2020, January). The relationship between trust in AI and trustworthy machine learning technologies. In *Proceedings of the 2020 conference on fairness, accountability, and transparency* (pp. 272–283).

Vygotsky, L. S. (1978). Socio-cultural theory. *Mind in Society, 6*(3), 23–43.

Webber, K. L. (2012). The use of learner-centered assessment in US colleges and universities. *Research in Higher Education, 53*(2), 201–228.

Xu, W. (2019). Toward human-centered AI: A perspective from human-computer interaction. *Interactions, 26*(4), 42–46.

Yang, S. J., Ogata, H., Matsui, T., & Chen, N. S. (2021). Human-centered artificial intelligence in education: Seeing the invisible through the visible. *Computers and Education: Artificial Intelligence, 2*, 100008.

Zhang, H. T., Park, T. J., Islam, A. N., Tran, D. S., Manna, S., Wang, Q., et al. (2022). Reconfigurable perovskite nickelate electronics for artificial intelligence. *Science, 375*(6580), 533–539.